NOTE ABOUT AUDIO FILES:
Since this book was published, all of the companion audio files are now available for download as MP3 files, rather than CDs. However, all the information and instructions in the book that refer to the CDs still apply to the audio files. Learn more about the audio files here:

http://hypnosishealthinfo.com/store/cd-set-becoming-slender-for-life/

"I'm on a diet, so I'll just have a salad—
a sixteen-ounce steak with french fries on
a bed of lettuce!"
~Hagar, ordering dinner in a restaurant

Becoming Slender For Life

self-hypnosis makes the difference

Roger Moore PhD

Published in the United States of America by
Maluhia Publishing
P.O. Box 101095, Bainbridge Island, WA 98110
www.slenderforlife.com
www.hypnosishealthinfo.com

Second edition, July, 2011 Printed in the U.S.A.
ISBN-13: 978-1517721374
ISBN-10: 1517721377

DISCLAIMER

As always, before beginning any kind of weight release program, diet change or exercise program you should consult with your personal physician. Especially if you have any kind of medical condition. Do not change medications without professional advice. The information in this book is general and not to be taken as professional advice for your specific health problems.

The very best weight release results occur when the Slender For Life™ Hypnotic Weight Loss Program in used in conjunction with visits to a licensed hypnotherapist. However, for people who do not have access to a hypnotherapist, using this book and the companion CD set offers an effective alternative. If you are not achieving the results you'd like working on your own, then you are encouraged to supplement the program with visits to a hypnotherapist.

When strictly following a starch-centered diet with the addition of fruits and vegetables for more than three years, or if you are pregnant or nursing, then consult your physician about taking vitamin B12 each day.

This program easily adapts to any recommendations from your physician. <u>You are ultimately responsible for deciding what foods you wish to include, eliminate or increase in your personal eating strategy</u>. The program is easily modified for any desired lifestyle as shown in Chapter Five.

Before you begin, go to **www.hypnosishealthinfo.com.** Sign up on the right side of the page to receive my daily blog posts. Highlight STRESS in the orange menu bar and click on the dropdown tab, Orange Blossom. Download Orange Blossom and listen daily for two weeks. **Orange Blossom is a free 27-minute stress reduction MP3 download** that is now a favorite of many and used daily around the world.

Prologue to the Second Edition

It is a rainy Labor Day in 2010, and I sit at the very same table in a rental cottage on the south end of Salt Spring Island, British Columbia, where three years ago I wrote the first edition of ***Becoming Slender For Life***. It's difficult to believe it's already been three years and yet so much has happened. Many people have read my book and the response has been so supportive.

Clients' comments have deeply touched my heart, as they've shared how much ***Becoming Slender For Life*** has meant to them. I receive emails from strangers telling me that for the first time they feel like they do have a chance of living at their goal weight. The exercises in Chapter Four seem to speak directly to the heart and open the door for long-lasting change. And chapter Seven has helped many folks continue on toward their goal at a moment when they were ready to give up. I love receiving your emails sharing your journey to your goal weight, so please, keep them coming.

In May of 2009, *Becoming Slender For Life* was honored with the coveted *Pen & Quill Award* by the International Medical & Dental Hypnotherapy Association. I am humbled and truly grateful to have my book chosen for this distinction.

I am more passionate now than ever about assisting people to lose weight. We have a global obesity pandemic that is *preventable*. Nearly one in three (32%, 23 million) American Children are obese or overweight. More than 80% of these children will likely be obese as adults. According to the World Health Organization, obesity is the top health problem in the world, overtaking AIDS. As a species, we are now 7 billion pounds overweight! At current rates, by 2015, 75% of Americans will be overweight and 41% will be classified as obese.

It is estimated that 80% of obese adults have at least one or more health concerns, such as: cardiovascular disease, diabetes, hypertension, fatty liver disease, osteoarthritis, gall stones, sleep apnea and certain cancers. For most children and adults, obesity is avertable and the health consequences are reversible with diet change, weight loss and exercise. As a nation, we cannot afford this needless health care crisis.

There have been some exciting recent developments in curbing the obesity crisis. Jamie Oliver and his Food Revolution have brought the childhood obesity epidemic and the outrageous school lunch program to prime time television. The result is that people are beginning to talk about this and similar food revolutions are brewing in communities across America. The Physicians Committee For Responsible Medicine (PCRM) has advocated a Healthy School Meals Act. In 2010 Congress passed a school lunch reform bill, but unfortunately it's not nearly extensive enough and is sorely underfunded. On a brighter note, First Lady Michelle Obama has initiated the *Let's Move* program to get our kids up and moving. Study after study shows that children who are physically active do better academically. Our nation is falling behind many countries in educating our children and providing for their health, and obesity is at the dead center of the reasons why.

It's time for each of us to take personal responsibility for our health and wellness. To me, the logical place to start is with what we put in our mouth. **Vote with your wallet.** Stores and restaurants stock and serve what we purchase. Stop going to fast food restaurants, and stop buying processed foods in the grocery store. Shop from the perimeter, where the fresh foods are located. **Start your own healthcare revolution by serving your family *real food***—food that looks like it was dug out of the earth, picked off a plant or bush or from a tree. When we consumers change, the food industry will adjust to our demands.

In *Becoming Slender For Life* I write that it's really all about creating a new relationship with yourself and a new relationship with food. All too often I hear: "When I lose weight I will be happy" or "My life will be better" or "I will feel better about myself." No—when you *decide* to be happy or create a better life or esteem yourself highly, then the weight will come off. Your weight does not dictate your emotions. **Your emotions dictate your weight.**

And there's the rub. Those of us who have obsessed on food (or any other drug of choice) don't want to feel. I still say *us*, even though it's been 15 years now since I let go of the weight. To this day I have my moments of not wanting to feel the hurt, the pain, the sadness, the fear, the anger, the stress or the thoughts that I am not good enough. Of course going down that old path leads to more pain and suffering. **When we don't allow the pain, we also deny the love and the joy.**

I remember in my sophomore year in college, I took a Zen Buddhism and Christianity course at Bethel College (now Bethel University) in St. Paul, Minnesota. In this course we read about the desire to *bolt*. It took me years to realize just how powerful this desire to bolt—to escape—really is. I see it from time to time with Slender For Life™ (and stop smoking) clients who just sort of disappear. They fail to show up one day for their session. They never return my calls and emails, and I never hear from them again. They've bolted. But where I really see it is in my own daily life and in the stories I hear from clients. I doubt a day goes by that I don't have an impulse to eat instead of feel. **Eating is a form of bolting.** If I eat that sweet pastry, or gorge myself at a meal, I won't have to feel.

In 1985, two of my closest friends and business partners were in a plane crash. Bill died in the crash, Bob died two weeks later. I had a ticket for the flight, but changed my mind and didn't go. Early in the morning, about an hour before Bob died in a Las Vegas hospital, I went out of his room in the burn unit to the vending machine and bought two packages of Hostess Cupcakes. In a matter of seconds I inhaled all four cupcakes. I just couldn't deal with the emotional pain anymore and that rush of sugar and fat numbed me out for a few moments.

I have never eaten another Hostess Cupcake. But from time to time, I do think about finding one. **Fortunately, that sort of desire is a huge wakeup call.** It's an alarm buzzer screeching at me to pay attention, to be mindful, to be conscious of what I am feeling and to allow myself to feel it. When I allow myself to feel the pain, I can grieve, I can hurt, I can be fearful and angry. I can cry and move on to what is next in my life. I no longer have to carry the weight of that pain with me. When I come out on the other side, I again

discover the love and joy that's always been available to me.

I tell clients that the self-hypnosis suggestion I give myself most frequently throughout each day is: *I am present and conscious in my body.* That simple suggestion reminds me to be aware of my feet on the floor, my butt in the chair and my breath as I exhale. From this place of consciousness and mindfulness, I'm aware of what I'm experiencing physically, mentally, emotionally and spiritually. From this space of awareness I will only eat when I'm physically hungry. If I'm truly physically hungry, I make healthy choices and I only eat enough to meet my body's needs.

My prayer for you is that you create a new relationship with yourself that is based on this moment—not on some story you lug around from your past. By being in this moment and realizing it's your own self-limiting beliefs holding you back, you learn to love YOU and learn to treat your body with the grace, compassion and dignity it so richly deserves. **This is what** *Becoming Slender For Life* **is all about.**

My best wishes,
Roger Moore
Roger@HypnosisHealthInfo.com

A Special Thanks

A special thanks to all my clients, you are my teachers. Thank you for your trust, your teachings, your tears and your laughter. You make it all worthwhile.

I am indebted to Charles Beeson, the creator of Slender For Life™ Hypnotic Weight Loss. I thank him for trusting me with Slender For Life™ and allowing me to take it into this millennium.

I am indebted to Dr. Topher Morrison for sparking my interest and for allowing me to believe. And to Dr. Melissa Roth for your friendship and honest straightforward guidance.

To Dr. John McDougall, thank you will never be enough—I owe you my life. Your kindness and guidance over the years are not forgotten.

I give my deepest appreciation to Oriana Green for her guidance and for making this book possible—and thank you for not letting me be stupid!

My love to my daughter-in-law, Dr. Nancy Miggins, thanks for loving me enough to be honest!

To my dog Malu, I miss you. You were a great companion. My prayer each day is to be the person you thought me to be. To my dog Luna, thank you for bringing a smile to my face and for making me take the time to play.

I am infinitely grateful to my wife, Marilyn, for her love, patience, understanding and hours of listening and reading. Her faith in me has been a source of strength for my heart and soul.

My thanks to my children Larry and Nancy, Shellee, Tim and Agnes, Josh and Lauren and my grandchildren Cassie, Alex, Kenna, Riley and Ellie whose love, hugs and laughter keep me going.

And finally, to my parents, I thank you for being who you are and for being such rocks of faith.

TABLE OF CONTENTS

For my love, Marilyn.
Thank you for being at my side.

WELCOME

To Slender For Life

Hi, I'm Roger Moore, PhD, Director of the Slender For Life™ Hypnotic Weight Loss Program. Mastering the issues concerning healthy weight has been both a professional and a personal mission. As a baby I cried a lot. Mom took me to the doctor and he said, "Feed him." Growing up, I was given a cookie anytime I felt anger, fear or sadness. I learned to use food to create feelings of love and acceptance, and I discovered how to use food to medicate or cover up uncomfortable feelings like hurt, anger, fear and loneliness.

As a result, I was overweight as a child and stayed that way into my young adult years. I didn't have the energy or coordination for physical activities. Whenever I dieted I could lose weight, but the moment the deprivation stopped, I always put as much or usually more weight back on. I finally realized that diets didn't work and I

I was overweight as a child

BEFORE

gave up. I felt hopeless and out of control. I promised myself I would never put myself through the pain of another diet. I figured I would just keep putting on the weight.

Then one day in a hypnosis class, I volunteered to be the subject for a weight loss demonstration. I didn't think it would work, but I began to notice some results. With several more hypnotic sessions, I changed my eating habits and I began to enjoy exercise. Over the course of a year I took the weight off and I have kept it off ever since—100 pounds of pain and lost energy. My waist size went from 44" to 32". I've been where you may be now, desperate for a lasting solution, filled with self-disgust and hopelessness.

When I was heavy I hated to sweat, yet it seemed I was always sweaty. I had folds and creases where dirt and lint collected, sports like skiing were awkward and difficult at best and clothes did not fit me properly. It was even difficult to tie my shoes. Worst of all, people treated me with condescension. Studies have long shown that overweight people are often perceived as less intelligent and that employers often view them as less competent, successful and intelligent than their co-workers. And now results of a five-year study by the British government released in 2006 show that gaining weight can indeed actually lower your intelligence! The study, published in the journal *Neurology*, found significant reductions in cognitive function for people with a body mass index of 30 or higher.

I've been where you may be now, desperate for a lasting solution

AFTER

But now—15 years later and counting—my life barely resembles what it did when I was fat. Hypnosis changed my life! I now love to workout and bike, I climbed Mount Rainier, I've completed five marathons and I participate in long-distance cycling events. Another result of my own journey is that I am passionate about assisting people in getting their excess weight off and keeping it off. The Slender For Life™ program can work for you too. I am rarely sick, I wear tight fitting clothes, and I now think of myself as a slender person. I am shocked when I see old photos of myself. I love the freedom that I have to hike, run and ride my bike. I have so much energy. Bottom line, I feel so much better about me!

Slender For Life™ was originally developed after seven years of research at Master Key Hypnosis Center in San Jose, California under the direction of Charles R. Beeson, C.H., R.H.A. Hypnosis had been used in weight release for over 50 years. Long-term follow up, however, showed no better results than the latest commercial weight release programs. It became his passionate challenge to create a comprehensive system using hypnosis that truly promotes change. I believe that basic objective has now been met.

I was certified as a Slender For Life™ Hypnotic Weight Management Specialist by Charles Beeson in February 1999. I saw the successful results of my clients and liked the program so much that my business, Abundant Living Resources, LLC, purchased Slender For Life™ on January 1, 2001.

Every week with Slender For Life™, I learn something new that improves the program, and so it continues to evolve.

In addition, I furthered my studies and earned a Doctor of Clinical Hypnosis degree. For my full resume, please see the back of the book.

Say goodbye to the hurt

You want to release your excess weight, not lose it, after all, things that are lost can be found!

Congratulations on your wise decision to use the Slender For Life™ Hypnotic Weight Management.System. You have obtained one of the most powerful weight release solutions ever made available. And, yes, I mean, *release*. You want to permanently release your excess weight, not lose it, after all, things that are lost can be found! The unconscious mind is very literal and it knows that if you lose something, you must go and find it. You never want to lug this weight around again! This program is designed to support you with putting an end to the hurt caused by being overweight. That's right, HURT. The emotional hurt from not being able to wear the clothes you want and look the way you know you can. The hurt from needing to opt out of physical activities with friends. The hurt and social stigma of being fat, chubby or pleasantly plump can destroy your self-esteem and self-confidence.

Sadly, the medical community is, for the most part, throwing in the towel with lifestyle changes when it comes to obesity. As reported in the Seattle Post-Intelligencer in 2004, this is the refrain heard from many medical doctors: "We can't get our patients to change their behavior—eating right and exercising—so we have to go strictly to the medications." More and more, overweight Americans are being prescribed drugs to treat the conditions that can lead to diabetes, heart disease and stroke. These are not drugs that help drop pounds. Instead, they allow people to maintain their unhealthy habits and sidestep early death. Medication is not the answer.

Art Caplin, a bioethicist at the University of Pennsylvania, put it this way: "The emphasis on drugs shifts responsibility from the individual, the food industry and society at large. People love to find a quick fix. They can say, 'Oh, well; I'm not indulgent; I'm just sick.'"

Being even moderately overweight can put you at serious health risk.

It puts significant strain on your heart causing angina and heart attacks. It can lead to hypertension, diabetes, high blood pressure, cardiovascular disease, gall bladder disease and some types of cancer. When you release your weight and keep it off, you reduce these risks.

It is true that genetics certainly plays a role in obesity. Some of us are more predisposed to obesity than those lucky individuals who eat what they want, when they want, don't exercise and don't gain weight. But we can't play victim to our genetics. Even though obesity is a familial trait, I am the one that chooses what and how much I eat as well as how much time I spend sitting on the couch. I can choose to eat more healthily, turn the TV off and be physically active.

Obese individuals face a number of extra health challenges, including cardiovascular complications, high blood pressure, atherosclerosis, thrombosis and more. Obesity interferes with the body's ability to properly use the hormone insulin and control blood glucose levels, putting obese individuals on the path to type II diabetes. Excess weight also puts additional stress on joints, increasing your chances that you'll develop osteoarthritis. Individuals who are obese are at greater risk for several forms of cancer. Sleep apnea is often a challenge for obese individuals, and women who are obese later in life are at an increased risk of developing Alzheimer's.

Overweight children are apt to become overweight adults, and they face many of the same complications as adults who become obese later in life. We have a crisis with our children today. Due to obesity, this is the first generation that has a shorter life expectancy than our own.

So congratulations on taking the first steps toward ending your hurt and becoming slender for the rest of your life.

Diets work—briefly

Sadly, in the U.S. it's normal to be overweight. **Sixty-five percent of the US population is overweight.** It is now *abnormal* to be at a healthy weight in this country.

Americans are sitting around and eating themselves to death, with obesity closing in on tobacco as the nation's number one underlying preventable killer. There are countless diets

You're going up against years of self-defeating habits, beliefs and values.

available today, and people can lose weight on most any diet, yet few people succeed in attaining their goal and *maintaining* that goal weight throughout their life. According to statistics from The National Eating Disorder Information Centre in Canada, 95 percent of people who lose weight regain it all within one to five years. Even people who have had stomach surgery struggle to keep the weight off and sometimes gain it back. The poster girl for gastric bypass surgery, Carnie Wilson, regained enough weight to land her on the Celebrity Fit Club show.

Now, if you're like most men and women who have struggled with their weight, you've already discovered that releasing weight is a relatively easy to understand process. Decrease calories, change your food choices and increase physical activity. You must burn more calories than you take in to let go of the weight, then you have to burn as many as you take in to maintain your ideal weight.

Easy to grasp. Not easy to do. Doing what is required in dieting often means deprivation, frustration and all of the physical and emotional discomfort that goes with it. You're going up against years of self-defeating habits, beliefs and values.

Then comes the day when, for whatever reason, you decide the diet is over. Slowly but surely you return to your comfortable old eating habits. Your exercise routine comes to a halt. The lost pounds and inches return. You wake up one day and discover you're still overweight. Worse yet, you weigh more than you did before you started your diet.

The ultimate solution

Imagine what it would be like if you could end your desire for sugary sweets and pastries? Imagine what it would be like if you replaced your preference for fried, fattening and fast foods with a greater desire for fruit, vegetables and salads? What would it be like if you could eat smaller portions and feel satisfied? If you really looked forward to exercise and loved it? What if you could stop stress, anxiety and boredom eating and could begin a new life of self-confidence and inner calmness?

If this described your behavior, you would be the thin person you want to be. And if these new behaviors became permanent habits, you could maintain your ideal new body forever, couldn't you?

But the plain truth is: diets are not the answer. It's not about the food. So if taking the weight off and keeping it off is not about the food, then what is it all about?

With the Slender For Life™ program you can eliminate packaged meals, pills, shots, fad diets and even counting calories. This program is not about those things.

This is about control. Your personal control over your eating habits, emotions and daily lifestyle. It's about you taking back your power; the power that you gave away to food, people, work, life's events and circumstances.

Your empowerment is created by learning how to use the marvelous powers of your mind. As a result, you can gain permanent lifetime control over your weight and be the attractive, healthy, energetic and slender person you were born to be.

The solution is self-hypnosis

Every once in awhile, the phone rings and I hear a former client say, "Roger, I've put on weight, I am out of control, I need to get back in there." I always ask, "Are you using your self-hypnosis?" Not once have I ever heard the answer "Yes." The answer is always "No." It seems that human behavior is such that we stop doing what works for us when we get comfortable—when we've met our goal—and then we wonder why we're in trouble.

You may not realize it, but we move from one trance to another trance all day long. You naturally enter into trance when you are bored and when you daydream. There are TV trances—the advertisers count on it—and of course driving trances. I bet you've had the experience of driving a familiar route and suddenly realizing you have no memory of how you got where you are. You were driving in a trance state, induced by the lulling of the motion and sounds of your car. Then there's the trance that we all experienced as school children

You may not realize it, but we all move in and out of trance all day long.

staring out our school room windows. Even our negative self-talk such as: *I'm not good enough, I'm too fat, I'm too old, too young, not smart enough* or whatever our negative myths may be, are also trances.

We do want to fit in, we need to belong, and the trance to be like everyone else is powerful. When others are dining on high-fat, high-sugar foods and high-alcohol gourmet meals, we want to do that too, and then we end up overweight. And then there are food trances. Eating too much too fast, losing yourself in chocolate trances, cookie trances, crackers and cheese trances.

All hypnosis is self-hypnosis. I, or any other hypnotherapist, can only be your tour guide. I cannot make you do anything you don't want to do. If I gave you the suggestion to rob a bank and bring me the cash, the only way you would ever entertain the suggestion is if you were already a bank robber. And if you were to really follow through on it, you still wouldn't bring me the cash. In order for hypnosis to work, the client and the therapist must be in agreement about the suggestion before it is made.

Hypnosis is not being out of control or being controlled by someone else.

With hypnosis you are not behaving gullibly, you are not weak minded or unconscious. Hypnosis is an awake state, a state of relaxation, and it is imaginative exercise for your mind. Hypnosis is bringing your conscious mind and subconscious mind into rapport. Hypnosis is the ultimate form of self-control. Far from reflecting any mental deficiency, the ability to be hypnotized is a positive measure. The more intelligent you are, the easier it is for you to enter into hypnosis.

I teach clients a one-minute self-hypnosis technique allowing them to take back the power in their lives. The power they gave away to food, to people, to work and to living a full life. Hypnosis is about taking back your power. Every person I am in contact with who has successfully used the Slender For Life™ program assures me they use self-hypnosis several times a day, every day.

Hypnosis is an awake state, a state of relaxation

I have no magic pill

My job is not to cure or to fix you. I have no magic wand or mystical fairy dust. All too often, clients come looking for a therapist who can magically solve their problems. And when that does not happen, the client blames the therapist and says hypnosis did not work. **Change has to be a change in your relationship with yourself.**

How to use this system

Go to **www.hypnosishealthinfo.com** and signup to receive my daily blog posts containing information on a variety of health and wellness related issues. You will find the signup on the right side of the page. Each post contains your Hypnosis Health Info Suggestion For Today. You will find a host of articles in the Article Library and many support tools in the Store.

CD NOTE

If you are working with a licensed Slender For Life™ weight loss coach, they will guide you with the reading of this book and assign which CD tracks to listen to.

If you are on your own, you will be most likely to have the best results by really absorbing each chapter and the appropriate CD tracks before moving on to the next. This may mean you spend several weeks on one chapter, and that's fine, but just be careful not to use this advice to remain stuck at a more comfortable point on the continuum to your goal. **Refer to the CD list at the back of the book for further instructions.** They are laid out in a progression designed to help you achieve your maximum level of success. If you are working alone, skipping around could very well sabotage your progress. If you want to read the whole book and listen to all the CDs quickly to get the big picture and then go back and spend more time with each one, that's okay, too. Though it's still not my recommendation for how to do this, I recognize that some of you just have to know where you're headed before you can immerse yourself in something new.

You can read the whole chapter then listen to the CD tracks or vice versa, or you may enjoy switching back and forth between them—it doesn't matter. What does matter is that you do both. The CDs are not an audio version of the book; they both have unique content. One is not a substitute for the other.

To start, you'll evaluate your readiness for change. Then you'll learn how to do self-hypnosis. Once that tool is in place, you'll uncover the challenges to your success that need to be resolved. After

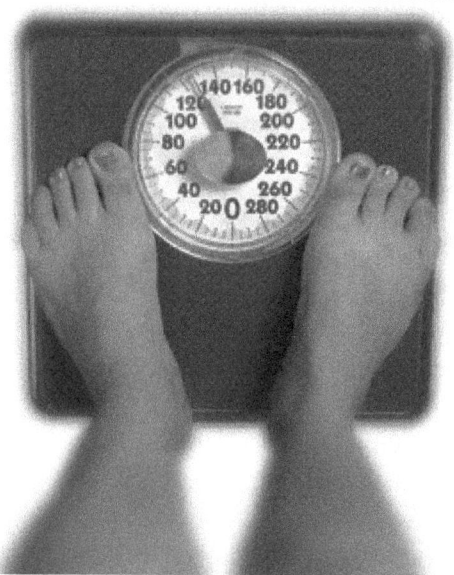

that, you'll examine the connection between your emotions and eating, and then you'll move on to discovering a better, healthier way of eating that will stop your food cravings. All along the way, listening to the CDs will enhance your learning experience, and you'll see how to create exactly the right hypnotic suggestions for yourself to support your healthy new choices. Ultimately, you'll understand how to stay with the program to reach your goal weight—and how to maintain it for the rest of your life.

Slender for Life™ has now worked for many men and women, and it can work for you. **I am convinced that using self-hypnosis is the key to maintaining an ideal weight.**

One of my former clients, Rhonda, sums up her experience like this: "It's working for me. I feel so much better and in ways I didn't even think I would. I'm more confident, because I know I look 'normal' now. No one classifies me as the overweight woman anymore. And some of my physical complaints have cleared up—notably bursitis in my hip. To say this has been a catalyst to change my life is an understatement!"

So, no matter how many times you may have failed at weight release and no matter what other programs you may have tried, you can be confident that you finally hold the key to unlocking your inner potential for successful weight release and lifetime weight control. **Let's get started.**

My Best Wishes,
Roger Moore, Ph.D.

Chapter One

Are You Ready To Be Slender for the Rest of Your Life?

Chapter One At A Glance
· You aren't alone—challenges we all face
· The biology behind our behinds
· Why this program is different
· Determine if you are ready and willing to change
· First, prepare for change
· Stop putting your life on hold
· A peek at your perfect life
· You have the power
· I dare you!
· Schedule and general instructions

The percentage of meals eaten or prepared away from home has increased more than 50 percent since 1970

What you're up against

Americans are among the fattest people on earth. Now, an estimated twenty-one million Americans over 60 are obese, a 43 percent jump from 2000. A whopping 64% of all adults in the U.S. are either overweight or obese, according to the National Health and Nutrition Examination Survey. "Americans need to understand that overweight and obesity are literally killing us," warns Tommy Thompson, former Secretary of the Department of Health and Human Services. Left unchecked, almost all Americans would be overweight by the year 2050.

Around the world, westernized people no longer eat as their ancestors did, or even as their parents did. Meals used to be prepared at home primarily using fresh foods and without adding much fat, salt, or chemical preservatives.

Today, most of us are too busy to prepare foods from fresh ingredients, so we purchase foods that are partially or fully ready to serve—foods processed with much added fat, sugar, sodium, and chemical additives.

The percentage of meals eaten or prepared away from home (restaurants, take-out) has increased more than 50 percent since 1970. Meals prepared outside the home are much higher in fat and sodium and lower in vitamins and minerals than home-cooked meals.

The challenges to losing weight are great, and there are many. Let us not forget impediments created by the food industry. Researchers at the University of North Carolina at Chapel Hill found the following:

- In 1977 the average fast-food hamburger weighed 5.7 ounces; in 1996, the average hamburger was 7 ounces, with 100 extra calories. (Hamburgers at non-fast-food establishments are now often smaller than 7 ounces.)
- During the same time period, sodas went from an average serving of 13 ounces to about 20 ounces.
- As of this writing in 2010, McDonald's medium fries have 380 calories and 20 grams of fat, and the large fries have 570 calories and 30 grams of fat. The McDonald's Angus Bacon Burger is a whopping 790 calories – 350 of them FAT!
- Homemade portions of most foods also have increased in size, with

the average American eating 50 to 100 more calories per serving of each food (or upward of 500 additional calories each day) in 1996 versus 1977.

· Candy bars and snack foods also have been super-sized, with even the smallest packages of some including more than one serving. Most consumers, however, equate one package with one serving.

Plates in restaurants have grown from ten inches to fourteen inches.

Many restaurant meals are now super-sized. A serving of McDonald's French fries ballooned from 200 calories in 1960 to 320 calories (late 1970s) to 450 calories (late 1990s) to the present 570 calories! What was once a 590-calorie McDonald's meal is now a whopping 1,550 calories. ONE MEAL! And McDonald's marketing goal is for every fast-food eater to consume a McDonald's meal twenty times a month! McDonald's is not alone in this. Plates in restaurants have grown from ten inches to twelve inches to fourteen inches. At a Mexican restaurant in Long Beach, California, I was served a portabella mushroom fajita on two 12-inch platters!

Between 1970 and 1994, the USDA reports, the amount of food available in the American food supply increased 15 percent—from 3,300 to 3,800 calories or by about 500 calories per person per day. During about the same period (1977–1995), average individual caloric intake increased by almost 200 calories, from 1,876 calories a day to 2,043 calories a day. No wonder 65 percent of the population is overweight!

And of course, there are the holidays, social nights out, eating in airports while traveling, family events and the list goes on. So this is our culture—this is the food trance in which we live. Choosing to be slender for life is abnormal in our culture. The norm is to eat and drink what you want, when you want and in the quantity you want.

 **At this point in time, it is *abnormal* to be at a healthy weight. It is abnormal to eat fruits, vegetables and grains and to stop eating when your body tells you it has enough fuel.**

If you choose to let go of the excess pounds, you'll likely have people around you who consciously or unconsciously try to sabotage you.

As reported in the *Seattle Post Intelligencer*, November 23, 2005, the Center for Disease Control and Prevention reports that the average adult male today weighs 191 pounds compared to 166 pounds in 1960, and is only half an inch taller. The average female weighs 164 pounds today, compared to 140 pounds in 1969 and is one inch taller.

The effects of this are all around us. Our cars have gotten bigger. Even the once 24-inch-wide coffin is being made wider and reinforced to hold more weight. Stretchers are being enlarged and reinforced. You can now buy extra wide reinforced lawn chairs. Airlines are reacting to the dramatic increase in the weight of their passengers. The average weight of a traveler has increased over ten pounds in the last decade. As a result, airfares have gone up to cover the increased amount of fuel needed. In 2000 the extra fuel cost was calculated at $275 million. Some airlines now require "customers of size" to buy two seats.

Obesity and the diseases associated with it were once relegated to kings and queens of Europe and the Alii of the South Pacific. **Today, we are a nation of gluttons. As Dr. John McDougall, MD would say, every breakfast has become Easter, every lunch and dinner have become Thanksgiving and Christmas and every bedtime a birthday party.**

journal exercise

Taking Stock

Journaling is a free and fun method of learning more about yourself and uncovering the underlying reasons why you do what you do. Think of it as peeling an onion—the deeper you go, the better the substance—and yes, there could be tears, but the good kind. The kind that signify you are getting at some core truths. Of course, your results will only be useful to the degree you are honest with yourself. Throughout this book you'll find lots of suggestions for journaling topics, all designed to help you dig down to your true feelings about yourself, how you got to this weight, why you stay there, what will motivate you to change, your feelings about food and so on. I guarantee it will be a fascinating journey! If you are a visual person, consider buying a special blank book to use and colorful pens, etc. to make the process more fun. Some people find it helps to set aside regular times to journal—early in the morning or late at night often work well. Or how about during your lunch hour—instead of dessert?

Take a few minutes to get real with yourself and consider these questions.

1. How many times in the last 30 days have you over-indulged during a restaurant meal or gulped junk food from a fast food joint?

_____

_____

2. How many separate items of obviously unhealthy food currently lurk in your house, car, desk and anywhere else you've hidden it?

_____

_____

It's important to admit your current eating patterns.

(We'll get to the fine points of what constitutes healthy food in Chapter Five.) It's important to honestly confront and admit your current eating patterns before you approach any process of change. Documenting your present reality will also be useful when you compare your progress in the months ahead.

One client, reported back to me after doing this exercise. "Even though I had already started buying some healthier foods and thought I was doing okay, I was shocked at how many items of worthless nutritional value I had stashed in my cupboards. I'd convinced myself that because I bought them in a health food store, my lemon cookies were healthful. And I even had treats stuffed into the glove compartment in my car. I guess I do still eat a lot of crappy food!"

The biology behind our behinds

At least researchers are beginning to understand what's behind this massive epidemic. Extensive research continues to be conducted regarding the addictive qualities of food. Yes, food can be addictive. While I doubt that you've ever heard of anyone addicted to broccoli, lettuce, carrots, grapes or bananas, people are easily seduced by foods that leave them out of shape and often in poor health.

In his book, *Breaking the Food Seduction*, Dr. Neal Barnard, M.D., tells us that whenever an experience provides more pleasure than expected, your brain releases a bit of dopamine, the brain's main pleasure-producing chemical. An unexpected food treat, a romantic flirtation—or anything your brain decides is a good thing—causes dopamine to lock onto your brain cells and build a *permanent* trace of where pleasure comes from. It keeps flavors, scents and sexual experiences alive in your mind and makes you want to experience them again and again.

During our cave dwelling past, food choices were limited, and our pleasure centers did not have a particularly challenging job. All they had to do was help us distinguish between a sweet, juicy ripe peach and one that was rock hard and un-ripened. But today, sugary, fatty, mouth-watering foods are everywhere, ready to bamboozle our senses and take us off course.

Today, for some people, the pleasure center is open for business 24/7.

 **Chocolate, cheese, cookies and doughnuts all stimulate the same part of the brain that responds to heroin. It feels good and we want more.**

This strong compulsive quality is the basis of an addiction. Would you rather have chocolate than sex? The same part of your brain that appreciates chocolate is also responsible for libido. When you eat chocolate , it stimulates opiate receptors in your brain and can become as habit forming—and what you may not realize—just as real as if you were addicted to narcotics.

So it's no wonder that releasing weight is a painful experience. Keeping it off takes ongoing effort. For some of us, our genetic predisposition is to seemingly gain weight just watching someone else eat that Krispy Kreme donut. I repeatedly hear, "I just want to eat like everyone else," or, "I just want to be like everyone else." Well, everyone else is overweight! To be at an ideal weight means living differently. It means eating and drinking differently. Our bodies were not created to eat high-fat, high-sugar foods and to sit at a computer all day and in front of the television all night. So with this harsh reality, how do YOU make changes in YOUR life when 65 percent of us are overweight?

There is a solution

You might be wondering exactly how does this program work? If you've been a veteran of the weight loss wars then you probably already know almost everything there is about taking weight off and keeping it off. The problem lies in DOING IT for the rest of your life! Knowledge by itself just isn't enough for most folks. That's why lifestyle behavioral classes and support groups don't work for most people.

The sky is green and the grass is blue. Let yourself feel how unsettling it is to read something so out of line with your inner perceptions. Feel the conflict created when new input is so opposite from what you've been taught all your life. This is what makes habit change such a problem. It's why will is powerless over imagination. When your subconscious mind must choose between deeply rooted emotions and logic, emotions will almost always win.

You need a deeper kind of mental approach to make critical changes to habits you've spent a lifetime establishing. The Slender For Life™ Hypnotic Weight Management System has been designed to support and guide you through making these changes deep within your own mind's internal computer—your subconscious mind. This system is made up of several strategies, that when combined, form the foundation for successfully managing your weight for the rest of your life.

As the first step, you'll master the art of self-hypnosis.

The techniques presented for practicing self-hypnosis are very powerful and easy to learn.

Mastering these techniques empowers you to reinforce your healthy new lifestyle habits for the rest of your life, plus you can use these same techniques to make changes in any other area of your life.

Hypnosis allows you to bring previously unattainable goals into reach. Don't worry about how to do it—this technique in self-hypnosis is easy to learn and use. It's natural and completely safe.

The use of self-hypnosis allows you to retrain your mind to easily and effortlessly adopt the behaviors you desire. You will simultaneously replace your habits, beliefs and mental roadblocks that prevent lifetime weight control. **When used correctly, you can use hypnosis to establish control by accomplishing the following:**

1. Let go of desire for fattening foods
2. Increase desire for healthy foods
3. Stop eating when satisfied (control portions)
4. Only eat to nourish the body
5. Reduce or eliminate emotional eating
6. Learn new stress coping skills
7. Put a halt to binge eating
8. Improve self-esteem and confidence
9. Motivate daily exercise
10. Modify your mental cognitive patterns to support all of the goals above.

Using hypnosis, you'll learn how to deal with emotional urges to eat.

Phyllis, who has gone down 80 pounds, had a typical reaction to the hypnosis part of the program. "Probably like most people, I was a little apprehensive at first because hypnotism was new to me. I was a big chocoholic—candies and sweets, a lot of diet sodas rather than water. Almost more than a craving was using food as a comfort thing, so that I would eat large quantities of it in an attempt to make myself feel better. Now my cravings for sweets are gone and I no longer use food for comfort."

The next step in our system is the identification and elimination of your mental barriers and roadblocks to making these changes. Behavioral psychologists refer to these mental blocks as cognitive patterns. These are your mental thought processes that dictate your self-limiting beliefs and values about food preference, eating habits, your physical appearance and self-image. These cognitive issues also include bad habits involving your coping skills when dealing with stress, anxiety and other emotions. Using hypnosis, you'll learn how to overcome your roadblocks and also learn how to deal with emotional urges to eat.

As the next strategy, Slender For Life™ recommends a ***flexitarian*** low-fat and high-starch eating strategy. Why low fat and high starch? It's healthy and it works. Throughout history, the healthiest people were the peasants. They ate fruits, vegetables and whole grains. They ate old European breads; they ate corn, rice and potatoes. The kings and queens ate the fatted calves and died of the diseases of obesity, cancer, heart attacks and high blood pressure.

In our era, Taiwan has a high percentage of healthy centenarians that live on root vegetables, rice and fruit. They use fish as a seasoning—not as their meal. One client likened this eating strategy to how her parents and grandparents lived. They killed a cow once a year and it fed a family of five for the entire year. When company came for Sunday dinner a chicken might be served. They lived from the garden in the summer and on root vegetables in the winter. I can hear the protests from everyone who bought into the low-carb craze, but if you read Chapter Five, you'll learn about different kinds of carbohydrates and why this really is scientifically sound and not just a different fad diet.

It's really all about getting back to a more natural, healthier way of eating where fats and sugars are treats—not the daily fare.

It may help to think of food choices as a continuum from horrible for your health to fabulous for your health, and starting from where you are right now, just start moving toward the better end of the spectrum, one food selection at a time. If you are deeply addicted to high fat and/or sugary, empty foods, you may want to make gradual substitutions and improvements. We'll discuss this in more detail in

Chapter Five. Despite the drama we've all seen on TV when the food police sweep in and empty someone's refrigerator and pantry of virtually everything they were used to eating, making a 180 degree change can be challenging for most people. If you don't have too many changes to make, you can probably be successful at making them all at once.

Lynn is the most extreme case I've encountered, and it's taken her a decade to clean up her act, but she's about 85 percent of the way toward her goal and much healthier for her efforts. "I grew up subsisting on junk food, and as soon as I was on my own, it's all I ate. I never cooked. I ate all my meals in restaurants, and I gained weight steadily until I was very fat and very sick. I never ate vegetables or salads—and I mean never. My idea of a vegetable was French fries or carrot cake.

"Finally, in my 40s, my sky-high cholesterol scared me toward change. But I was too far gone to make wholesale changes, so I just started making a few substitutions at a time. Every January I made a new list of what I eat, and when I compared it to the previous year's list, I could see I was making progress. I worked with a nutritionist to learn how to rethink my eating, and I dared myself to experiment more. I even started cooking for myself.

"I can live very nicely as a flexitarian."
~Lynn

"The key for me has been to never say I can't have a certain food. Deprivation doesn't work for me. I may only eat carrot cake once a year now, but knowing I <u>can</u> eat it makes all the difference for me. I can live very nicely as a flexitarian. I've gone from guzzling four cans of Coke a day to sipping on one serving of watered down fruit juice as my afternoon treat. I've gone from living on frozen TV dinners to preparing vegetable- and starch-dominant dishes. I still eat some meat, but it's not the star attraction anymore, and I often have meals that are meatless. My energy is so much better and all my tests come back in the normal range now."

By following the guidelines in this book as an ideal, you should experience maximum weight release and enjoy considerable increase in your energy level. You may also notice improvements in your general health. Slender For Life™ clients attest that making changes using this eating plan is the EASIEST program of all to follow.

Pam writes, "I thought this was going to be hard. I thought no way am I giving up meat and cheese. But this week I have had no meat and no cheese. My food has been great. I feel better and I have more energy. I think this is doable!"

I have never known anyone to experience anything but positive effects from making this a lifetime eating philosophy.

Blood sugars usually become regulated in as little as three weeks, blood pressure lowers, people with irritable bowel syndrome and fibromyalgia report they are doing better and people with arthritis say that they are experiencing less pain.

The eating strategies I recommend are derived from plans designed by Dr. John McDougall and Dr. Neal Barnard, both medical doctors and nationally known experts in nutrition. In the Appendix I'll also give you lots of resources for further exploration of this topic, including books by both doctors.

CD NOTE

These strategies are supported by the guided hypnosis sessions provided on the companion CDs. Repeated listenings in conjunction with your own self-hypnosis exercises provide the keys to making Slender For Life™ work where all other diet plans fail. Not only will you be able to attain your goal weight, but you will be bolstered in your ability to maintain your perfect weight for life.

Finally, you'll learn new attitudes about the role of physical activity in your weight release strategies. Before you turn up your nose and sink deeper into your easy chair, at least read Chapter Six with an open mind. You may notice that so far I've avoided discussing the "E" word. Well, here it comes: exercise does NOT have to be torturous. Just because Janice enjoys getting up at dawn to run for five miles every day, doesn't mean that's the answer for you. When you read all the suggestions I offer, I really believe you'll be able to find something you can wiggle into your day—so to speak.

So are you willing to change?

Diets focus on the physical aspects of losing weight. Eat a certain regime of food and you lose weight. When the diet is over, the

Weight loss is much more than a physical matter.

weight comes back on because there was little or no behavioral change. As with any transformation, weight loss is much more than a physical matter. Change must occur in every area—physically, mentally, emotionally and spiritually. We are on a physical, mental, emotional and spiritual journey.

In order for change to occur, you have to *want* to change and you have to be willing to do the healing work. Just buying a gym membership or reading a book is not enough. You have to show up and put in the effort. In fact, the true work occurs out in the real world, (not in my office) and it can be painful, rather like growing pains. When my granddaughter Kenna was ten, she told me one day that her legs hurt. When I asked why, she replied, "It's growing pains." She's rapidly growing tall and slender and her body strains to keep up, and sometimes it just hurts. Well, so do the strains of growing mentally, emotionally and spiritually. Making changes, like letting go of your weight, is apt to be a painful experience—but certainly well worth the effort.

Any change, even going on your dream vacation or moving into your dream home, has a level of stress involved. Often, when faced with pain (stress, hurt, anger, fear, sadness and so on) we turn to our drug of choice to not feel this pain. This drug of choice may be food, alcohol, tobacco, sex, pornography, gambling, shopping, the Internet, shoplifting or any other addictive behavior. When the drug is taken away, we then get to experience the pain.

It's really not about the food—food just muffles your pain.

"With hypnosis I am happier with myself. I am more outgoing and I don't have that crazy feeling that I need to eat junk food."
~Carmen

Once you substitute healthier coping skills, you won't need to treat food as a drug and it will then be easier to make better choices about what you eat.

Fourth grade teacher Carmen was willing to change, and she released her final 40 pounds (of a 130 pound loss) with the Slender For Life™ program. She now says she is "happier, calmer and more confident. I was shy and could not fit into airplane and theatre seats. People looked at me funny and I suffered in my head. With hypnosis I am happier with myself. I am more outgoing and I don't have that crazy feeling that I need to eat junk food. I now eat healthy, have more energy and I am more focused. People admire what I have done and I refer my friends to Slender For Life™. When asked how she felt about her improved appearance, Carmen replied, "A million, million, million times better—happy, happier, like it doesn't solve everything, but a least when I look in the mirror it makes me feel that at least one big thing is going right... no more Lane Bryant and seat belt extenders for me!"

We're all born without defenses; we develop mental and emotional defenses as we get older. It's a good thing that we do. Without the protections of these mental and emotional shields, we'd be constantly bombarded by undesirable feelings and external threats, both real and imagined. Defensive reactions allow us to avoid, temporarily at least, what we cannot confront and let us get on with our lives.

But we pay a price for these necessary psychic protectors. They alleviate pain but distort and disguise our experiences. They don't resolve problems, although they may help us momentarily feel better, and they can hurt us in the long run. Not only can these defenses prevent us from seeing our problems, they become habit. We become tolerant to our pain and accept it—in a way it's comfortable because it's familiar. It's what we know and to step outside of what we know is uncomfortable and scary. This is another kind of trance that prevents us from getting what we say we want in life. These fixed ideas and tolerance to pain become comfortable—familiar.

No matter how painful it is to be overweight, the fear of change and the fear of the unknown is often greater.

Sometimes we contemplate change. We're aware our defenses aren't working very well for us, but we aren't yet ready to act. Change threatens our very identity and asks us to abandon our way of being. Change threatens our security. What we know is familiar and we are not ready to venture into the unfamiliar. And, what if we fail in making change? This is a fear that can paralyze and prevent change. One client, Jackie, wrote, "I thought that I came here to release my weight, like letting go of a balloon. But when I opened

We become tolerant to our pain and accept it.

my hand, the whole bunch of balloons were released. Now I don't know who I am."

I've had people call for information about weight loss and then use every excuse from parking to money to avoid actually scheduling or showing up for the consultation.

Choosing to lose weight or making any other change in your life takes preparation and perseverance. Many changes—quitting smoking or drinking, releasing weight, reducing stress or becoming active—involve a kind of psychic surgery that is as serious as many lifesaving operations. The date you set to start your weight reduction program is as important as one for coronary bypass surgery or chemotherapy. People fail to arrange enough time, energy and money to lose weight. They may have taken years to put the weight on and spent thousands of dollars in sweets and fatty foods. Yet they think that with one session they'll magically change their behavior, lose the weight and keep it off.

HOT

Experts reveal that weight-loss clients have the best chance of maintaining their goal weight when they are actively involved in a weight-loss program for 22 weeks or more.

POINT

Some of the most successful Slender For Life™ clients will leave their initial consultation without signing up, because they realize they have preparatory work to do first. They tell me they are going to think about it and talk with their spouse or partner. They go home and look at their work and family schedules and plan when they'll attend their appointments with me, when they'll get in their exercise, listen to a 30-minute CD, plan their menus, shop and prepare healthy foods and how they'll handle any family resistance to eating more healthily. Then with their groundwork done, they start their work with me with many of the pitfalls removed.

Stop weighting for your life to begin

That's not a typo. Weight often equals wait. When you carry extra weight, you can fall into the habit of putting events, dreams and goals on hold until you are slimmer. For example, Kathy put off dating for years because she couldn't imagine anyone would find her attractive. Jim failed to pursue his dream of becoming a motivational speaker because he couldn't bear to be stared at. Shirley never spoke up at business meetings even when she knew she had valuable ideas, because she feared drawing attention to herself. As a result she watched her less-talented co-workers be promoted right past her. All these people were weighting for a slimmer future to really live their lives. What are you weighting for?

journal exercise

What are you avoiding?

What things have you put off because of your weight? What new activities have you failed to pursue? What new people have you been afraid to approach? Which business ventures have you avoided? What dreams have you parked in your freezer right behind the Haagen Dazs? As painful as these admissions are, they also can become your motivation for change.

_____

_____

_____

_____

_____

_____

_____

What do you really want?

Discovering how to increase your motivation can be challenging. It fascinates me that when I ask a client how her life will be different or what her life will be like at her ideal weight, she is often stuck for an answer. She has no idea. Even people who have never been to Phoenix have an easier time describing to me what it would be like to visit Phoenix. They talk about hot desert sun, mountains, cactus and cowboys. But try to get them to describe in detail about life at their ideal weight and their eyes glaze over and they go into shut-down mode, as if it's inconceivable to imagine being slim.

And instead of focusing on what their life will be like at their ideal weight, new clients will focus on a goal weight. Often I hear, "I'd be happy if I only lost 50 of the 150 pounds I have to lose." They are too afraid of failing again to allow themselves to think about actually attaining and maintaining their *ideal* weight.

journal exercise

Picture your life

So please take a few minutes and envision how your life will feel at your ideal weight. Focus on activities that you could do at your goal weight that you can't do now. Playing down on the floor with your grandchildren—and getting right back up with ease. Walking for several miles every day—with eagerness and delight. Fitting comfortably into an airplane or theatre seat, tackling a big remodeling or landscaping project. How do you want to be living your life in the years ahead? What do you want to be different?

_____

_____

_____

_____

_____

_____

You do have the power of choice. This is a gift of options you can give to yourself—it's a gift of freedom—a gift of choice. The choice to be able to train and climb Mount Rainier, run a marathon or enjoy a rewarding intimate life. There is a genuine power in knowing that if you want to do something physical, you can. For 65 percent of Americans, that choice is not an option. They do not have the option to say "yes" or "no" to certain physical activities. They simply can't do them. The good news is that whether you are 12 or 80, it's never too late to lose weight and benefit from a healthy lifestyle.

The goal is to face your challenges in life, experience your feelings, no longer needing to *eat* them. The goal is to let go of your mistaken identity, no longer hiding behind your weight. The goal is to become your true self, living the rest of your life at your ideal weight.

It's really not about the food; it's not even about reaching a goal weight. It is about embracing a conscious relationship with yourself. It's about taking back the power you gave away to food, to people, to circumstances. It's about allowing that hidden part of yourself to be seen, heard and felt in the real world. It's about vulnerability. Using hypnosis, you can reclaim control over your life and shift out of an unconscious trance into consciousness.

Are you likely to slip back into your old unconscious trances? From my perspective, yes—as long as you have a pulse. However, with the proper tools and awareness, you can make the choice to return to a more healthful path. **Change is never complete, it's never finished. Change is your journey in this life.**

Your ideal weight goal

A 72-year-old woman should weigh about the same as her ideal weight at age 22.

What would be your perfect, ideal weight? You can determine this with your medical doctor or use your own judgment. Your ideal weight is not a stepped down, baby-step goal, but rather your best weight for your gender, height and body frame. Your age is really not a factor. The popular idea that it's okay to weigh more as you get older has been clinically disproved. A 72-year-old woman should weigh about the same as her ideal weight at age 22. Arguments that support the old myth are just a way of rationalizing poor eating habits and may be denial of a health-threatening problem. It is, though, perfectly all right to create mini goals along the way. In fact, it's a

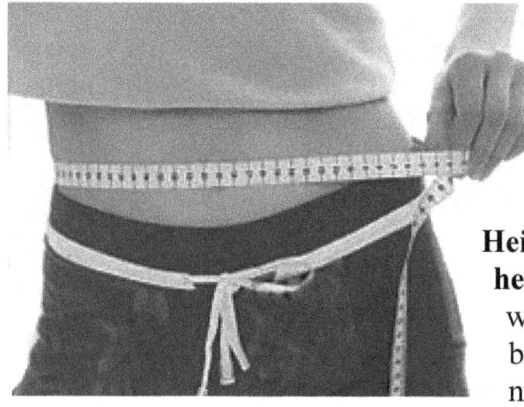

good idea to have small goals over short time frames if you have a lot of weight to release. A hundred pounds can seem overwhelming. While losing two pounds in one week feels doable.

Use the Metropolitan Life Insurance Height and Weight Table on the next page to help determine your weight goal. Select a weight number on the lower end of your bracket. Many medical experts believe these numbers to be on the high side, since the table was last updated in 1983. Next, determine how much weight you need to release to reach your weight goal.

One of my clients shared with me this other way of naming what she was experiencing. Never underestimate the power of the specific words we choose...

I AM SLIMMING!

"My mother grew up in England and she told me that they never referred to losing weight, they called it slimming. What an empowering word. It feels so much more freeing than 'losing weight'."

STANDARD METROPOLITAN LIFE INSURANCE HEIGHT/WEIGHT TABLES

Women

Height	Small Frame	Medium Frame	Large Frame
4'10"	102-111	109-121	118-131
4'11"	103-113	111-123	120-134
5'0"	104-115	113-126	122-137
5'1"	106-118	115-129	125-140
5'2"	108-121	118-132	128-143
5'3"	111-124	121-135	131-147
5'4"	114-127	124-138	134-151
5'5"	117-130	127-141	137-155
5'6"	120-133	130-144	140-159
5'7"	123-136	133-147	143-163
5'8"	126-139	136-150	146-167
5'9"	129-142	139-153	149-170
5'10"	132-145	142-156	152-173
5'11"	135-148	145-159	155-176
6'0"	138-151	148-162	158-179

Men

Height	Small Frame	Medium Frame	Large Frame
5'2"	128-134	131-141	138-150
5'3"	130-136	133-143	140-153
5'4"	132-138	135-145	142-153
5'5"	134-140	137-148	144-160
5'6"	136-142	139-151	146-164
5'7"	138-145	142-154	149-164
5'8"	140-148	145-157	152-172
5'9"	142-151	148-160	155-176
5'10"	144-154	151-163	158-180
5'11"	146-157	154-166	161-184
6'0"	149-160	157-170	164-188
6'1"	152-164	160-174	168-192
6'2"	155-168	164-178	172-197
6'3"	158-172	167-182	176-202
6'4"	162-176	171-187	181-207

journal exercise

Are you ready?

The true first step is deciding if you really are ready to begin this program. Taking off your excess weight and keeping it off is apt to be the most difficult and exciting, challenging and rewarding journey of your life. I've mentioned fear several times already, and I will continue to talk about fear. **Ask yourself these tough questions.**

· Are you ready to be treated differently?
· Are you ready for more attention, especially personal or sexual?
· Can you afford a whole new wardrobe…or several, as your body shrinks?
· Will your fat friends feel betrayed?
· Will fat family members reject you?
· Will there be more pressure put on you at work to succeed or contribute more?
· Will you be pushed into new roles?
· Will you end up with loose skin and want plastic surgery?

_____
_____
_____
_____
_____
_____
_____
_____
_____
_____

These are real issues in people's minds; issues that paralyze many people and prevent them from obtaining their ideal weight. Too often we make up stories to answer these questions that hinder weight release and then live our lives by that script—and then we get to be right about it!

So ask yourself: **Are you ready to reconcile your old inner self with your transformed outer self?** You can live your life in the miserable comfort of the familiar or step out into the unknown and experience the pain <u>and</u> joy of life.

While living on Maui, I would go to a sacred place called Kipahulu. A mountain stream cuts its way through the boulders of Haleakala and flows into the ocean. At Kipahulu there are pools of water surrounded by high rocks. My son Josh and I would climb up about 25 feet onto these rocks. Already nervous about the height, we'd stand on a ledge and prepare to jump off. To enhance the experience, we'd declare the jump to be about a particular goal. The goal could be anything from creating greater financial abundance, getting better grades in school to enhancing relationships. As we made our declarations, our knees would be knocking. We felt both the fear associated with height and the fear of accomplishing the goal we'd just declared.

We'd step out…there was a moment of suspension in the air…followed by the fall and immersion in the cold pool of water. When we surfaced and took our first gasps of air, every cell of our bodies radiated—we knew we were alive. We knew we were experiencing life. I have never experienced a more alive feeling.

How about you? Are you ready to step into your fear?

Are you ready to take off your excess pounds and leave the weight forever?

Are you ready to experience living life to the fullest? Are you ready to be different than 65 percent of the U.S. population who is overweight? If so, read on…Slender For Life™ is for you.

Are you ready to live life to the fullest?

At **www.slenderforlife.com**, (look on the right side of the page) you can download and print out your own "I Am Slender For Life™" card. Then each night as you get into bed, pick up your card and touch your forehead with it, holding it so you are looking slightly upward and read out loud or silently to yourself "I am slender for life." Lay the card down, snuggle in and begin counting backward silently until you fall asleep—starting with a higher number if you are not already drowsy.

         10 ... *I am slender for life*
          9 ... *I am slender for life*
          8 ... *I am slender for life*
          7 ... *I am slender for life*
          6 ... *I am slender for life*

The goal is for your last thought of the day to be: "I am Slender For Life."

So if you've decided you are indeed ready to change your life by releasing your weight for once and for all, then I think you'll find the next step both fun and empowering. Let's go get inside your head!

CD NOTE

      **But first, if you haven't yet done so, be sure to start listening to the CDs. See the instructions in the back of the book, or follow the instructions of your Slender For Life™ weight loss coach.

CHAPTER TWO

Is Your Mind open?

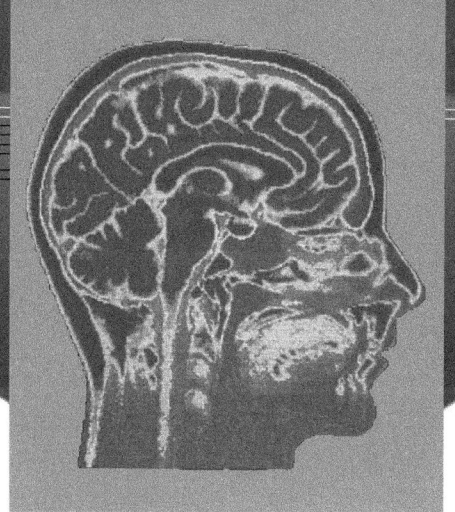

Chapter Two At A Glance
· Understanding hypnosis
· You already know how to go into trance
· The power of the stories you tell yourself
· Your brain explained—really!
· You're always in control
· Debunking myths about hypnosis
· It all depends on your attitude
· Learning self-hypnosis
· Think of all the things you can do with it
· Creating reminders and suggestions
· Going even deeper

Congratulations for making it this far in the book—that means at least some part of you feels ready to consider changing your weight forever. Even if you haven't really made up your mind to try the Slender For Life™ system, I encourage you to at least read this chapter so you'll see how simple it really is to master self-hypnosis—and discover how many ways you can apply your new skill to better your life. Spend as much time with this chapter as it takes for you to become adept at self-hypnosis. Rushing forward without this skill in place will undermine your success.

What hypnosis is—and isn't

The Slender For Life™ Hypnotic Weight Management Program is a structured method for you to change your thinking. If you are like many of my clients, all you know about hypnosis are the misconceptions popularized in movies and on television and the great myths that are told by people who have never studied or experienced hypnosis.

Frequently, people fear they will be controlled by me or someone else and that they will be out of control. It is even taught by some fundamentalist Christians that hypnosis opens one up to Satan himself! As a Christian, it is obvious to me that anyone promoting such misconceptions is uneducated in the facts about hypnosis. From my perspective, mindless eating is trance. And being in that mindless eating state, a gluttony trance would seem to be of Satan. I wonder what is more of the devil; being in control of yourself or out of control in a trance of gluttony. I am astounded at the number of overweight Christians who fear hypnosis. They are in fear of a God given solution, when they should be in fear of the problem.

Modern day methods and applications of hypnosis have made it a trusted and valued discipline of the healing arts, social sciences and human services. Old-time myths and misconceptions about hypnosis have given way to allow for responsible professional uses that have been a major benefit to thousands of people for many years.

The use of hypnosis was approved for medical use in 1958, and is now being taught at major universities and respected learning institutions across the country.

Hypnosis has proven applications in medicine, dentistry, psychology, obstetrics, counseling, law enforcement, habit management, pain control and in virtually every area of education. Major hospitals are now including hypnotherapists on their staffs.

In the September 27, 2006 issue of *Newsweek* magazine, Dr. David Spiegel of Stanford University School of Medicine, wrote: "One of the interesting ironies about hypnosis is that old fantasy that it takes away control. It's actually a way of enhancing people's control, of teaching them how to control aspects of their body's function and sensation that they thought they couldn't."

**"One of the interesting ironies about hypnosis is that old fantasy that it takes away control."
~Dr. David Spiegel**

There are unlimited applications for hypnosis in self-improvement for both personal and business use. Ellen DeGeneres spoke on her talk show in 2006 about overcoming a long-standing cigarette addiction with hypnosis and in the December 31, 2006 Parade magazine, she said that hypnosis worked and she will continue using it. Professional, Olympic and collegiate athletes use hypnosis to enhance concentration and performance. More and more sports teams employ their own hypnotists and even provide training to their players in self-hypnosis techniques. Jan, a tri-athlete, successfully used hypnosis for style correction, speed and strength. She reported back to me that she exceeded her time goals.

The use of hypnosis in sports has been around for hundreds of years. In the 1956 Melbourne Olympics, the Russian Olympic team took no less than 11 hypnotists to develop mental clarity and help the athletes with visualization. With hypnosis it is possible to communicate with the unconscious mind in order to promote healing or even speed up a slow metabolism. You can use hypnosis to create new conditioned responses as well as to change your perceptions of things like food and exercise. Repeated reinforcement makes it last.

> **Never in recorded history has there ever been any danger linked to hypnosis. Hypnosis is fun, feels good, and is relaxing and beneficial.**

In the December 2006 issue of *O, the Oprah Magazine*, in an article titled: Losing Weight: The Mind Game, Aimee Lee Ball writes that "Because the hypnotic state is characterized by heightened concentration and responsiveness to instructions, proponents say it can help break routines, separate a desire to eat from the impulse to act on it, and imprint new eating patterns on the subconscious mind." She goes on to quote Deirdre Barrett, PhD, of Harvard Medical School: "What hypnosis does is get around having to wait for change." Ball interviewed a number of clinicians who described their success using hypnosis for weight control. Then she quoted Debbie Competello, who shared her success story: "I had allowed food to be the controlling element in my life. Nothing else mattered. Hypnosis was important in getting to some of the underlying issues." After a lifetime of failed diets, Debbie was finally able to release 163 pounds.

"proponents say it can help break routines, separate a desire to eat from the impulse to act on it"
~O Magazine

Often clients may not even feel hypnotized. A very light state of trance is all that is necessary for real change to occur. Hypnosis is so normal and so natural and so familiar that when we go into trance it just feels like the same old thing that we have done before, even in deep trance. For most clients, a light trance is all that is necessary to obtain results.

We are always in trance and move through various states of trance throughout the day. Driving long distances often puts us into a daydream state we call highway hypnosis. You drive your car subconsciously while your thoughts are somewhere else. If you've ever lost track of time while watching TV or listening to music you have been in light hypnosis. The advertising industry counts on it. When you are listening intently to someone with rapt attention, you are in trance.

Many people come to a hypnotherapist thinking there is something about trance that is different than their normal state of consciousness, but this simply is not the case. **A light trance feels no different from relaxation. No matter how deep into trance one goes, there is a feeling of familiarity. Do not expect to feel hypnotized. Do expect to feel relaxed.**

Louise's reaction to her first experience of hypnosis is typical. "It was so much easier than I thought it might be, and so relaxing. When it was over, I felt like I'd just had a refreshing nap. Very mellow, very enjoyable. I didn't have any trouble wanting to do it several times a day."

> **Almost everyone goes into a light state of hypnosis several times a day.**

So what's your story?

We move in and out of trance all the time. **My definition of hypnosis is taking control of the trance that you are in.** We each have our own stories, our myths about ourselves, about our lives, about the people and the world around us. One Sunday morning, as I was carrying our suitcases to the car in Vancouver, British Columbia, I saw a bumper sticker that read, "Don't believe everything you think." That says it all. We hold our myths, our truths, to be sacred, yet all too often these truths are fairy tales—perhaps, even horror stories that we have made up—and then we live our life according to these fables.

Here is what I mean. When I was 8 years old, my dad sold his 160 acre farm—all the cows, pigs, chickens, lambs and my horse. We left the big farm house and the wide open spaces of southern Minnesota for a small apartment above a motel that he bought in Iowa. I did not want to move. It was explained to me that my brother, who was 17 years old, did not want to farm and was moving to San Diego after graduation. And since I couldn't do the work he did, and my dad didn't want to do all the work himself, the farm had to be sold.

But what I *heard* was: I'm not good enough, I'm not capable and it was my fault we had to sell the farm. For many years, *not good enough* ran my life. For far too many years I lived my life with this perception. I accepted evidence that I was not good enough and added it as proof to support my perception.

One day many years later at a family reunion, one of my uncles asked my dad why he sold the farm. He replied that my brother didn't want to farm and that I was only 8 years old at the time. An 8-year-old could not do the work of a 17-year-old and that at the age of 45, my dad didn't want to do all the hard work himself.

My jaw hit the floor. Oh my god I thought—all these years I believed it was because I wasn't good enough, and it was really about the fact that an 8-year-old cannot do the work of a 17-year-old. **In that moment, my perception, the myth that I had been living was shattered.**

All thought, all memory and all emotion occurs and is stored in every cell of your body.

Reinforcing these fables we create is our cellular memory. As you will see in the next section when we go on a field trip through the brain, all thought, all memory and all emotion occurs and is stored in every cell of your body. The smell of a cherry pie baking or the sound of a parent's voice can instantly rocket us back into childhood—into that trance where you experience thoughts and emotions of an earlier time. It could be as simple as a 6-year-old falling out of her tree house and running to her mom for comfort. Her mother holds her and kisses her and soothes her tears with a Hershey bar. Here she is, held and comforted in love, reinforced with the sugar rush of the opiate receptors receiving that heroin-like stimulation. And all of this anchored with mom's arms wrapped around her. This type of experience can become a pattern of desire and response that is triggered whenever the girl—and later the woman—needs comforting. And each reoccurrence adds to her cellular memory and her associations with whatever food(s) she was consoled with. In Chapter Four I'll give you exercises to uncover your own stories about food.

Looking around in there

So let's look at how your mind works. (Refer to the diagram on the next page.) We all have a conscious mind and a subconscious mind. The *conscious mind* protects your subconscious mind from the outside world. The conscious mind is the rational, analytical part of the mind. It's the thinking, judging part of the mind that expresses your free will. It is our ability to rationalize that keeps us sane.

As long as we can rationalize our behavior, we will do it. When we can rationalize having a cookie, we will eat the cookie. Our rational mind invents reasons to make it okay to eat a cookie, even when intellectually we know that the cookie may be full of fat and sugar, which slows us from letting go of excess weight. As long as your rational mind can create a reason for your actions, you will continue the behavior.

> **The rational mind does not need truth—only reasoning. When actions can no longer be rationalized, change will occur.**

Willpower also resides in the conscious mind. Most people diet with willpower and of course they fail. To diet with willpower, you have to focus on power: you must keep constant vigil on your behavior. The second that you lapse in consciousness, the subconscious mind will automatically kick in with the old behavior patterns. Willpower is not part of the internal mind and it cannot create internal change. When willpower and imagination meet, imagination wins. Imagination is part of the subconscious mind.

The next component of the conscious mind is *temporary memory*. Temporary memory is where we store names, phone

As long as we can rationalize our behavior, we will do it.

HYPNOSIS AND THE MIND

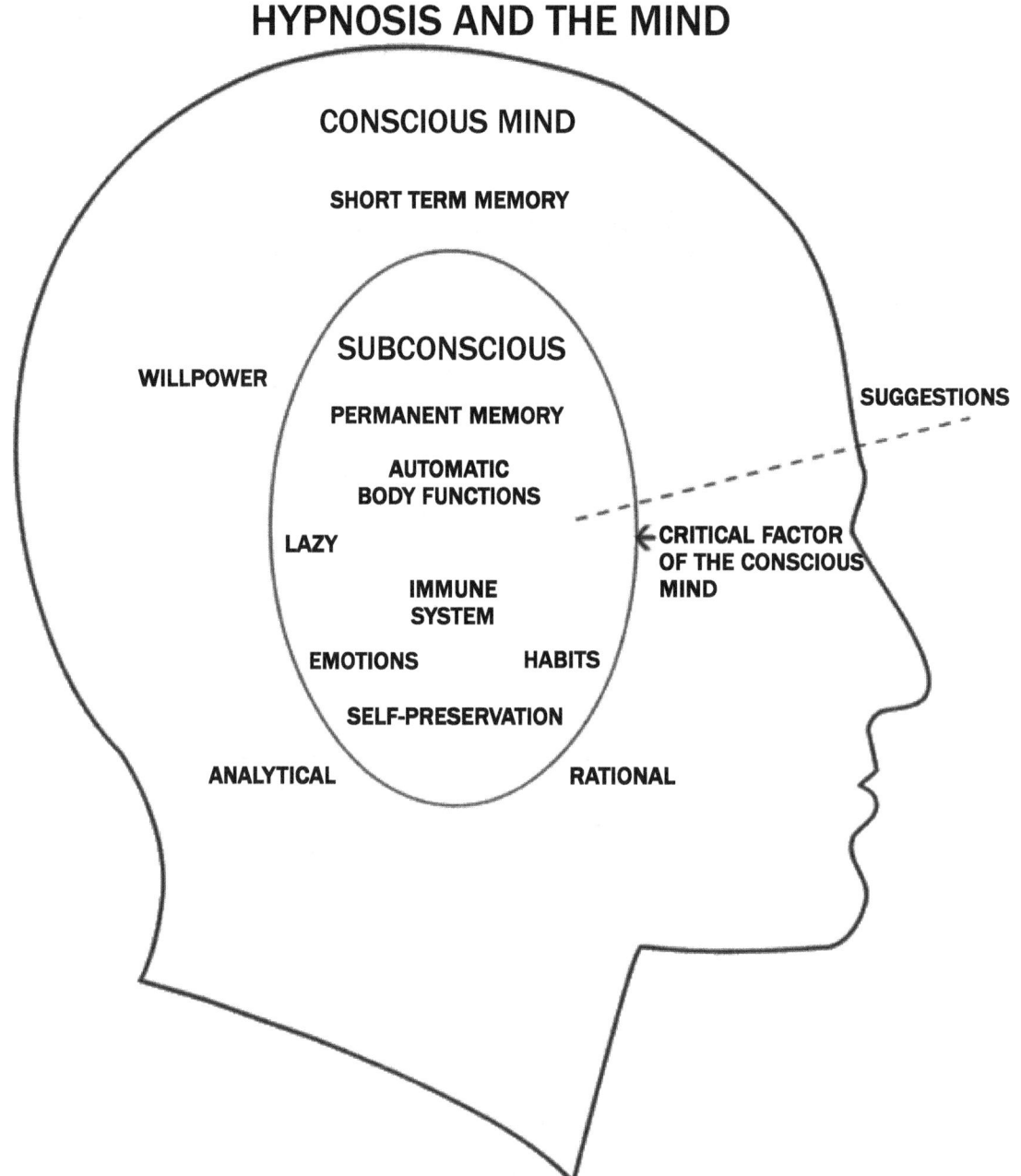

CONSCIOUS MIND

SHORT TERM MEMORY

WILLPOWER

SUBCONSCIOUS

PERMANENT MEMORY

AUTOMATIC BODY FUNCTIONS

SUGGESTIONS

LAZY

← **CRITICAL FACTOR OF THE CONSCIOUS MIND**

IMMUNE SYSTEM

EMOTIONS   **HABITS**

SELF-PRESERVATION

ANALYTICAL   **RATIONAL**

Hypnosis is the bypass of the critcal factor of the conscious mind with selective thinking

numbers, birthdates and where we left our car keys. This temporary memory is nothing compared to the permanent memory of the subconscious mind. In fact, the conscious mind is weak when compared to the power of the subconscious mind.

The *subconscious mind* is the most powerful goal achieving tool we have. And yet, your subconscious mind cannot judge; it is not a seat of reasoning or creative consciousness. Judgment occurs in the conscious mind. The subconscious mind is a stimulus-response device. When an environmental signal is perceived, the subconscious mind reflexively activates a previously stored behavioral response—no thinking required. The subconscious mind is a super computer loaded with a database of programmed behaviors and resides within every cell of the body. Some of these programs are genetic and most are acquired through our developmental learning. A suggestion placed into the subconscious mind will powerfully produce results.

The subconscious mind operates in a world of interior impressions. Its meaningful reality consists of ideas and images of that world. The subconscious world is where the heart is, and its reality is completely subjective. It can never be adequately grasped by objective knowledge or directly observed by another person.

No one else can ever give your subconscious mind enough love, nor will there ever be enough comfort food to soothe your subconscious mind. This love and comfort can only come from you.

Imagination is your perception of or orientation to the world. Is your glass half full or is it half empty? Are you cheerful and excited about life and living life to the fullest, or are you fearful, filled with anxiety and imagining the worst? Imagination is not about truth. It's just a perception. Once a perception is installed in the subconscious mind, the subconscious mind accepts it as fact and makes it so!

Again, imagination is your perception of the world. It is

your identity. This perception is a point of reference that determines your direction. If you imagine the world as fearful and filled with anxiety, you will experience fear and anxiety. If your perception of yourself is that of a fat person, you will be fat. If you believe that you are not good enough, you will live your life as not good enough. Consciously, you may set a goal to lose weight or to improve your self-esteem. But if you don't believe you can be slender, if you don't believe you are already good enough, you will never achieve your weight loss and self-esteem goals. All the willpower in the world will get you nowhere.

Real change occurs when the old perceptions in the subconscious mind are changed to match those of the conscious mind. Or, as famed hypnotherapist Dr. Milton Erickson, MD put it; the subconscious mind must be in rapport with the conscious mind.

"...these molecules of emotion regulate every aspect of our physiology."
~Dr. Candace Pert

The subconscious mind is also home for our *permanent memory*. All information that we have seen, heard, smelled, tasted and experienced kinesthetically (both internally and externally) is stored in permanent memory. As neurobiologist Dr. Candace Pert has proven, neuropeptides—the chemicals triggered by emotions—are thoughts converted into matter. Our emotions reside physically in our bodies and interact with our cells and tissues. According to Pert, "these molecules of emotion regulate every aspect of our physiology. A new paradigm has evolved, with implications that lifestyle changes such as diet and exercise can offer profound, safe and natural mood elevation."

If all memory and all emotion occurs and is stored in every cell of your body for future use, then your body really represents a cooperative effort of a community of about fifty trillion single cells. While each cell is a free-living entity, together they accommodate the wishes and intents of the central voice; what we call mind and spirit. You have a thinking body; this is the permanent memory. This is what makes you who you truly are. You are the sum total of all your past. **You will think your next thought, act your next action and feel your next feeling based upon everything that has happened in your past.**

Emotions, the ones that feel good and the ones that feel bad, reside in the subconscious mind. This is where you feel. Your emotions affect your health, and that includes your body weight. As you know, nature abhors a vacuum. When you feel empty, you consume. People consume with food, cigarettes, drugs, shopping, sex, gambling and many other vices.

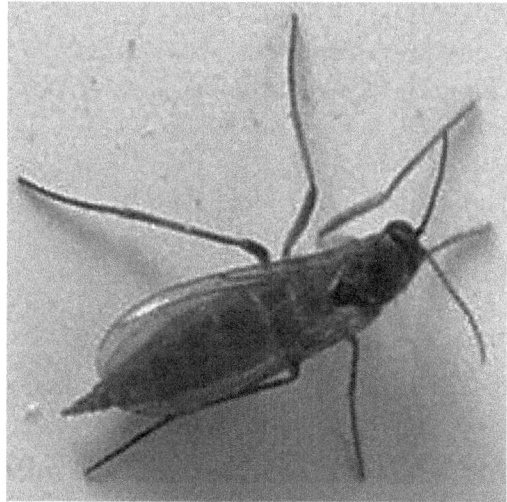

The subconscious mind is the *protective mind*. Its primary directive is to protect you from dangers real and imagined. Phobias and panic attacks are the subconscious mind's way of protecting us from dangers that are imagined—they are not real dangers. The subconscious mind wants you to feel secure. Unfortunately, security is familiarity. If you are used to feeling anxious, it is familiar, it is known—and as miserable as the anxiety might be, it is secure. You know what it feels like. For you, being overweight is what you know, it's secure.

If you're accustomed to eating frequently so that you're never hungry, the experience or even just the thought of being hungry creates anxiousness. When we use food to numb out, to not feel, then when we do experience anger, hurt, fear or sadness, it's unfamiliar. These emotions don't match our inner perceptions of how life should be and thus we feel insecure.

We use perceptions to judge life experiences. If new experiences synchronize with our perceptions we feel very secure, the world agreed with us. Conversely, we feel very insecure when life experiences do not agree with our perceptions.

The most important part of the conscious mind, the *critical faculty*, has everything to do with internal change. The critical faculty is part of the conscious mind but gets its directions from the subconscious mind. The subconscious mind cannot judge a suggestion. If a suggestion reaches the subconscious mind, it will

Your emotions affect your health, and that includes your body weight.

accept that suggestion as fact and make it so—no questions asked!

A first-time suggestion will be scrutinized by the critical faculty, which exists to protect the vulnerability of the subconscious mind. It takes all suggestions and compares the suggestion to the perceptions we hold on the subject of the suggestion. If a new suggestion is not in accord with our perceptions, the critical faculty prevents the suggestion from entering the subconscious mind. If the suggestion is found to be in accord with our perceptions, the critical faculty allows the suggestion to enter the subconscious mind.

The more times a suggestion is either accepted or rejected, the more powerful the perception becomes. Each acceptance or rejection reinforces our perception. This is known as *compounding*. Through that compounding, our belief in the accumulating perception grows proportionately stronger. This reinforces our human need to be right. In other words, we gather proof to reinforce what we believe to be true. If we believe that we are not good enough, then we live our life as not good enough and get to be right about it!

Since we want to accept only evidence that supports what we believe to be true, habit change becomes very difficult. We want to do what is known and familiar—not something new and unfamiliar. This is why imagination is stronger than willpower.

When it comes to new ideas and behaviors, our subconscious mind is like a blank computer disc. It has incredible storage capacity, but nothing has been entered into the data bank. So there is no data to judge against. If there is nothing to judge against, there is no critical faculty! The critical faculty cannot function until it has something to judge new input against. The very first viewpoint we consider on any specific subject, topic, or idea, goes into the subconscious permanent memory unjudged. Then instantly, you now have a perception on that subject. Now there's something to judge against. And no matter whether it's right or wrong, good or bad, that first impression goes into the subconscious mind uncensored and (only because it got there first) becomes the perception against which everything is judged for acceptance or rejection.

Let me give you an example: People who grew up prior to the 1960s were surrounded by smokers. In the movies, cigarette smoking was portrayed as cool and sexy. No one thought tobacco could kill us. And despite the fact that the Journal of the American Medical Association first reported links between smoking and cancer in 1950, it was another 14 years before the U.S. Surgeon General issued a statement advising against smoking. That generation of people had the most difficult time believing that smoking was indeed bad for them. **Their critical faculties had accumulated too much evidence to the contrary.** Even today, if your first contact with smoking is perceived as positive, it can be tough to change your mind about it.

Putting hypnosis to work

With hypnosis, we bypass this critical faculty. People live their lives playing a hypnotic tape in their subconscious mind that is often giving them negative messages and self-limiting beliefs. With hypnosis, we have the opportunity to change that inner dialogue. It's like taking out an old cassette tape and putting in a new one. You can seize control of your thoughts and change your behaviors by giving yourself new messages.

With hypnosis, much of what we are doing is undoing old habit patterns, old perceptions—and beginning new habit patterns and creating new perceptions. It changes the lens through which we view the world. More importantly, we are creating a new relationship with ourselves.

So how do you create a new relationship with yourself using hypnosis? It's a return to consciousness—mindfulness. The return to consciousness is allowing yourself to experience both the pain and the joy in life.

It is to really be alive: to love and to fear.

None of us lives in a sterile world. Even with our best intentions and best efforts, we slip into old trances, old patterns of behaviors, back into unconsciousness. Life is a tapestry of trances, but most of us are letting everything and everyone else choose the colors and pattern in the tapestry and then we complain about what we create.

"Life is a web of trances, ranging from light to the deep."
~Adam Crabtree

In *Trance Zero*, Adam Crabtree writes, "Traditionally, the phenomenon of trance has been associated with a special state called hypnosis. There is no basis for believing that these phenomena are limited to this special trance state. We all have the capacity to produce these phenomena, and we can experience any of them at any moment in our everyday existence. So, as it turns out, the phenomena of trance are simply the phenomena of life."

Crabtree believes that we are constantly going in and out of trances of various kinds, and he further states that "Life is a web of trances, ranging from light to the deep."

With hypnosis, you are always in control, even though it appears that you are giving up control.

What you are really doing is shifting control from the conscious level to another part of yourself, allowing the conscious mind and the subconscious mind to work together. Working together, powerful results may be attained. The conscious mind was formed to deal with life in the world and puts practical focus on the present moment with immediacy and urgency. The subconscious mind concentrates on the inner world and is aware of the whole range of inner experiences.

With hypnosis (all hypnosis is self-hypnosis), you are exercising control over yourself. Hypnosis is a path to a destination. Your focus simply changes from the conscious to the subconscious world. The conscious mind deals with rationality and determination. Reason dominates conscious experiences and willpower provides the force to get things done.

Hypnosis is not power over another person.

Just making a conscious decision to change is not enough. Willpower only goes so far. Dr. Shelley Stockwell, describes it this way: "Thought, behavior, and emotion originate in the subconscious mind. If you ask your conscious mind to change a pattern that has its origin in the subconscious mind, it's a little like calling in a plumber to fix your electricity."

Your subconscious mind's world is very real. Its realities have a quality of presence and vividness every bit as insistent as that of the physical objects and people of the conscious world. In fact, the subconscious reality often seems more real than that of the conscious world. For example, in my 20s I was a college graduate, president of corporations and employer of 100 people, yet I was living my life as not good enough, not capable enough. Regardless of my real world, my inner-world reality was *not good enough.*

And though with hypnosis you are exerting control over yourself, hypnosis is not power over another person. It is a complex interaction, a cooperative act between the hypnotherapist and the client. It is two people cooperating for a mutual end, which is to establish better communication with the unconscious mind. The hypnotherapist is just the facilitator. Only you can hypnotize yourself. Hypnosis is not a "do to" process, rather, it is a "do with" process. **Hypnosis is the induction of a profound change in your state of consciousness through a cooperative flow of energy and ideas.**

You are always in control. All hypnosis is self-hypnosis.

A client in hypnosis will not:
1. do anything he would not normally do while awake
2. do anything that violates a moral or ethical issue for him
3. do anything outside the context of the hypnosis session. That is, if you are working on food issues, you won't suddenly decide to quit your job or end your marriage.

Myth Breakers:
* Hypnosis is not sleep.
* You are totally aware of everything.
* You're in complete control.
* You cannot be made to do anything.
* All hypnosis is self-hypnosis.

What the mind accepts, the body carries out

Your hypnosis sessions can be enjoyed by listening to the companion CDs, and by using the Light Switch Technique tracks. For maximum effectiveness, the Slender For Life™ system uses both passive and active approaches to self-hypnosis.

As you participate in your hypnosis sessions you will feel very relaxed. Your hypnotic experience will be unique to you. Clients describe their hypnosis sessions as vacations, meditations and pure relaxation. The relaxed state that you ultimately achieve may feel like you were awake in a dream. In this state you may experience different physical sensations that are quite normal and are associated with deep relaxation. These feelings may include heaviness in different parts of your body, tingling in your hands, face or toes, a light or floating sensation, a feeling of detachment, and sometimes, involuntary muscle twitches. Sometimes clients describe feeling loose and limp, and sometimes they describe warm, tingly sensations. For me, it's a trip to a Maui beach.

Do not be alarmed if you feel these sensations. Just let them be an indicator of feeling relaxed.

Ben—whose old downfall was restaurant food—found it easy to learn the techniques and has become a big fan. "Self-hypnosis and relaxation are great skills to have in general. Using this program of self-hypnosis, the weight comes off almost effortlessly, yet slowly enough to be safe. You can eat anywhere with confidence that you can make the best choices for yourself. And you don't have to clean your plate!"

Importance of attitude

So that you receive all the wonderful benefits from your hypnosis sessions, you should have a positive attitude and a willingness to accept responsibility for your outcome. Your attitude absolutely contributes to your success in this program.

Your attitude absolutely affects your success in this program.

It's important to remind you that hypnosis will not *make* you do anything. If you are in conflict or indifferent during your hypnosis session, hypnotic suggestions will tend to lose their effectiveness.

At the end of a weight loss consultation, I frequently hear, "I guess I will give this a try." In *Star Wars*, Yoda told Luke Skywalker that "There is no try…do or do not." Goals that we "try" to achieve in life usually end up in failure. The attitude behind the word "try" often translates into failure in our subconscious mind.

The right attitude is one of positive belief and expectation. When you are listening to hypnotic suggestions for change, you want to create and maintain the positive attitude of: "I want that. That's for me. I know that it works!"

By doing this, you get to be empowered, rather than a victim of your circumstances. I often get the impression that people are waiting for me to wave my magic wand and fix them. (While I do have a Mickey Mouse Magic Wand, it's good only for laughs.) When you approach your hypnotic sessions with a positive attitude, then you are empowered to get the results that you want in your life.

CD NOTE

It's as simple as flipping a switch

Your next step with the Slender For Life™ System is to master the art of self-hypnosis. Using your CD (if you purchased the complete package—otherwise you can learn it from reading this chapter and by going to **www.hypnosishealthinfo.com** and clicking on Self-hypnosis and Light Switch in the orange menu bar) where you'll learn how to use hypnosis by imagining turning off a light switch. After you feel comfortable using this technique, you can begin giving yourself hypnotic suggestions.

web extra

Many of my clients believe that learning and practicing this technique to eliminate their mental blocks and change their eating habits is one of the most empowering parts of this program.

On the CDs you will be guided into a relaxing state of hypnosis and taught how to create a visualization, or mental image of a light switch. As you listen to the CDs, just pretend or imagine what is being discussed. Don't try to make anything happen. Your mental attitude should be one of positive expectation and allowing the process to unfold naturally.

Let me explain the difference between the three light switch tracks. The first one ("Learning") explains how it works. The second track ("Using") guides you through it, and the third track ("Practicing") gets you started and doing it on your own. After you have completed the tracks Learning the Light Switch Technique and Using the Light Switch Technique, continue with Practicing the Light Switch Technique, which shows you how to practice your self-hypnosis technique and subjectively measure your results. Now this is important. Everything you achieve is enhanced and developed further each time you practice the technique. Do not become discouraged. Nobody does this perfectly in the beginning. Have fun with it and enjoy the relaxation.

The one-minute exercise you learn on Practicing the Light Switch Technique is the foundation of the technique. Practice it every chance you get. If you do it five times throughout your day, that's only five minutes. Also, once a day for the first week of practicing the one-minute light switch technique, listen to the track Self-Hypnosis Deepening.

This track guides you in deepening your level of relaxation. You are in effect, programming your subconscious mind to enter a profound state of deep relaxation, and one of the deepest states of hypnosis. Following these instructions conditions your mind to enter this state at

You are in effect, program-ming your subcon-scious mind to enter a profound state of deep relaxation.

will—simply by closing your eyes and imagining turning off your light switch. In this relaxed state, any tension, fear or anxiety is tremendously reduced and more than likely will disappear completely.

Once you have become comfortable and consistent with entering this beautiful state of relaxation, you are ready to begin giving yourself hypnotic suggestions and using the Power Minutes which are found in the orange menu bar at **www.hypnosishealthinfo.com**. (Hover the cursor over Self-hypnosis and Power Minutes will drop down).

web extra

The possibilities are endless

You now have the means to unlock your potential in almost any personal endeavor.

Write your hypnotic suggestion on a small card or piece of paper. Read your statement over at least five times, then drop the card, close your eyes, and turn off your light switch. The mental image, affirmation or positive statement for a new behavior is absorbed deep within your subconscious mind. Detailed instructions on how to do this are on the following pages.

You now have the means to unlock your potential in almost any personal endeavor. Using hypnosis you can take strokes off your golf game, improve your concentration and memory, enhance sports or work performance, stop smoking or eliminate any bad habit, increase sales performance, improve relationships and interpersonal corporate communications. And of course, you will use your new skill to become slender by creating new attitudes and habits around food and exercise.

SELF-HYPNOSIS INSTRUCTIONS

Basic Method

You can't simultaneously read these instructions and do these techniques, so these written instructions are provided as a reinforcement of the audio instructions. (If you don't have the CD set, you may listen to these instructions here: **www.hypnosishealthinfo.com/self-hypnosis** .) With the CDs, be sure to begin studying self-hypnosis with the track "Learning the Light Switch Technique." (You can also go to

web extra

www.hypnosishealthinfo.com and click on Self-Hypnosis and then Light Switch in the orange menu bar.)

1. Place yourself in a SAFE and COMFORTABLE position.
2. GIVE YOURSELF A TIME LIMIT (one minute).
3. Raise and lower your index finger. When your finger touches whatever it is resting on, close your eyes and drop into a deep state of hypnosis. TURN YOUR LIGHT SWITCH OFF.
4. While you are in hypnosis DO NOT THINK ABOUT THE TIME. Your subconscious mind does that for you.
5. Emerge when you have the feeling that your time is up.

Light switch technique

Let's begin by practicing just getting into trance. First, you are going to look at your watch, a clock, your computer or your cell phone and note the time both in minutes and in seconds. Learn to use hypnosis in one minute. You can take several one-minute periods throughout your day. Most of us would struggle to find time for one fifteen-minute session, let alone several fifteen-minute sessions. If you've ever had the experience of waking up just before your alarm clock goes off, it's the same thing. Ask your subconscious mind to let you know when a minute is up.

Imagine going down an endless staircase of relaxation.

Then imagine that your finger is a light switch that magically controls all the muscles in your body. You and you alone control your light switch. No one else can turn you on or off. Only you can do that. When it is off, do not move. If you want to scratch an itch or answer the phone, simply turn your light switch back on.

When you are comfortably seated, raise your index finger and when you are ready, close your eyes, lower your finger and shut off your light switch. (I suggest using your index finger to represent your light switch. You may choose to use a different finger, your whole arm, or tap your foot—just use some physical signal.)

Upon shutting off your light switch, imagine an endless staircase of relaxation. Imagine that as you descend these stairs, each step down takes you deeper, deeper, 100 times more deeply relaxed.

Go to your favorite, relaxing place. For me it is Paipu Beach on Maui. I can feel the straw mat under my back and the heat of the sand coming up through that mat and the heat of the sun on my body. I hear the cardinals in the bushes behind me, the coconut leaves rustling in the breeze and the waves crashing. I smell the sweet scent of plumeria mixed with the salt air, and I am quickly very deeply relaxed. Do this for one minute. For our purpose a minute is roughly 55 to 65 seconds. (Don't get hung up on exact timing.)

You do not need to climb back up the stairs, but you do need to turn your switch back on as you open your eyes. Don't worry about your thoughts or where your mind goes at this stage. This is not meditation, where you are trying to eliminate mind chatter. Later, when you add suggestions, your mind will have something to focus on. But for now, just experience being in your favorite place.

When your subconscious mind lets you know a minute is up, turn on your light switch and see how close to a minute you came. Like all skills, the more you practice, the better you become.

Connect your self-hypnosis with activities you do every day.

Practice self-hypnosis five times a day every day

You need reminders and you need to anchor or hook this to other activities that you are already doing. Great anchors are brushing your teeth, putting your watch on in the morning and taking it off at night, a morning snack, lunch, an afternoon snack and bedtime teeth brushing. Connect your self-hypnosis to activities you do every day. If you hook it to going to work, you will do it Monday through Friday, but then miss the weekend.

If you're the sort of person whose best intentions vanish into your daily tasks, then you might want to make one self-hypnosis minute mandatory as your very first action each day. That way you know you've gotten you day off to a great start. If you are working on eating suggestions, doing your light switch technique right before each meal can be effective in keeping your eating plan front and center in your thoughts.

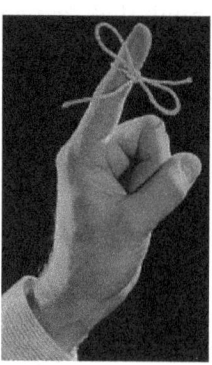

Create reminders. Sticky notes work great. I kept sticky notes in my Franklin Planner for two years before I realized I was doing it on my own. Don't expect to retain this as a new behavior in just a few days or even weeks. One of the best reminder ideas I've heard from my clients is to put a sticky note for each hypnosis minute on the left side of your bathroom mirror and/or your computer monitor. Throughout the day as you do your self-hypnosis, move one note to the right side of your mirror or computer monitor. Some women use hoop bracelets. They will have five on one wrist at the beginning of the day and by the end of the day they are on the other wrist. Other possibilities are five buttons in a pocket or five pebbles on one side of your desk that you move to the other side. **The bottom line is, find a reminder system that will work for you.**

Be sure to practice your light switch technique in loud noisy places such as riding the bus, sitting in Starbucks or by turning on the TV and radio at the same time at home. (It's okay to close your eyes in public. No one will notice, and if they do, they won't care!) If you can only do this in a quiet place with soft music in a comfortable chair, then it's not a functional tool. You want to be able to use self-hypnosis at work or in an airport. Sometimes the only place you can find to use your light switch is while sitting on the toilet—and I hear from moms with young children they may not even get to do that alone!

I recommend to my clients that they practice their light switch technique for seven days before adding in suggestions.

Be sure to practice your light switch technique in loud noisy places.

SELF-HYPNOSIS
Hypnotic Suggestions and Imagery

You should now be able to enter into hypnosis entirely by yourself. The next step is to formulate your own hypnotic suggestions. There are several important points you should consider before beginning.

Tips for creating suggestions

1. Keep suggestions short and concise.
2. Use only positive words. Do not use "no," "not," "don't," etc. (Your subconscious mind does not grasp a negative qualifier and you might get the opposite result.) Focus on what you do want. Never: "I don't crave chocolate." Instead, "Fruit is my snack of choice."
3. Keep vocabulary simple. A 6-year-old child should be able to understand it.
4. Practice using "I" statements, "You" statements and "He/She" statements and see what works best for you. For example: I feel my body becoming healthier every day; You are enjoying eating foods that promote weight release; She keeps her promises to herself about healthy eating.
5. Use only two or three suggestions per session when using the light switch technique.
6. Use only present tense words. Never use "will," "want to," "going to" or "like to".
7. Use action words such as "enjoy," "love," or "desire."

Examples
· I love and enjoy exercise.
· Exercise is my favorite activity of the day.
· As a result of my exercise, I am calm, relaxed and have more energy.
· I love fruits, vegetables and whole grains.
· Fruit is my snack of choice.
· I only eat enough to meet my nutritional needs.
· It is okay for me to leave food on my plate.

· I drink six or more glasses of water each day.
· Water is my drink of choice.
· I am calm and relaxed.
· I sleep soundly and restfully throughout the night and I wake in the morning relaxed, refreshed and excited by the new day.

web extra

You may also want to go to **www.hypnosishealthinfo.com** and in the orange menu bar highlight Self-hypnosis and click on **Suggestions**.

Specificity

In the middle of a forest, there was a hunter who was suddenly confronted by a huge, hungry bear. In his fear, all attempts to shoot the bear were unsuccessful. Finally he turned and ran as fast as he could. The hunter ran and ran, until he ended up at the edge of a very steep cliff. His hopes were dim. Seeing no way out of his predicament, and with the bear closing in rather quickly, the hunter got down on his knees, opened his arms, and said, "Dear God! Please give this bear religion!"

The sky darkened and there was lightning in the air. Just a few feet short of the hunter, the bear came to an abrupt stop and glanced around, somewhat confused. Suddenly, the bear looked up into the sky and said, "Thank you, God, for this food I'm about to receive…"

The moral is, be careful what you ask for! Both in writing suggestions and in goal setting it's important to be specific in what you want and to make sure you really do want it.

In writing suggestions for self-hypnosis, you must be specific. If you used the suggestion: I create more abundance in my life, you may be intending financial abundance but your unconscious mind might start packing on more fat. So let's modify it to: I create more financial abundance in my life. The problem is still lack of specificity. Your unconscious mind is like a computer. It is only as smart as the operator, and it only does what you tell it. (And it does do what you tell it!) You might walk down the street, see a penny, reach down and pick it up, and the unconscious mind checks off having accomplished more financial abundance! It did exactly what you told it. A specific suggestion would be: I maintain a million dollars or more in my bank accounts. Now that's specific! Here are some more examples.

Too vague:
I eat good foods.
More specific:
I only desire to eat foods that I know contribute to my health.
Too vague:
I work out a lot.
More specific:
I enjoy at least 30 minutes of exercise every day.
Too vague:
I drink plenty of water.
More specific:
I enjoy drinking eight glasses of water every day.
Too vague:
I lose weight easily.
More specific:
I easily release at least two pounds of fat every week.

web extra

At **www.hypnosishealthinfo.com** in the orange menu bar you can again highlight **Self-hypnosis** and click on the last drop-down tab, **Hypnosis Suggestions.** Every daily suggestion I have used since 2008 is listed there for your use. Feel free to use them as they are written or modify them for your use. **The intent is that they give you ideas for wording your own suggestions.** Throughout this book you will also find suggestions for your use.

Be careful what you ask for— you may get it!

When setting goals, not only do you want to make sure the outcome is what you really want, you must also be willing to do what is required of you on the journey to that goal. A number of years ago I wanted to open four hypnosis offices. I already had two and thought I wanted two more, so I set out on the journey to open two new offices at the same time. Fortunately, I used self-hypnosis and "turned the clock" forward six months and then five years to view my life with four offices. I didn't like what I saw. When I looked at what I had to do and the things that I had to give up to open two new offices at once, I didn't like the pace I had to work at, the time removed from being at home with my family. When I looked five years ahead and saw the pitfalls of running four offices, I knew then that I was unwilling to achieve this goal. Too many times previously in my life I had gotten excited about a goal and achieved it, only to discover I didn't want it after all. Be careful what you ask for— you may get it!

HOW TO GIVE YOURSELF SUGGESTIONS

1. Write one to three suggestions on a piece of paper.
2. Place yourself in a SAFE and COMFORTABLE position.
3. GIVE YOURSELF A TIME LIMIT.
4. Hold suggestions in one hand and read them out loud or silently to yourself five times slowly, concentrating on each word.
5. When you begin to read your suggestion(s) for the fifth time, raise your index finger. When you read the last word of the suggestion, lower your finger and drop into a deep state of hypnosis. TURN YOUR LIGHT SWITCH OFF.
6. While in hypnosis, do not think about or try to direct the suggestion. Just relax. You may find the words of the suggestion floating around in your mind. They may be out of order. That's okay. Just stay relaxed. Focus on the OUTCOME. (You at your ideal weight, etc.).
7. Emerge when you feel your minute is up.

You may wish to use this alternative method:

For the first two weeks use only one suggestion per week. After the first week, you may change the suggestion and use this new suggestion for a full week.

For the third and fourth week you may give yourself a different suggestion every day, but not more than one suggestion per day.

CD NOTE

After the fourth week you may give yourself up to three suggestions each time. Occasionally listen to the Self-Hypnosis Deepening Track on your CDs to establish and maintain deeper levels of hypnosis.

Method for using
Self-Hypnosis Deepening

1. Get into a SAFE and COMFORTABLE position.
2. Press the PLAY button on your CD player.
3. Raise and lower your index finger. (DO NOT GIVE YOURSELF A TIME LIMIT. THE CD WILL BRING YOU OUT OF TRANCE.) TURN YOUR LIGHT SWITCH OFF. Drop into a deep state of hypnosis, and just follow the instructions on the CD.
4. The track, which lasts about 16 minutes, will guide you out of hypnosis at its completion.

Power Minutes

web extra

Power Minutes are 1 to 4 minute MP3 downloads available at **www.hypnosishealthinfo.com/self-hypnosis/freeaudio**. Power Minutes have become very popular, and even I am surprised how much I use them. Written Suggestions is a very active process. Sometimes it's nice to be more passive—just kick back and listen—but you don't have time for 27 minutes of Orange Blossom. Well now there's a 3-minute version of Orange Blossom. **Feel free to participate in the fun:** please email me your scripts for your own Power Minutes. I will tweak them, record them, send the recording to you and post it at Hypnosis Health Info for all to enjoy.

Now play with me for a moment.

Imagine you are making a movie about your life. The stage is filled with the various parts or aspects of yourself. At times, getting in and out of the director's chair is your scared, hurt young child aspect. At other times, the critical parent part of you is calling the shots. Or maybe a rebellious, angry or self-righteous part of you takes over. Imagine how chaotic this movie—or your life—would be with so many different parts of yourself fighting for control. Sometimes, all it takes is the scent of a favorite childhood food and instantaneously, you enter the trance associated with that experience—and an aspect of yourself who has no business directing your current life gets into the director's chair. Each of these aspects has its own agenda, and this play or movie can become a disaster.

With hypnosis, you are placing the loving, nurturing adult part of yourself in the director's chair. You are bringing the conscious and subconscious minds together, working for a common goal. Working together, creating a powerful movie where you can achieve what you want in your life. With hypnosis, we can do what Adam Crabtree describes as entering that state of being absorbed in whatever is appropriate at the moment, but with a readiness and ability to shift to another focus naturally as needed. We can be mindful in the moment—conscious. As he says, "In life we move from trance to trance, from focus to focus. This roving of attention can be random and chaotic, or it can be coordinated and meaningful."

"I have reached my goal weight, but more importantly, I have made slight mental changes through mindfulness."
~Janice

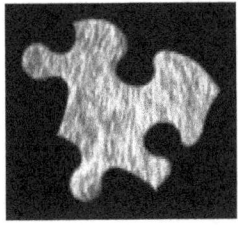

Janice says she has found the missing piece to her yo-yo puzzle and found peace in her heart by using this program. "I have reached my goal weight, but more importantly, I have made slight mental changes through mindfulness. Self-hypnosis is a great practice, and I learned to trust the trance. Good things will happen to you if you can let yourself go 'under' and 'open.'"

I tell my clients they can come see me once a week, every week, for the rest of their lives. Or, they can listen every day to the CDs I give them or become dependent on themselves. We are exposed daily to all sorts of hypnotic suggestions: to the baked goods in the coffee shop; to high-fat, high-sugar foods and large portions in restaurants; to birthday cakes, holiday foods and those McDonald's commercials on TV. We either choose the trance we are in, or we remain stuck in the 65 percent of the

population that is overweight. Self-hypnosis is the way to success and will make adopting and sticking to your healthy new lifestyle very doable.

But first we have to blast away some roadblocks. **In the next chapter we'll uncover—and eliminate—the excuses you've been giving yourself all these years.**

Smart Phone Apps

This is for all you smart phone users. On my iPhone I have a free app called **RxmindMe**. It is intended to be used to remind you to take your prescriptions. I don't take any medications, but it sure works great for reminders to use your Light Switch Self-hypnosis. I have it set up for 5 reminders per day; I call them Light Switch 1, Light Switch 2, etc.

The second app I use for the Light Switch is called **Awesome Note**. It's a note pad with folders you can color coordinate with different titles. My folders are titled: Exercise, Health, Business, Personal and Relationships. In each folder I create notes that contain my hypnotic suggestions. I write only one suggestion per note. So if the one-minute self-hypnosis I want to do is about long-distance training on my bike, then I'll select notes from the Exercise folder.

I didn't think that I would ever give up my color coded index cards, but my iPhone has changed all that. **I'm loving how easy this is to set up and to use. Give it a try.**

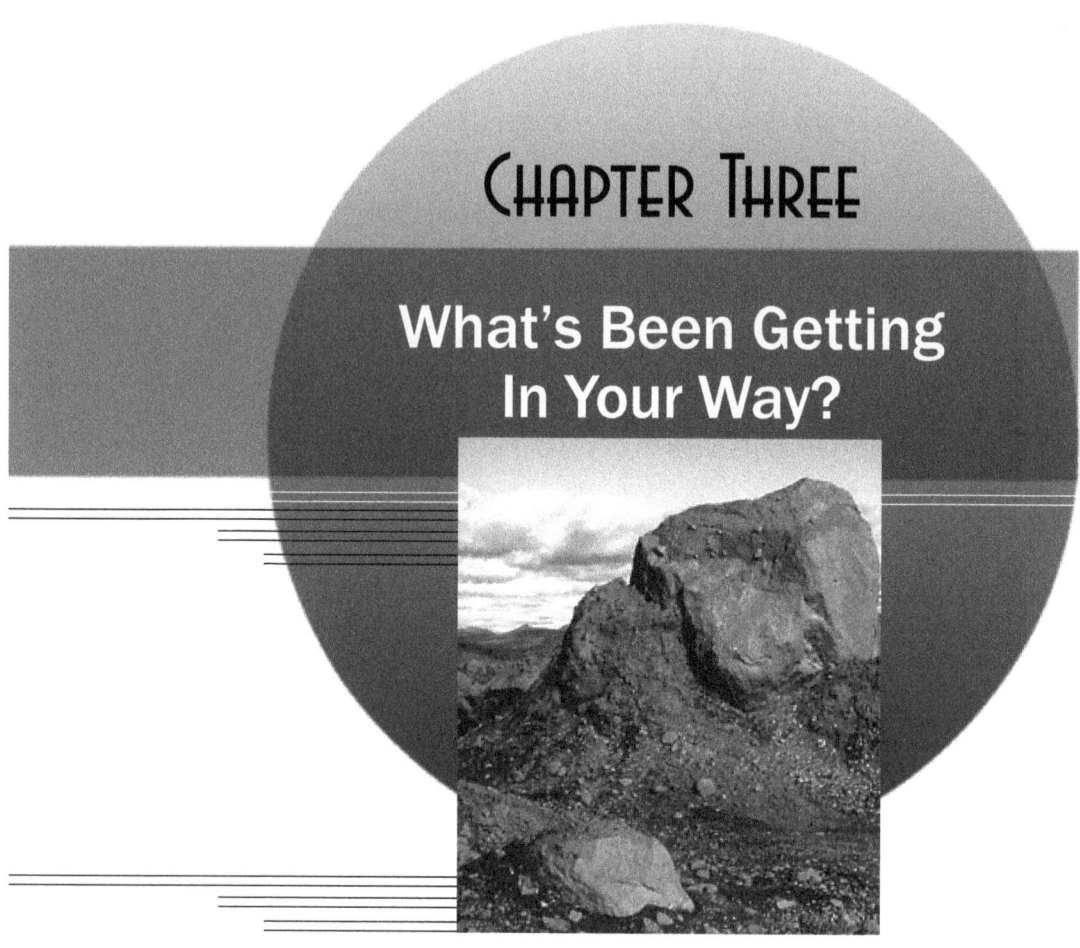

CHAPTER THREE

What's Been Getting In Your Way?

Chapter Three At A Glance
- Understanding the challenges of permanent weight loss
- Tackling the pain/pleasure problem
- Dealing with family and peer pressures
- Finding other ways to reward yourself
- Shutting down negative mind chatter
- See yourself slim
- Setting realistic goals
- Reveling in your imperfection
- Looking behind your protective layers
- Discovering your emotional motivators
- Hypnotic suggestions for eliminating roadblocks

Now that you've learned some self-hypnosis skills, it's time to put them to work confronting–and conquering–the roadblocks that have kept you from attaining and maintaining your ideal weight. You may be surprised at some of them. I'll get into some specific ones–and their solutions–in a bit, but first I want you to understand some general challenges that most of us are up against on this journey.

Your path to becoming slender for the rest of your life will be one of, if not the most, challenging journey of your life. It can also be one of the most rewarding experiences in your life. That's certainly been true for me.

In 1977 I studied chemical dependency at the Vern Johnson Institute and St. Mary's Hospital in Minneapolis. I was beginning my training to be a drug and alcohol counselor, though my career later took a different turn. While in this training, I began to think that I was an alcoholic. There were only two times in my life where I was actually drunk and overall I didn't drink very much, but I recognized in myself the feelings and behaviors of an addict. Confused and struggling for many years, I was later clinically diagnosed with depression. I never could adequately describe how I felt to therapists or to anyone else.

Today, I realize my addiction was not with alcohol, it was with food. Technically, food is not an addiction. With addictive behavior there is an element of choice in the development of the addictive behavior. But you have to eat food. You can't survive without food. It s a regulated form of behavior. The brain defends you from not eating. You cannot stop eating simply because you choose to stop eating–excepting those rare zealots who starve for a cause. You've got to continue to eat in order to survive. The brain protects you from starvation, and does it with remarkable resolve. Having said that,

I do treat weight loss as an addiction; in fact I consider it to be the most difficult of addictions to overcome.

I can send former smokers out the door after one session and they never smoke again. An alcoholic can stop drinking, attend Alcoholics Anonymous, and never drink again. Food was my drug of choice, but I don't have the luxury of never eating again. If losing weight was as simple as never eating again, weight loss programs would be out of business. But imagine telling a smoker that in order to survive he'll need to have three puffs on a cigarette every day. He'd be back to a pack or more a day in no time.

The pain of dieting

There s no getting around it—letting go of weight is apt to be a painful experience for those of us who used food as a drug. (Though using self-hypnosis techniques will make this journey easier, you are still apt to experience some emotional pain during the process.) In the past, when painful issues came up, we ate to numb out, to not feel, to feel what we wanted to feel or to fill a void. Marilyn put it this way: 'I was trying to get in control of my emotional state by getting in control of my eating, rather than my emotions.' When food is no longer used for emotional purposes, our issues are in our face. We have the opportunity to do the healing work and leave the weight of the pain—and the pain of the weight—behind. For some, it s just too painful, and they give up on the program and themselves and go back to self-medicating with food.

Since we chowed down our first wooly mammoth around the campfire, food has been an ingredient of social, holiday and religious customs throughout the world. Every mother has used food to nurture her children. We gather for meals and break bread together. But today, our attention often shifts to the food, and we forget the people we are eating with.

At least twice each day going to and from my office, I walk past an ice cream store. I have never been inside, but I have spent time standing outside watching the customers. I have been fascinated watching slender people sit in groups of two or more, often with a small cup of ice cream and several spoons. They look at each other, they are engrossed in conversation, and their ice cream is melting. Next to them, the overweight customers devour large portions of ice cream with lots of toppings. They are usually alone. If they are with someone, there is little to no conversation, and they're usually looking away from the person they're with–and there is no danger their ice cream will melt.

Too many of us are living to eat rather than eating to live.

Food should be pleasurable, it should taste good, it should be wonderfully presented and it should be fun. But too many of us are living to eat rather than eating to live. People today are suffering from mental, emotional and spiritual dis-eases of the heart, and often they re using food to stimulate those parts of the brain that are meant for relationships–talking, flirting and just being together. If foods can work on the very parts of our brain that are designed for warmth, friendship and love, no wonder loneliness leads to overeating, drinking or drug use. A vicious cycle develops; the more weight you carry, the less likely you are to be active. The less active you are, the more isolated and lonely you become. A bowl of rocky road ice cream becomes a quick and easy way of masking the loneliness.

One client wrote on her intake questionnaire that she loved having "parties in her mouth" and feared giving these up. Dis-eases of the heart come in all shapes, forms and disguises. Dieting is an uncomfortable experience in and of itself for most people, just as any change can be painful.

Then there are all the familiar rituals of food to reconsider. Stopping at Starbucks and getting the morning latte; indulging in that morning Krispy Kreme donut; lunch with friends at work; that trip for the Snickers bar in the afternoon; enjoying a glass of wine with cheese while preparing dinner; and the cookies late at night when everyone else is in bed and the house is finally quiet.

And few people want to be different from everyone else, so with 65 percent of us overweight, the norm is to eat as only kings and queens used to, which makes traditional dieting very hard to do. And then you add the physically addictive qualities of food to all the mental and emotional discomforts, and you can really have a tough road ahead.

It s not uncommon to have clients come in to their first or second session angry. Often they verbalize they re upset about the eating strategy, or they don't like something about our introductory kit. Sometimes this anger starts as soon as they make the decision to start the program. From time to time I overhear new clients creating all kinds of scheduling obstacles with office personnel or even tell us that it's up to us to call them the day before their sessions to remind them of their appointment. Well, guess what?

 Having to give up the way you've been eating can make you angry. Who wants to give up old eating habits? People want to eat what they want to eat, when they want to eat it.

Letting go of weight means changing many beliefs about who we are.

"Other people eat that way. Why can't I?" they ask. It's tough to be different when 65 percent of the American population is overweight.

So if losing weight is an uncomfortable experience, how do you imagine finally taking control? After losing 100 pounds, in the October 3, 2005 issue of Newsweek, Arkansas Governor Mike Huckabee revealed: "I knew that I was not living a healthy lifestyle, and I wanted to change it. But I'd lived this way a long time, and I didn't think I could change. People have to believe that the benefits of healthy behavior outweigh–no pun intended–whatever benefits they perceive in overeating and under exercising."

Yet letting go of weight is much more than just changing what and how much we eat. Letting go of weight means changing many beliefs about who we are, how we behave and what we look like. Letting go of weight means we can no longer hide. But there s no escaping pain. Choosing to be overweight means choosing the different sorts of pain that go with that and accepting that pain is your normal, permanent state.

What are you hiding behind?

After my Slender For Life clients completed their initial individual sessions, we used to do a weekly group session while they progressed toward their ideal weight goal. One week the scheduled topic was fat. I had my prepared notes. I had the hypnosis script ready to go. I was all set. One man, I'll call him Bill, was sharing his experience of recently being stuck in a pattern of up a pound or two, down a pound or two. I asked what that was all about. "I don't know," he responded, "I wish I knew." We had been there before. Bill had a pattern where he would drop three to five pounds, and then gain one or two pounds. He was down 59 pounds and had another 50 pounds to go. Often, his excuse was work-related stresses.

Then I asked about his identity, if he thought of himself as a 180-pound person or a 239-pound person. What unfolded was a captivating discussion about our false self and our authentic or real self. Bill believed that the excess weight was part of his identity, a part of who he was as a person. **Weight was used as an excuse to distance himself from his partner and to insulate himself from friends and family**–to keep them from getting too close. He used eating as an excuse to take a break at work and to self-medicate when stressed. **Bill used weight to keep from being the big V: VULNERABLE.**

We began to discuss the authentic self and this false self. With tears in their eyes, others in the group started sharing about rejecting their authentic self and even hating their authentic self just as they hated their body. Some stated that they had no understanding of their real self. Wanting to find a way to illustrate this concept, I drew a diagram on the white board. (See next page.)

We talked about hiding behind the weight and hiding behind false beliefs that we held to be true about ourselves. Embracing the authentic self was so foreign to what most of us were taught that it seemed wrong and even selfish.

A different kind of identity issue came up in a consultation with Robert, who is in his 70s. He told me that he was a former bodybuilder. As a younger man, he was big and strong; he felt powerful. He associated personal power and strength with size. Today he is no longer a body builder, nor is he physically strong. In fact, his excess weight had weakened him. He was big all right, but fat

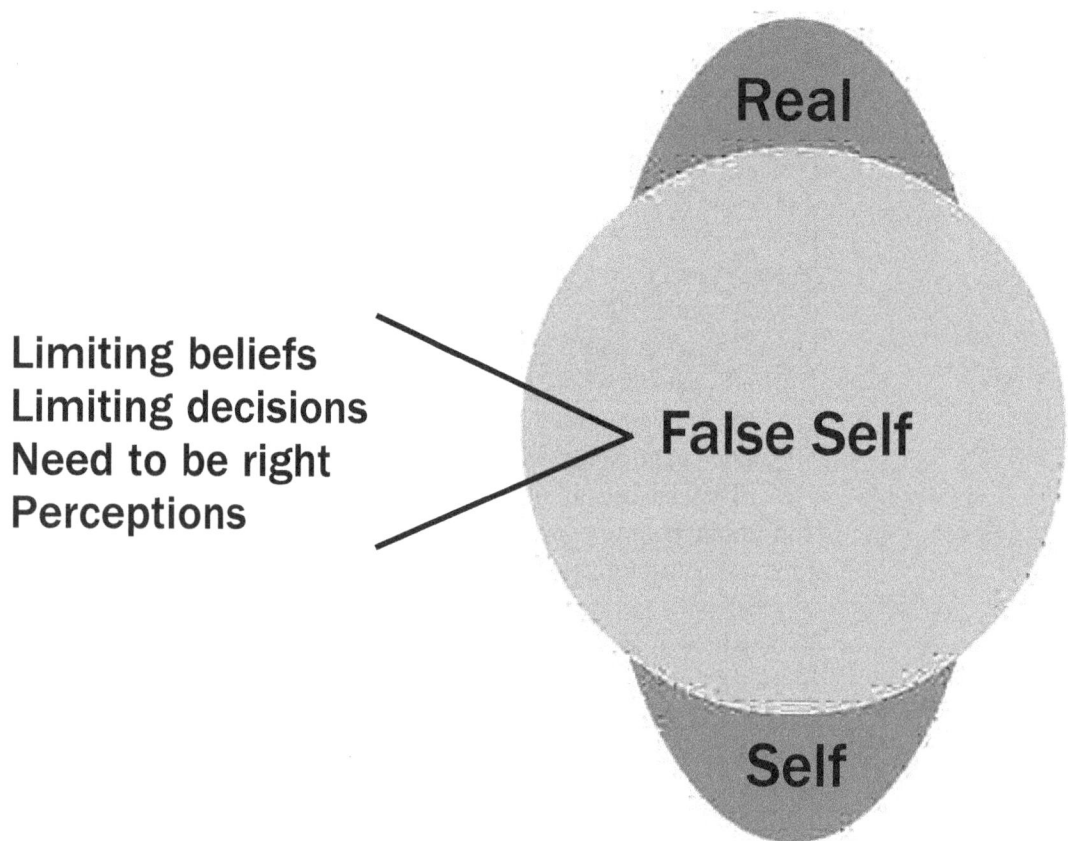

Limiting beliefs
Limiting decisions
Need to be right
Perceptions

Real

False Self

Self

had now replaced muscle. Robert's fear was that if he lost his excess weight, he would be small–which meant that he was weak. I am sorry to say that Robert chose not to do Slender For Life, his belief that being at a healthy weight meant that he would be weak was just too ingrained.

And then there is the issue of our family's and friends' perception of us. When we as individuals begin to change, we are no longer what our family and friends believe us to be. And when we don't meet their expectations, that alters their understanding of the world, and they often don't like that. They want us to be who they think we are, and they'll work hard at keeping us as they think we are. It s just like crabs in the crab pot: one crab starts to climb out, and the others pull it back in. Being who we truly are is challenging and often risky. Some may ask: Who do we think we are to believe

The uncon- scious mind is like my office computer. It s powerful and yet it s an idiot.

that we have the right to make choices and to believe we are worthy? The reality is: Who are we not to be worthy? As Nelson Mandela said, "It is our light that frightens us."

I pointed out to the group that of course there is another issue. The unconscious mind is very powerful. It creates exactly what we believe to be true; holding on to the perceptions we discussed in Chapter Two. If we believe that we are unworthy, the unconscious mind will deliver unworthiness. The unconscious mind is like my office computer. It's powerful and yet it's an idiot. My computer is only as smart as the operator, which has certainly been the bane of numerous tech support people I've called for help over the years. Often I can't get my computer to do what I want it to do, because I don't know how to do it! It's that old cassette tape I mentioned earlier playing the same old song. Until we change what we believe to be true, we will continue to create the false self.

In hypnosis, I ask clients to imagine an infinite source of love, healing and light above them that shines into their heart, moves to their brain, and then moves through every cell of their body, illuminating all the darkness within them. It's as if they've been wandering around in a dark scary cavern all these years, tripping over unseen, frightening objects. Then one day, they discover a light switch and they realize that this is not a dark scary cavern, but a beautiful cathedral filled with all the gifts, talents and resources they need for this lifetime. Everything they need is within them.

journal exercise

What cave have you been in?

Now ask yourself:

- How have your own self-limiting beliefs kept you from your true self?
- What aspects of your true self have yet to find expression?
- What does your true self know about you that others don't?
- What hidden talents or gifts would you like to share with others?

_____

_____

_____

_____

_____

_____

_____

_____

The answers are all in there

So what can you do about the dis-eases of the heart, the mental and emotional discomfort that drives people to sugar and fat? You need to make a choice. You can either do what everyone else does and continue putting on the weight, or step out of the multitude and start living differently. The key is to step out of the pack without anyone knowing it.

> Changing your relationship with yourself and with food is a gift you are giving yourself.

If you're lucky, there are two, maybe three people in this world who will truly support you. For most of your family and friends, it is none of their business–so don't tell them! You do not need anyone telling you that one fried chicken dinner won't hurt you.

I remember when I was in my 20s my wife and I went to Iowa to visit my grandmother and my great aunt. I had lost about 30 pounds (I was still significantly heavier than I am now). My great aunt took one look at me and tore into my wife, accusing her of not feeding me and not taking care of me. Her tirade was followed with a meal of pig's feet, beans and fresh homemade white bread. Sad to say, after that experience I very quickly put on more than 30 pounds.

Families can be roadblocks, and now we'll look at the most common ones people face on this path to becoming slender for life. The good news is–each one comes with ways to leap right over it.

There are better rewards than food

Food is often used as a way of rewarding yourself for a job well done. Whether it's completing a big project at work or just scrubbing the toilet, many people use food as a special treat. On your journey to becoming slender for life, it's essential that both long-term and short-term rewards be developed that are safe, healthy and ecological on all levels. Trading food rewards for maxing out your Visa card or gambling online are not safe, healthy and ecological.

Solution to using food as a reward:

Rewards can be surprisingly simple, such as leaving your desk and walking to the water fountain, going for a stroll around the office building, enjoying the ritual of making hot tea, or curling up with your dog and a good book. Immediate rewards such as a cup of tea are more useful than long-term rewards. Seeing yourself looking great a year from now at your ideal weight in your new bathing suit on a white sand Maui beach is a great long-term reward. But when the stuff is hitting the fan, that Snickers bar will win out over that fantasy of the beach every time.

journal exercise

How have you used food as a reward?

Recall some instances when you used food as a reward. See if a pattern develops. Are there certain situations where you are most apt to crave a food reward? They are likely to be times when you are emotionally aroused. Having a confrontation with a demanding boss is much more likely to trigger a desire for food rewards than simply cleaning your house.

Now make a list of typical events that trigger your need for food rewards, leaving space to write after each one. When you are done, after each event write a new kind of reward that would be more appropriate than food. For example, holding your ground with your boss and not acting like a doormat might get rewarded with a weeknight outing to a movie, or perhaps a trip to the bookstore to browse for something on self-empowerment, or maybe you'd rather have a massage. The key is to match the reward to the level of achievement. Only you know what that is for you.

_____

_____

_____

_____

_____

_____

_____

_____

_____

_____

_____

Then, keep this list in mind the next time you catch yourself thinking about a food reward, and enjoy a healthier alternative instead.

Andrea was working on her self-esteem issues and came up with a fun reward system that emphasized the new self-empowerment she felt. "Being a very visual person, I wanted to honor important benchmarks in my progress with something tangible–to replace the chocolate cakes I used to bake for myself. So I decided to buy a long gold chain necklace that I'd wear every day and add small heart charms for every accomplishment. Each charm was different and had some connection to the achievement. Some had tiny gemstones and others engraved words. For a weight-loss milestone I added a diamond heart. I can wear this necklace under my clothes so no one has to know–or ask me to explain it. The heart charms rest right above my own heart as a constant reminder of my progress. I have so much fun shopping for each new addition to my necklace, that I totally forget about the chocolate cake I'm not eating!"

Silencing negative chatter

Think about a time in the recent past when you either ate too much or you gained weight, and try to recall your self-talk. For instance: *What's the matter with you? You're no good. You'll never be successful at losing weight. You can't keep any commitments.* Negative self-talk is trance. Now, remember, Dr. Candace Pert has shown us that all thought, all memory, all emotion occurs and is stored in every cell of our body. What we are working with is cellular memory. It is very real to you.

Margaret was talking about the voice in her head that was telling her: "This is too hard... you will never be successful." For Stan is was: "I've failed at every weight loss attempt I've ever made, why should this be any different?" And Sue had been hearing the same refrain her entire life: "You'll never look like your sister, you'll never be as pretty and as thin as she is."

We all have mind chatter and too often it is negative.

We all have mind chatter and too often it is negative. Fortunately there are tools for working with this chatter.

Solution to negative chatter: bring to mind your negative chatter.

Is it your voice or someone else's? Now take this chatter and turn it into a cartoon character like Daffy Duck, a Teletubby, Bugs Bunny, Porky Pig or Olive Oil. What happens to the power of that chatter? It becomes comical, doesn't it? Now bring it back again in its original voice, get it running in your head and then imagine it emanating from your big toe. Again, the power diminishes. Finally, bring it back one more time in its original voice, get it running and then shrink it down to the size of a postage stamp. If you are right-handed, place it in the far left hand corner of the room on the floor. (Left-handed people place it in the far right hand corner of the room on the floor).

What happened? It's gone, isn't it?

All three of these techniques are Neuro-linguistic Programming (NLP) techniques. They are

Just as you need to become more conscious of what you eat, you need to become more conscious of what you think.

powerful interrupters to get you out of the negative trance of that chatter. And yes, when you are in that chatter, you are in a trance. Is your alarm clock a pleasant sound? Mine isn't! How about the smoke detectors in you home? Mine are loud and obnoxious. Alarm clocks and smoke detectors are wakeup calls, attention getters. You need to break that trance just as an alarm clock shatters your sleep. You need to create a call to a different action.

As I said before, one of the chatters that ran my life was "Not good enough, Roger." No matter what I did, it was never enough. It would get so that I would stop trying to do things because I kept raising the bar, and I could never be successful. To this day, there is not a day that goes by that I do not hear "Not good enough, Roger." But where it used to be an anchor, it's now a friend—it's my wakeup call, a call to action. The message now is "Stop coasting, Roger, be your best. Be enough."

What is the opposite or positive statement that can be created from your negative chatter? For example, if you typically tell yourself: "I can't win…every time I try something new I fail," then the next time you start to run that tape, replace it with a positive counter statement. Such as: "I am a winner…I have wonderful ideas that produce great results." Or, if you say to yourself: "Why bother with dieting…I always regain the pounds I've lost," think instead: "I now have the tools and ability to permanently release my excess weight."

The key is to learn to monitor your thoughts so you catch these insidious negative thoughts before they become further ingrained in your subconscious.

Just as you need to become more conscious of what you eat, you need to become more conscious of what you think. **So fill out the chart on the next page and refer to it often, until you master the skill of monitoring—and replacing—your negative mind chatter.** Some of your positive replacements may make good hypnotic suggestions, and/or you may want to carry an index card with them in your pocket or purse. Some people like to post these positive affirmations where they can be reminded of them throughout the day.

Negative thought	Positive replacement

Ten-minute exercise

Here's a slightly different approach to try. When critical thoughts are running through your mind, for ten minutes write the opposite of every negative thought as fast as you can. It's okay to repeat the same opposite message. If the thoughts are: "I am a failure" and "I am a fat slob," then write: "I am succeeding at releasing this weight" and "I am slender, trim, healthy, and I look fabulous!"

You can take control of your life

The reality is, no one else is telling you what or how much food to put in your mouth.

Clients regularly tell me that they "know it all" when it comes to nutrition. They've read every book and tried every diet and have still failed to keep the weight off. Their knowledge of what they should do, coupled with the many past failures makes it almost impossible to believe they could ever be in control of what they eat, how much they eat and ultimately, their weight. There is often fear of "one more failure." I've had people leave a consultation in tears without starting Slender for Life™ because they do not have the strength to endure one more failure. For some, not trying is far less painful than one more potential failure.

This lack of belief in your ability to be in control can be an impetus for failure. It's almost as if some people are waiting for failure to happen or looking for an excuse to fail. People who don't believe they can be in control tend to give up on themselves easily.

Solution to feeling out of control:
One of the hypnotic suggestions I use is: "You are the one in control of what you eat, how much you eat, and ultimately your weight." The reality is, no one else is telling you what or how much food to put into your mouth. **The means to seize control is self-hypnosis.** As I've said, I believe that hypnosis is learning to be in control of the trance you are in. By starting out each day with suggestions like the following ones, you have an excellent chance of learning to control your behavior.

- I am present and conscious in my body throughout the day.
- I am in control of what I eat, how much I eat, and ultimately my weight.
- This time I am changing my life for the better, and I succeed at creating a healthy body.

CD NOTE

In order to succeed in anything in life, it is necessary to first have confidence and belief that you can and will succeed. The CDs contain tracks that have been carefully created to increase your self-confidence to provide an amazing level of inner control, as well as melt away the dis-eases of the heart and improve your long-term success. See the Emotion Trigger Track. (CD #4 tracks 2 & 3.)

Can you see yourself slender?

It's difficult to be committed to something you can't even imagine. If you had difficulty in Chapter One visualizing yourself slender, then that can also be a kind of roadblock to your success. Here's a tip to try. Prior to releasing my own excess weight as an adult, the last time I weighed my current weight was in grade school. I had no clue what I would look like at 150–155 pounds. That was unimaginable to me. When I envisioned myself, it was with 100 extra pounds.

Solution to lacking a clear image:
So that I could begin to create an image in my mind's eye of

myself at my ideal weight, I finally found a photo of a man in an underwear ad that was about my height and frame size. I put that photo on my bathroom mirror so I could focus on that image of myself every time I brushed my teeth. You can do all sorts of creative things with your images: make a treasure map, a dream board or a collage. Use images from magazines, or even better, old pictures of yourself at your goal weight if you have them, or you can Photoshop yourself thin on your computer!

There is no way to diet perfectly

Some people try to diet perfectly and want a specific diet plan to follow. They want to get out their food scales, their measuring cups and start counting calories and grams of fat. The ultimate result of perfectionism is failure.

There is no way of dieting perfectly. There is no way to follow any eating strategy perfectly. Give it up. It can't be done.

You just do the best you can. Even when you try to make healthy choices, you can't count on what will be served when eating out. I've avoided dairy products for years and have gotten pretty good at easily ordering in a restaurant. Once on a road trip my wife and I stopped for lunch. I ordered a fake-egg, cheese-less veggie omelet—but it was served to me with hollandaise sauce slathered all over the top of it! I have ordered pasta with tomato sauce and veggies, only to discover there was cream in the tomato sauce. I have even ordered a veggie wrap with "no cheese and no dairy" and my first bite was a mouthful of sour cream. When I walked back to the counter, the young girl who took my order replied: "But that's just sour cream." Apparently she didn't know sour cream is a dairy product! So you learn to scrape off what you don't want and you move on.

Many of my clients are nurses. I have the greatest respect and admiration for nurses. They work long hard hours, often in hospital units that are understaffed. They seldom get a bathroom break and meal breaks are often impossible to take. When it comes to dieting, nurses are some of the most difficult perfectionists to work with. Of course, one of their skills and strengths is perfectionism. Perfectionism is essential to their job. They must be exacting in which patient they are administering medications to, giving the right medication and correct dosage. But when they turn their perfectionism on themselves, it bites them on the backside.

None of us is perfect, and we need to get over it.

Joan's story goes something like this: It's the fourth work day of the week, she put in several hours of overtime the previous three days and today is looking no different. She's tired, has had no time with her family and little sleep. She's been on her feet for hours; she is seriously hungry and hasn't had the opportunity to take a lunch break. There are M & M's and an open bag of chips at the nurse's station, so as she runs by, she grabs a handful of each. Though she's only been a Slender For Life™ client just over a week, her sense of failure is overwhelming. Since she feels she's blown the day, she gives up and eats whatever is easily available. "What's the use? I will never be successful with weight loss anyway," she rationalizes to herself.

In her next session we discussed her perfectionism and the places in her life where it served her and the places it did not. Over the following weeks, Joan became more loving and accepting of herself and she treated herself—and her body—with love, dignity and respect. She created a new relationship with herself, one that allowed her to obtain her ideal weight and one that allows her to maintain her ideal weight to this day.

None of us is perfect, and we need to get over it. The real challenge, certainly, is learning to love ourselves and to forgive ourselves.

Another way perfectionism sabotages us is when we set goals that are unattainable. A mental attitude of creating unreasonable and impractical expectations for yourself in both your weight release results and in any kind of program you may use or join, will only lead to heartbreak. At the first indication of not living up to your high perfectionist ideals, you may be ready to quit. Since it's impossible for anyone to do this or any other weight release program perfectly, it's unlikely you will be the first!

Solution for perfectionism:
Realistic, attainable goals are crucial for weight release success. Focusing on letting go of two pounds this next week is so much more imaginable than shedding 50 or 100 pounds. Exercising three or four times a week is doable, and anything more than that is a bonus. For most people, a goal of daily exercise, while beneficial, is a setup for failure.

journal exercise

Nobody's perfect–not even you!

If bells are going off in your mind telling you that this is one of your issues, **try journaling about your desires for perfection**. Ask yourself what happens when you are less than perfect—which, let's face it—has to be all the time! Ask yourself why you're so hard on yourself. Wouldn't it be nice to be more gentle with yourself by setting realistic, attainable goals? That way you can experience the joy of meeting them and end the punishing cycle of perfectionism.

_____

_____

_____

_____

_____

_____

_____

_____

_____

You may want to first try setting realistic goals for something less emotionally charged than weight loss. For example, if you've always been the kind of person who has to have her home in spotless order at all times, experiment with more flexibility around cleaning schedules. I promise you, the sun will still come up tomorrow even if you go to bed with dirty dishes in your sink. Once you learn to relax around other aspects of your life—and enjoy all the free time that creates!—try being less demanding of yourself when it comes to your eating program. It doesn't have to be a pass/fail situation. You can do well for a week, then slip up a bit one day and still make overall progress. You will never attain perfection, so you might as well stop trying right now.

95% Focus on the progress you are making and not perfection. Ninety-five percent perfect is good enough. Always have a plan to get back on track should you ever catch yourself deviating from your eating and exercise strategy. Forgive yourself if you slip up.

Stop Judging Yourself

My take on forgiveness is to not focus on the act, but on the judgments we hold about the act. Too often I hear forgiveness described as a sort of fairy tale about an incident—making it okay that we just ate a whole package of Oreos. But it isn't okay and it will never be okay. Still, we don't need to judge ourselves for it either. I encourage clients to leave their whips with me in my office. They don't need them anymore.

Rosalie and I were talking one afternoon about forgiveness. This 50-year-old woman carried a great deal of guilt and self-judgment about her actions and choices that she'd made as a teenager and as a young woman in her 20s.

She also talked about her father and his behavior toward her as a child growing up. We discussed how forgiveness too often comes across as making actions okay, that what happened was okay, when it really wasn't. Or forgiveness may turn into creating a fairy tale about the past. Or else it appears as if you're rewriting history to exclude what really happened. If you were abused as a child, how do you forgive the abuser? Somehow, "I forgive you for abusing me" doesn't seem very authentic. And if you've just eaten the entire pint of Ben & Jerry's, it is difficult to make that okay.

> By letting go of the judgment we free ourselves from the continued abuse of the action.

Solution for self-judgment:

I suggested to Rosalie that forgiveness should be focused on her, that is was time to stop punishing herself for things she did 30 years ago. Self-forgiveness can be a powerful, loving process. Self-forgiveness separates who we are from our actions and judgments.

The real issue is your judgment. Your judgments of yourself and your judgments of others are what poison your psyche. By letting go of your judgments, you can put the past behind you and move on. By letting go of the judgment you are not making your behavior or someone else's behavior okay, you are ending the negative mental self-talk.

I learned about forgiveness at the University of Santa Monica. This is the first approach that ever made sense to me. When clients are self-flagellating about how terrible they are, I encourage them to take out a piece of paper and do this exercise.

Fill in the blanks:

I forgive myself for judging myself as _____
_____.

In the blank line, you write the judgment. For instance, I would write: I forgive myself for judging myself as not good enough. I forgive myself for judging myself as fat. I forgive myself for judging myself as having no control.

Next, you write a person's name and the judgment you hold of them. I forgive myself for judging _____
as_____.

Examples: I forgive myself for judging my spouse as abusive. I forgive myself for judging Bob as hurtful. I forgive myself for judging Mary as skinny.

You see, our actions are our actions. They occurred, right or wrong. Whether these actions occurred one minute ago or 30 years ago, it is our judgment about the action that eats at us, that decimates our self-esteem. It's not up to us to judge, and by letting go of the judgment we free ourselves from the continued abuse of the action. Some people have experienced inexcusable acts of abuse. But many years later, they are the ones carrying on the abuse—not the abuser. What happened, happened. There is no need to pretend it didn't. But what hurts us now is our judgment about what happened. Our job is to let go of the judgment.

Uncovering protective layers

Imagine believing that an activity is not safe physically, mentally, and/or emotionally and then going ahead and doing it—for the rest of your life! Now that's a challenge!

There are so many reasons why people use food for protection—and I'm convinced now that men use food for protection as much as women do. Often clients are unaware—even shocked—when they realize their weight is protecting them from something, and that they really don't want to let go of their excess weight. It's as though they have two different warring halves. One side wants to release the excess weight, and the other side wants to hang onto the instant satisfaction that sugary, fatty foods provide.

Rachel talked about her "evil twin" who was there to protect her. She eventually created a new relationship with her now "loving twin." The job of this "loving twin" is to protect her in ways that serve her best health and interests today.

A common excuse I hear from both men and women is that when they were thinner (and almost always when they were much younger) they were sexually promiscuous. And now their fear is that if they get to a healthy weight, they will again be promiscuous.

Sylvia is a delightful woman in her late 70s who had 60 pounds she wanted to let go of. In one of her sessions I asked her if it was okay for her to release her extra weight...did she need to keep the extra pounds. She looked stunned, but only hesitated for a moment when she began telling me about how she loved her husband of over 40 years and had a monogamous relationship with him. But she also explained that she'd been sexually promiscuous as a young adult prior

There are so many reasons why people use food for protection.

to meeting her husband. Sylvia realized she feared that if she was at her ideal weight, she would again be attractive to other men and cheat on her husband. I asked her if she was the same person today as she was in her 20s and asked what she had learned through life experiences. I also asked if she was presented with the opportunity now, would she really cheat on her husband. "No!" she emphatically replied, "I love him…of course I wouldn't do that!" This is one of those moments where I can see a client's neurology changing as that shocked looked comes over her face, and she realizes what an unfounded fear she'd held on to.

People who have been sexually abused, both men and women, frequently use excess weight to protect themselves from others. Several gay men have shared with me that by being overweight they are protected from AIDS, as no one wants to have sex with a fat man.

The reasons people believe they need to keep weight on are limitless and extend far beyond physical and sexual abuse. People hide out, keeping others safely at a distance; they use weight to have an excuse to keep from doing something, such as cleaning the house or going to parties. Some people even rely on their excess weight to draw attention—when it's difficult for them to move, they can get others to wait on them. Ultimately, they all avoid vulnerability.

Another common protective excuse is, *If I'm successful attaining my ideal weight, what else will I expect of myself?* Or, *If I'm successful at reaching my ideal weight, what else will others expect of me?* Louis understood this well, once he realized he was using his morbid obesity to keep his sons at a distance. He'd never been particularly athletic, and he didn't enjoy playing catch and other sports with his children. His weight was his excuse for not playing sports. By the time his two boys were in grade school, Louis had eaten himself out of close relationships with his sons. They were so embarrassed by his appearance that they had stopped asking him to come out and play with them.

What else will I expect of myself?

When Louis finally understood that he was missing out on a lot more than shooting hoops in the driveway, he had all the motivation he needed to change his lifestyle and get out of his recliner.

Donna is an attractive woman in her late 50s. She was about 40 pounds overweight and was embarrassed by her appearance. She turned down social events, parties and fund raisers because of her embarrassment. Donna had been very socially active, yet she didn't particularly enjoy the social scene. Even though she was overweight, she was well liked and highly respected and continued to receive social invitations. She realized that without her extra fat, she would no longer have an excuse not to attend those social functions. Happily, Donna did reach her goal weight and did learn to say "No" to unwanted social events.

And then there are issues surrounding attention.

Women often feel uncomfortable having men notice them. Sometimes husbands will sabotage their wives (or wives will sabotage their husbands) so that no one else will be attracted to them.

Sometimes simply being noticed is uncomfortable. A common feeling is, "No one will notice me when I'm fat. I can hide." And some people are uncomfortable being complimented when they do lose weight. They don't want the attention and wonder why they're receiving it just for weighing less. There is sometimes anger over this attention as they wonder, "What was wrong with me as a person when I weighed more?"

The extra fat meant she had time to grieve in peace.

For Lori, who packed on over 100 pounds in under a year coping with the death of her partner—and sadly, also the next person she got close to—the extra fat meant she had time to grieve in peace without fending off more eager new men. In two years she doubled her weight and finally felt safe from unwanted attention. The real trouble started several years later when she thought she was ready to release the weight. Until she made peace with the role her weight had been playing in her life, it was absolutely impossible for her to keep the extra weight off, because she had convinced her unconscious that the extra weight was a wonderful, useful thing.

Solution for protective layers:
First it's important to do some self-examination to determine if you're holding onto weight for protection. Awareness is the first step. Sometimes all it takes is a light bulb moment to be ready to release long-held weight.

journal exercise

What are you hiding?

To uncover what you might be protecting yourself from, journal about these words and what they mean to you:

- protection
- safety
- vulnerable
- exposed

_____

_____

_____

_____

_____

_____

_____

_____

_____

Another way to think of your extra weight is as armor.
So what battles are you preparing for, against what demons are you defending yourself? If you could snap your fingers and be slender, what would you be afraid of?

Then, if you decide this is one of your weight issues, you can take the next step. When it comes to being sensitive about attention, the real issue is learning to give and receive attention to and from yourself. It's important to recognize that the common denominator in all your relationships is you. You are the only one who shows up in all your relationships. If you're uncomfortable receiving attention, ask yourself: What is it about you that is uncomfortable? What is it about you that you're denying? What is it about you that you're rejecting? It's only by accepting and loving you and your body as it is right now that will you ever be able to give the self-care that will allow you to make healthy eating choices, exercise and ultimately let go of your excess weight.

The number one job of your unconscious mind is to preserve your body. Milton Erickson would call it bringing the conscious mind into rapport with the unconscious mind. You can learn to dialogue in a healthy way with the various parts or aspects of yourself and integrate these parts of yourself so that they all work together in supporting you in obtaining your goals, and this is a technique we'll explore in Chapter Four.

> If you don't want to release your excess weight—If you believe it's not safe for you to lose the weight—then there's a part of you that somehow benefits from being overweight.

If you believe it's not safe for you to be slender, then long lasting weight release will be almost impossible. If you determine that this describes your situation, then I urge you to schedule some sessions with a qualified therapist who can guide you in releasing these negative emotions that no longer support you.

You may need to release weight, but do you have the motivation?

Now that I've identified many common roadblocks to weight release success and given you numerous tools to combat them, we need to look at the biggest boulder of them all: a lack of true motivation.

I guess maybe I'll give this a try . . . I know I should lose weight . . . it would be better for my health. These are typical half-hearted reasons I hear to release weight. And then there are the reasons for failure like: "Oh, this it too hard." or "I'm too busy or stressed to do this now."

While you may have a NEED to let go of the weight, the real question is: How motivated are you? Without the motivation to live the rest of your life slender and healthy, you will diet and then just put as much or more weight right back on. **Arriving at your goal weight is**

a mile marker; it is not the end of the journey. You must focus on living the rest of your life as slender and healthy.

Need is defined as something that is essential or vital. In terms of weight control, a need to lose weight would include reasons related to health, relationships (when weight is affecting them), self-esteem, number of pounds overweight, etc. Motivation is defined as your incentive, desire or drive to take action to make a change. Regardless of the need to make a change, you may not have the motivation to accomplish the goal.

HOT

Motivation is the one essential ingredient to successful weight control. Motivation is stronger when fueled by a high need to lose weight. However, when the pounds drop off, so does the need to lose weight. This, in turn, may reduce or eliminate motivation to continue healthy eating habits.

POINT

Commitment may fade when a level of comfort is reached. I see this both with people who have large amounts of weight to release and people who have only 20 pounds to shed. A person who has 100 pounds to release may slim down 50 or 60 pounds and feel great. They feel the best they have in years. Their blood pressure is down, their blood sugar is down, they can get up off the floor. They feel great! And then the motivation to continue on disappears. They wonder how could life be any better than this. And before long, they stop doing the work as their attention has drifted to other matters.

Being commitment-challenged means you may have had problems in the past keeping focused on doing what you need to do to release your excess weight and maintain your ideal weight. You may have treated weight release much the same way as you treat a common cold—you took some medicine and temporarily changed your behavior. But soon, you're right back to your same old poor habits. This is classic dieting mentality. This pattern reveals that you desire the end result, but you have not yet become resolved to really want to change your bad eating habits for the rest of your life. You're content with depriving yourself of foods you believe you enjoy just long enough to obtain results, then, for whatever reason, you stop dieting, old habits return and with them all your lost weight.

You would think that health would be a great motivator to lose weight. Sadly, it is not. I am sure you've seen someone on the street with an oxygen tank and a cigarette. Even this obvious health need to quit smoking is not enough to make some smokers quit. Telling people that if you don't change your diet or quit smoking, you are going to have a heart attack is not that motivating in the long run, because it's too scary to think about it, so they don't. When someone has had a heart attack, they will do anything you tell them for about a month or two, and then the denial comes back and they often go back to their old patterns, because they think it's too hard or too scary.

I am reminded of Mike, who goes to the same gym I do. Mike comes in about twice each week to work out with a personal trainer. He's a highly successful businessman in his 60s. He travels around the world and winters in warm climates. Mike is overweight, has high blood pressure and has had heart surgery. He has a high need to lose weight. He knows he should and is always talking about it. When he is here on the island during the week, he loses a pound or two. But come the weekend or a few weeks of travel, and he returns to his high-fat gourmet meals with wine, and his pounds return. Mike is not motivated to give up the immediate gratification of the "good" life for a potentially longer life of health. He is not committed to losing weight.

In the United States we spend an astonishing $1.8 trillion a year on health care; this represents 15 percent of the gross domestic product (GDP). The vast majority of this money is expended by a relatively small percentage of the population for diseases that are, by and large, behavioral.

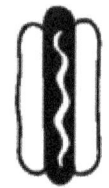

Why do we resist changing our behavior so very strongly?

For example, two million people a year have coronary artery bypass surgery or angioplasty to treat their heart disease, at a cost of $30 million. These procedures, in and of themselves, rarely prevent heart attacks or prolong life, because the affected vessels get clogged up again and again. Doctors tell their patients that if they drink less alcohol, eat less, stress less and get more exercise, they will live longer and not need repeated surgeries. However, research has shown that 90 percent of all people who have bypass or angioplasty don't change their behaviors. Ninety percent!

Why do we resist behavioral change so tenaciously? Why, even at the risk of death, do we hang on to such dysfunctional behavior?

Because the facts speak only to our conscious minds, and our subconscious minds have a different agenda

Behavioral change only comes about when our emotions get involved. Feelings, not facts move us beyond our old limitations. Dr. Dean Ornish, the distinguished founder of the Preventive Medicine Research Institute in Sausalito, California, has a world-renowned program for cardiac patients, which includes psychological, emotional and spiritual dimensions. Dr. Ornish finds almost 80 percent of his patients stick with their lifestyle changes and safely avoid bypass or angioplasty surgery. He says it's not fear of dying that motivates people to change, it's getting a new vision of life.

> You need to believe you can feel better, not just live longer. Joy is a far more powerful motivator than fear—it's not change or die, it's **change and live!**

So what is your compelling reason to be at your ideal weight? What will your life be like at your ideal weight? What will your life be like at age 80, if you live from now until then weighing 130 pounds instead of 200 pounds? What would it be like at age 80 to go on vacation in Italy and walk the streets of Rome weighing a youthful 130 pounds, instead of sitting in a wheelchair in a senior care facility weighing 200 pounds? Do you want to spend your later years being sedentary, or would you prefer to take your grandchildren to Disneyland and enjoy it with them?

Solution for lacking motivation:
The motivational answer is to discover what it is about living the rest of your life at your ideal weight that makes eating fewer cookies worth your effort.

journal exercise

Welcome to the rest of your life
To do so, consider the following questions.
- What is it about living the rest of your life at your ideal weight that makes drinking less wine worth your effort?
- What is it about living the rest of your life at your ideal weight that makes exercising, shopping, buying and preparing healthy meals

and snacks worthwhile?
- What activities would you like to enjoy when you are 75 or 80?
- What activities could you enjoy now if you were at your ideal weight?
- How would your social life change if you were at your goal weight?
- Would you make different career moves at a lower weight?
- Do you think you'd be perceived as more valuable as a thin person? Would you earn more money?
- Would you be more fearless, more adventurous at your target weight?

_____

_____

_____

_____

_____

_____

_____

_____

_____

_____

_____

_____

With the advantage of self-hypnosis, you'll have a much greater chance of success.

Yes, there is a price to be paid to get to your ideal weight. You must burn more calories than you take in. And to maintain your ideal weight, you must burn all the calories you take in. There is no other way. That basic formula of weight loss in unchanging—though with the advantage of self-hypnosis techniques, you'll have a much greater chance of succeeding than you've ever had before. But without the motivation to live your life at your ideal weight, the pain may be far too great, you may not believe you can be successful, you might quit the first time you cheat, you may cling to your reasons for being overweight, and you could create even more stress in your life and eventually fail to achieve your ideal weight.

52 Reasons

Take time right now and begin listing 52 Reasons for being at your ideal goal weight. One or two words are all you need. (Look

What are YOUR reasons?

better. Play with grandkids. Walk around Italy in my 80s. ....) **I urge you to use a pad of sticky notes and write one suggestion per page.** Each week for the next year post a new reason why being at your goal weight is more important than a cookie or why going for that walk is more important than the Today Show. Keep yourself motivated – even when you only have a few more pounds to release. Don't cheat yourself and stop short of your goal.

So are you committed to do what it takes?

Unfortunately, many weight-loss clients are not committed to making any real changes in their eating and exercise habits. It seems that most are looking to hypnosis as a magic pill to lose weight while maintaining their unhealthy eating habits and lack of exercise. This attitude is not a commitment: Let me drink the Slim Fast, get this weight off, and then I can go back to McDonald's and my ol' buddies Ben and Jerry. I describe true commitment as: I see this as a lifelong change in my relationship to myself and my relationship with food.

In the first weight loss session, I hand out the following written homework assignment called My Slender For Life™ Commitment. I ask that clients complete their Commitment over the week, make a copy for themselves and bring it to their second session. **These questions are specifically ordered so that you start with ten years from now and work your way back to the present**. I urge you to put your heart into completing this commitment that you are making to yourself. Put time and effort into this, do not rush through it.

web extra

You can download a printable version from **www.slenderforlife.com**.

Before beginning, go to **www.slenderforlife.com** or **www.hypnosishealthinfo.com**. On the right side of the page you will find a short video titled Remember When. Watch this video prior to completing your Commitment.

If you are working with a Slender For Life™ licensed weight loss coach, be sure that you make a copy of your Commitment. Keep one copy for yourself and keep it updated. Take the other copy to your second session. If you are reading this book on your own, feel free to email me your commitment (roger@hypnosishealthinfo.com) and I will be happy to read it. **Remember, this is a COMMITMENT you are making to yourself**.

My Slender For Life™ Commitment

Please write your health and wellness goals on separate paper or on your computer. Keep a copy for yourself and bring these goals with you to your second session. There is not enough room on this paper to answer these questions. Put some time and thought into your responses. Your goal is to live the rest of your life at your ideal weight. What will your life be like at your ideal weight? How will you feel about yourself? What physical activities will you be doing that you can not do now or how will your physical activities improve? **Make sure that you sign and date your commitment.**

Goals for Ten Years

Goals for Six Years

Goals for Three Years

Goals for One Year

Goals for Six Months

Goals for Two Months

Goals for One Month

Goals for One Week (What is it that I am willing to do to release at least two pounds this next week)

What are my obstacles?
Things That I Have Been Unable to Start

Things That I Have Been Unable to Change

Things That I Have Been Unable to Stop

Healthy Things That I Am Unwilling To Do To Meet My Weight Release Goal

What My Life Will Be Like In Ten Years If I Reach My Goal

What My Life Will Be Like In Ten Years If I Do Not Reach/ Maintain My Goal

Write out 52 Reasons for being at your goal weight. Post one each week for the next year. (Bring a copy of this as well.)

Your goal is to live the rest of your life at your ideal weight.

Here are some examples of what clients have written:

Michael wrote: **Goals for Three Years:** "In three years I will be 60 years old, slender and physically fit. I will be in good enough shape to train and climb Mt. Rainier. I may decide that I don't want to climb Mt. Rainier, but then it will be my choice. Right now, I do not have a choice; I am too fat to climb."

Joann wrote: **Goals for Ten Years:** "I have weighed 135 lbs. with ease for almost ten years. I have no physical problems. My joints feel like I am in my 20s or 30s. I take numerous trips every year that center around physical activity, such as hiking, biking, skiing, walking. People mistake me for a woman much younger in years. Overeating, eating more than is good for me or more than my body needs, food cravings for sweets—these are habits from the distant past that I haven't felt in years and years. It's almost like that was another person who felt and acted that way. If people describe me to someone, they call me 'that slim woman who loves to exercise.' My ability to reach and maintain my weight has spilled over into other parts of my life. I have abundant energy and confidence. I pursue activities with gusto. I have the kind of body where my clothes look elegant, no matter what I have on. I can be dressed in jeans and a tee shirt, but they look chic on me."

Joan continued on: **Goals for Six Years:** "I have weighed 135 for almost six years. I still remember that it was 2006 when I first made the commitment with Slender For Life™. Now it's 2012. Some days it seems like just a very short time ago that I was worried about my weight, overeating, suffering from food cravings. Other days it's hard to imagine that I was ever that way. I still catch my reflection in a mirror or window and marvel that it's me. I think to myself: Hey, I'm not walking along worrying that I look too fat and wanting to make my self invisible."

> **"I feel so good that I don't even think about eating any other way."**
> ~Joan

More from Joan: **Goals for One Year:** "I reached my goal of 135 lbs. Many friends and my husband kept thinking this was just a phase I was going through and soon I would begin eating fish and steaks again. I try to explain to them that it is not hard, that I feel so good that I don't even think about eating any other way."

What my life will be like in ten years if I reach my goal: "I will look much younger than my age. I will feel fantastic and vibrant and active and sexy. I will be healthy physically and mentally. I will have a life that includes a lot of physical activity. I will feel that I can go anywhere, do anything without feeling shy or inhibited by anything. I will have assumed the identity of a vibrant, good looking, active person. It will feel natural to me. I won't even think about living any other way."

What my life will be like in ten years if I do not reach my goal: "I will probably have health and joint problems, unable to get around so well. I will be grumpy because I won't like the way I look and feel. That will make me angry, and I will not love myself. I will look older and not feel very sexy. I will feel inhibited in trying new things in life. I will feel self-conscious about my body. I will limit things that I do, like visiting our friends in Hawaii, because I might have to appear in a bathing suit. I will feel like I failed."

Sonya wrote: **Goals for six years:** "I am turning 50 in the best shape of my life. I run, hike, participate in athletic events, keep up with my husband and am generally active every day."

Sonya added: **Goals for three years:** "I have kept my weight off and am strong and fit. I can take on hikes with steep elevation gain and celebrate the view at the top. I have completely redone my wardrobe with hip, stylish clothes, size 8. I can shop in New York with my husband for the latest trends, knowing I will find clothes to fit. My husband can buy clothes for me…something he has wanted to do since we met."

More from Sonya: **Goals for one year:** "I HAVE REACHED MY GOAL: For the first time in my life, on New Years Eve, I don't make a resolution to lose weight. I am where I want to be. I am fit and strong. Exercise is no longer a should but something I look forward to. My relationship with food is healthy: food is a fuel and the most important tool to ensure I don't get heart disease and die young. My body is fit and strong, and I am wearing a sexy black dress that drives my husband wild!"

Sonya added: **Goals for six months:** "I no longer feel deprived when I pass up rich or fattening food. I feel good knowing that I am fueling my body with what I need to live a long life. It has gotten a lot easier to have the right food on hand. It is summer and I am wearing shorts and swimsuits, hiking and swimming and have had enough weight loss to believe that I really can reach my goal."

"My eating patterns have become second nature."
~Lynn

Lynn wrote: **Goals for ten years:** "I'm the coolest 62- year-old grandmother. I weigh 125 pounds." **Goals for three years:** "I have maintained my ideal weight. What a success! Food has totally ceased to be an obsession. Nutrition, exercise, self-hypnosis are automatic daily routines. Medication for hypertension is minimized or unnecessary."

Lynn added: **Goals for one year:** "Almost there. My goal is in sight. I look and feel great. I'm motivated to continue to my goal. I'm proud of what I am accomplishing. I am no longer pre-diabetic. My doctor is impressed." **Goals for two months:** "My eating patterns have become second nature. I enjoy my food choices and my exercise routine. I sleep well and expand self-hypnosis to help relive stress."

What my life will be like in ten years if I reach my goal: I will be healthy, slim, happy, looking and feeling great, not old and creaky; I will have broken the family history cycle of adult onset diabetes and heart disease."

Lynn summed it up like this. **What my life will be like in ten years if I do not reach my goal:** "I may not be here. I will have diabetes and heart disease."

Stay focused on what you say is really important in your life.

I discovered the following quote on my cup one day while enjoying a cup of coffee: "The irony of commitment is that it's deeply liberating—in word, in play, in love. The act frees you from the tyranny of your internal critic, from the fear that likes to dress itself up and parade around as rational hesitation. To commit is to remove your head as the barrier to your life." ~Anne Morriss (on a Starbucks cup)

Consider your Slender For Life™ Commitment to be a work in progress. Keep your head out of your way and stay focused on what you say is really important in your life. Periodically, revisit your Commitment and update it. Remember, it is your motivation that will propel you to be slender for the rest of your life.

Eliminating mental and emotional roadblocks using self-hypnosis

Of course using your One Minute Light Switch Self-Hypnosis with written suggestions is a powerful tool for taming those tigers. Here are some suggestions you can use or adapt for yourself.

Mental and emotional pain
- My new eating habits are more and more comfortable each day.
- The child in me is no longer responsible for what I eat. The loving, nurturing adult part of me is in control of my healthy new eating choices.
- I release myself from unhealthy holiday traditions and create new traditions that support me in my goals.
- I desire to release my excess weight more and more each day.

- It is now easy for me to think in a way that creates my ideal body.
- I am in control, even when others are eating unhealthy fattening foods around me.
- I enjoy eating low-fat, healthy foods more and more each day.
- I only feed myself healthy foods and positive thoughts.
- I give thanks each day for all that is right in my life.
- It's okay to release the weight.

Creating success
- I am successful in obtaining and maintaining my ideal weight.
- I have infinite control of my eating habits.
- I create my ideal body with my thoughts and my actions.
- A craving is just a thought. Like all thoughts, I create it, I can control it, I can change it!
- I command my body to release the excess weight.
- It is now easy for me to behave in a way that creates my ideal body.
- A craving is just a thought, and I am in control of my thoughts and emotions.
- I am successful, because I am a success.
- I am assuming the thoughts, deeds and actions of a physically fit, happy and healthy person.
- I am making the right choices to release weight and change my eating habits.
- I indulge in appropriate behaviors.
- I allow myself to achieve and remain at my ideal weight.

Perfectionist expectations
- I forgive myself for judging myself as not good enough.
- 95 percent perfect is good enough.
- I forgive myself and instantly get back on track.
- I am free to give and receive unconditional love.
- I focus on my positive results and not perfection.

Secondary gain
- As I become more slender and attractive, I am becoming more self-confident and more self-assured.

- I am protected by my protective shield.
- Others around me do not bother me or disturb me.
- I am at peace with the world and everyone in it.

Commitment
- I am motivated to live my life at my ideal weight.
- I choose to be happy, healthy and physically fit.
- I obtain and maintain my ideal weight throughout my life.
- It is up to me to create my ideal body and I am doing it!
- I am committed to my weight release goals.
- I succeed with my weight release goals. I am committed to changing my eating habits—permanently—for the rest of my life.
- It is time for me to release my excess weight forever.
- I really want to eat only food that is healthy and nutritious.
- I give my body permission to release my excess weight.
- My determination increases more and more.

Practice using these techniques and select the one or ones that work best for you.

 Remember, there has been a negative dialogue going on in your head most of your life, but this negative dialogue is just plain silly. However, there is nothing silly about having a healthy, loving and nurturing dialogue with yourself.

I really believe one of the reasons we're on this earth at this time is to learn to be the loving, nurturing adult for that part of us that is hurting, so that we can be loving and nurturing to ourselves and to others. Until we give ourselves love and acceptance, there will never be enough love from our spouse, children, family, friends—and certainly not from food—to meet our needs.

To recap, in this chapter I talked about overcoming these roadblocks to weight release:

- Using food for rewards
- Negative mind chatter

- Feeling out of control
- Inability to see yourself slender
- Needing to be a perfect dieter
- Self-judgment
- Hiding behind protective layers
- Lacking real motivation

If you know or suspect there are other roadblocks in your own path, then I encourage you to do the following journal exercise

journal exercise

What's in your way?

Get into a relaxed state and ask your subconscious mind what barriers you have placed in your own way. How long have they been there? Why did you place them there? What will it take to remove them? If you have difficulty getting answers, you can also try asking yourself these questions just before sleep, along with the suggestion that you will know and remember the answers when you wake.

_____
_____
_____
_____
_____
_____
_____
_____
_____
_____
_____
_____
_____
_____
_____
_____
_____

CD NOTE

I realize that the work of this chapter will require of some readers the biggest leaps of progress. So if you are having strong reactions to some of the material in this section, please take some time to journal about them and keep listening to the Emotion Trigger CD Track. There is no timetable for this weight release journey. Take as long as you need with each step in the process, until you feel ready to continue. If you experienced a lot of "bingo" moments in this chapter, I do think you'll find a lot of help in Chapter Four, in which I'll show you many ways to overcome emotional eating and stop eating as a reaction to stress.

So when you're ready, put down that bag of Doritos and discover some healthier ways to nurture yourself.

Chapter Four

Do You Understand Why You Eat What You Eat?

Chapter Four At A Glance

- What are you stuffing?
- How to counteract food cravings
- Discover your true cravings
- A look at your phantom life
- What do your downfall foods symbolize to you?
- How to stop worrying about the future
- Understanding your hunger
- Becoming a more mindful eater
- How to feed your inner child
- Getting a grip on stress
- Hypnotic suggestions for emotional and stress eating

Now it's time to address the two biggest challenges most overweight people face: eating for purely emotional reasons and eating as a reaction to stress. Both are major causes of obesity. You may find yourself eating when you're not physically hungry, as a reaction to feeling upset, sad, lonely, angry or fearful. In addition, stress eaters often eat when they're bored.

When you feel a negative emotion that you would describe as sadness, anger, fear, shame, guilt or hurt, you are probably experiencing a physical feeling of tension or anxiety. These feelings can be TRIGGERS that initiate your conditioned response to eat. Almost everyone does this to some extent. Many of us have been programmed since we were babies to associate love, comfort and security with food and eating. If this habit is extreme enough to affect your weight, the techniques in this chapter can facilitate your change.

Normal reactive emotions can be controlled and modified through self-education, psychotherapy, hypnotherapy, counseling or even medications in certain cases. If negative emotions are severely compromising your quality of life, you should discuss the problem with your hypnotherapist or other mental health professional. It is imperative, however, that you also allow yourself to *feel* your emotions—all of them—in a healthy way. It's okay to be angry, sad, frightened, joyful, powerful and loving. **Remember: stuffing your emotions often equals stuffing yourself with poor food choices, becoming over-stuffed by eating too much.** A good visual reminder of this bloated feeling is Poppin' Fresh (aka the Pillsbury Doughboy), who really doesn't have anything to giggle about.

What do you really crave?

Does this sound familiar? Here you are, less than an hour since you last ate and you have your head in the refrigerator or you're heading down to the vending machine or to Starbucks. You have that feeling that you want something—almost as if something is missing. Perhaps you're feeling something you don't want to feel, and a muffin is your drug of choice to squelch it.

This is your opportunity (that I discussed in Chapter Three, page 64) **to *experience* the pain.** The food is merely the mirror reflecting what you're feeling that you don't want to feel. The old

behavior is to eat. The new behavior is to experience the pain, to heal and to no longer have to carry the weight of the pain around with you—creating a new relationship with yourself.

Add this dieting tension to the stress of a bad day and weight control becomes next to impossible. Food, the very thing that is used to reduce tension and make you feel better, can now feel like the very thing you need to deny yourself.

We have learned by adaptive behavior that when we're needing friendship and love, food works as a substitute to stimulate the deepest part of the brain that would normally be activated by interacting with others. Many of us have substituted a bowl of chocolate ice cream for spending time with family and friends, and as a result, we find ourselves becoming more and more isolated. This spreading isolation and loneliness can lead to overeating, alcohol abuse or drug use. And once these addictions start, they develop a life of their own.

journal exercise

Where's your life?

Can you recall any social opportunities you have opted out of in the past year? Even casual invitations to go out after work with colleagues or to a movie with friends? Are the barstools too tiny or the movie seats too tight? Or do you feel stared at in public social situations? Are there cultural activities you've wanted to attend but haven't? Perhaps the auditorium seats are too narrow? Can you think of any groups or organizations you've been reluctant to join— possibly because you feel some shame, embarrassment or self- consciousness about your appearance? How about dating—has that been on hold too? Make this list as detailed as you can. Then ask yourself how long this avoidance has been going on. When you are done, read the next paragraph.

_____
_____
_____
_____
_____
_____
_____
_____
_____
_____
_____

The list you just compiled is a picture of the life you're not leading, a vision of your heart's desires manifested as lost opportunities. This list represents fun, joy and intimacy you aren't having. These are days of your life you can never get back. (But you can commit today to reversing the trend, so that a year from now you won't be able to make a similar list.) If you didn't fill out the Commitment Form (see Page 94), do it now.

As I have said, comfort eating was a major issue for me. One of my fondest memories as a young boy on the farm was of my grandmother coming to visit. She would come and live with us for weeks at a time, and she made the best cinnamon rolls. I remember sitting at the kitchen table with her rolling out the dough. I would play in the dough, making snakes and snowmen and monsters. We would talk and laugh. The whole house smelled of yeast and cinnamon. It was a time when I felt unconditionally loved and unconditionally accepted.

For many years after Grandma died, I couldn't get enough cinnamon rolls. I can still smell the aromas from Three Sisters Bakery

When I smell baked goods, my heart skips a beat!

in Wailuku, Maui. They made cinnamon rolls almost as good as Grandma's. I used to go in there at least once a day and get at least one cinnamon roll, sometimes two or three and sometimes twice a day.

Anytime I felt the least bit unloved, the least bit unaccepted, I wanted cinnamon rolls, or other bakery treats. I went looking for Grandma's "food is love" comfort foods. My association of love and acceptance was anchored to the smell and taste, as well as to the opiate rush that high-sugar and fatty, refined-flour foods provide.

Thanks to hypnosis and the other healing work that I have done, I still love the smell of a great bakery and especially the smell of cinnamon and rising yeast, but I no longer have to eat the rolls. When I smell baked goods, my heart skips a beat! I love that smell and I would never *not* want to love that smell. Today, when I walk into a coffee shop or bakery, I can enjoy the sights and aromas, think of Grandma and feel absolutely loved, and walk out completely satisfied with a cup of coffee.

Solution for food cravings:
Here are two very powerful and effective Neuro-Linguistic Programming (NLP) techniques that you can use to stay in control.

Postage Stamp

You learned a variation of the postage stamp technique in Chapter Three, and here is another use. Imagine a cinnamon roll (or whatever food or beverage craving you want to diminish). You can smell the cinnamon, sugar and the yeast. It's still warm and the frosting is slightly runny. Your fingers are sticky and your mouth bursts with sensation as you taste the dough, sugar and cinnamon.

Next, imagine stepping out of that scene and turning it into a photograph of you with the cinnamon roll. Make the photo either all white, gray or black and shrink it down to the size of a postage stamp. If you are right handed, visualize it in the far left hand corner of the room on the floor (if you are left handed, put it in the far right hand corner of the room on the floor). Now notice that the desire for the cinnamon roll is gone.

This technique can also be put to good use when dining out.

Even if you're having the best meal of your life, there is no need to overeat. Once you reach the level of fullness that is enough fuel for your body, just Postage Stamp the remainder of the meal and you'll feel totally satisfied without having to clean your plate or pick at it until it's taken away.

What's on your desktop?

You can now resist temptation when it is at its highest.

web extra

Follow the steps above to recreate the image and sensation of whatever food craving you want to overcome. Imagine sitting down at your computer and you find an icon of that cinnamon roll on your desktop. Notice where it is—is it in the upper left, lower left, upper right, lower right or center of the screen? Is it bigger, smaller or the same size as the other icons? What does it look like?

Now think about a food that you absolutely hate; for me, it's canned green peas. I can't stand the smell, the taste, the texture, the look or the memories associated with canned green peas, (though I do love fresh peas).

Again, imagine that on your computer desktop you find an icon of canned green peas—is it in the upper left, lower left, upper right, lower right or center of your screen? Is it bigger, smaller or the same size as the other icons? What does it look like?

For me, the cinnamon roll is big and in the center of the screen; the peas are smaller and in the lower left quadrant of the screen. Imagine clicking on the cinnamon roll and dragging it down to the icon of peas. The closer it gets to the peas, it takes on the look, smell, taste and texture of the canned peas. Now the desire for cinnamon rolls is gone. You can use this with any food or beverage (imagine pouring a glass of Green Pea wine!)

Go to **www.hypnosishealthinfo.com** and in the orange menu bar highlight Weight Loss. The drop down tab is What's On Your Desktop? Click on that. You'll find a visual version of this tool. Use it to learn how you can turn down that desert tray at the restaurant.

These are power tools you can use when standing in line at the coffee shop or passing by the bakery section in your grocery store. With these techniques, you can now resist temptation when it is at its highest—when those fattening foods are literally in your head by way of their aromas.

The tool in the next section is a writing exercise and will take more time, but the payoffs can be tremendous.

Food really is a metaphor

Janice, a 58-year-old artist, was amazed at what she learned about symbolic eating. "My number one indulgence meal has always been a burger and fries. When I tried to figure out what they symbolized to me, I suddenly remembered that when I was 7 years old and allowed to walk by myself to a neighborhood burger stand, that was where I spent my first-ever allowance. We never had French fries at home, and rarely even burgers, so both were real treats. And I associated them with my initial steps of independence. Ordering a burger and fries was my first taste of freedom—no parent was around to tell me I couldn't have this meal. And I now realize that even though I've eaten many thousands of burgers with the ever ready fries, each time there was also an extra jolt of joy attached, because **I was subconsciously celebrating my independence**. As an adult, I don't really need to do that anymore, so I can imagine releasing that food craving now that it's been drained of importance."

Due to the unusual circumstance of her name, Candice had an easy time figuring out her food addiction. "Until I was 21, I was always called Candy. And no surprise, I ate a LOT of it! As my very name, candy was always in my awareness. I felt like I could never get enough of it. Nearly every day I took my 35 cents lunch money and skipped the school cafeteria for a trip to the corner store where I bought seven nickel candy bars instead. (Hey, it was the 1950s, and those nickel candy bars were bigger than the dollar bars today.) And yes, I ruined my teeth in the process. **What I see now is that there was a profound lack of sweetness in my life**, I experienced my parents as bitter and sour, and my little girl mind was trying to find any way I could to sweeten my life. As an adult, it's been especially difficult to resist during the holidays, as I also associated crystal candy dishes full of bright ribbon candy with other people's Hallmark-happy homes. Now I realize the truth behind those fantasy images, and I can walk away from the candy aisle."

journal exercise

What does food symbolize to you?

List all your downfall foods, ones you know (or suspect) are bad for you, then write about each one. Key into the olfactory memories (the smells, which are our strongest), tell the food's history in your life, it's role in your life, when and where you first ate it, who you were with and so on. See what each food symbolizes to you (comfort, independence, feeling special, etc.). A variation would be to write your life story with food, your earliest memories about food; ask your parents what they recall about your eating habits as a young child, what things you liked or disliked.

_____

_____

_____

_____

_____

_____

_____

_____

_____

_____

_____

_____

In examining what associations you made long ago with your favorite comfort foods, see if you can't separate them from the foods themselves. Perhaps you connect fried chicken to family picnics, and those were the rare exceptions when your father seemed to relax around you. Now, instead of driving through KFC whenever you miss your dad, give him a call or talk about him with a family member, or enjoy old pictures. Eating fried chicken won't recreate those good feelings—in fact, quite the opposite. **It boils down to gaining awareness about why you crave what you do, so you can diffuse the power that food has held over you.**

Stop worrying

This common behavior can easily lead to mindless eating. You can probably recall worrying about an upcoming event and watching your fears dissolve once it was over. Worry over a future event is sometimes called *anticipatory anxiety*. The uncertainty of the outcome can create all sorts of fears as well as a negative future fantasy. This type of anxiety can also cause insomnia. It can even escalate into a full-fledged feeling of panic.

Solution for mindless eating:
The good news is, you can release this kind of anxiety in just a few moments using the following exercise in mental imagery.

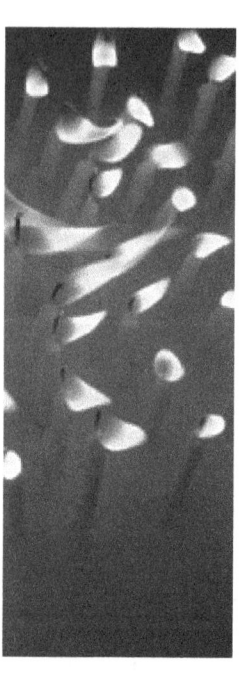

Close your eyes and visualize the following:
1. Imagine that all your past memories exist on a timeline extending outside your body. The direction in which your past originates is best determined by asking yourself: In what direction is my past? (Your answer is intuitive.) Or, the name of my first grade teacher is____. Notice the direction the thoughts come from. Or it may help to visualize a row of numbers representing each year of your life and just notice whether the row begins on the left or the right, above or below.
2. Now ask yourself: In what direction is my Future? Or try imagining your 100th birthday celebration and notice from what direction that picture comes.
3. Next, imagine the successful completion of the event that is causing you the anxiety. Imagine the best possible outcome that is for the highest good of all concerned. Be right there in this scene looking through your own eyes. Engage all your senses to really experience this event. Notice the last thing that has to happen so that you know this event is successful. Then, step out of this scene so that it

becomes like a snapshot of the successful completion of the event.

4. Now imagine floating up out of your body so high above the timeline of your life so that your timeline is only an inch long.

5. Then float into the future to the event you're worrying about.

6. Release the photo of the successful completion of the event down into your timeline.

7. Now float fifteen minutes further into the future past the event and float down into your timeline and face toward the present time.

8. Notice how everything between the present and the future event aligns itself to support the successful completion of this event. Notice that you feel no anxiety.

9. Return back to the present. You have just created a positive future fantasy.

Are you really hungry?

In Chapter Three I described scenarios using food as a drug—to numb out, to not feel. The alternative is conscious eating. **Conscious eating is mindfulness. Conscious eating is checking in with your body and determining if you are truly physically hungry.** If you are not hungry, then allow yourself to sit with the discomfort and with the notion that something is missing.

journal exercise

Where does it hurt?

I invite you to allow your pain and face these questions:

· What am I feeling that I don't want to feel?
· What am I not feeling that I want to feel?
· What's missing in my life?

_____
_____
_____
_____
_____
_____
_____
_____

To uncover what's really bothering you, try this. With your dominant hand, write about your mental and emotional hunger. Then switch and write with your non-dominant hand and allow your hunger to reply. (It's important that you don't make this about spelling, punctuation, grammar or even readability. Perfectionists, do not get all hung up about doing this perfectly.)

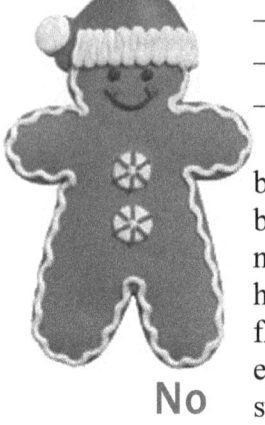

No amount of cookies could substitute for being with my family.

For example, Theresa shared how she was upset last year because she was unable to go home for Christmas. She found herself baking double batch after double batch of every holiday cookie she'd made as a child. She recalled how they didn't taste good at all and how she checked her recipes to try and figure out why they had no flavor and why they didn't seem at all sweet. "After I did this exercise, I realized the obvious answer: no amount of cookies could substitute for being with my family, and there wasn't enough sugar on earth to sweeten my loneliness last year." If Theresa ever has to miss another family event, she'll be emotionally prepared—and know not to seek joy in oatmeal lace cookies.

Go to the movies

When you do experience losing yourself in a pint of Ben & Jerry's, a box of chocolates, a batch of cookies or a bag of chips, it can be a great opportunity for healing. The next exercise is another good way to counteract a lack of mindfulness and food trances.

As soon as you become aware that you are eating for emotional reasons, imagine being in a movie theatre up in the projection booth next to the projector and looking out the little window. Look down into the theatre at the top of your own head, so that you are *watching yourself*. In fact, also imagine you are seeing yourself watching a movie. There on the screen is a film of you gobbling down the ice cream, cookies or whatever food you just consumed unconsciously. Really notice THAT *you* up there on the screen

Really notice THAT *you* up there on the screen doing the emotional eating.

doing the emotional eating. Get in touch with that character on the screen, and really connect with what you are thinking and feeling.

Now, how old is that little boy or girl on the screen? What is that part of you thinking? *I'm not good enough, no one cares, it's not safe.* What is that part of you feeling (anger, hurt, fear, sadness)? Did you experience yourself as a child up on the screen? If not, then think about your earliest memories of these same emotions you experienced on the screen. Often, the answer is you were less than 10 years old. It makes no difference how wonderful a childhood you may have had. It makes no difference whether or not you were overweight as a child or if you ate emotionally as a child. What is it that this little boy or girl really needs to feel safe—is it love, attention, what?

The story can go something like this: A 3-year-old is running down the sidewalk, trips, falls and scrapes his knee. Grandma scoops him up in her arms, puts a Scooby Doo bandage on it, kisses away the tears, holds and comforts the toddler in her arms of unconditional

What is it that this little boy or girl really needs to feel safe?

love and feeds him one of her homemade chocolate chip cookies. This is powerful stuff! Here we have grandma's unconditional love, we have the physical anchoring of the hug, as well as the refined flour, sugar and chocolate stimulating the same opiate receptors as does heroin.

And here we are today, a few years later still falling and scraping our knees. Grandma is no longer picking us up, but the accessibility to chocolate chips cookies is more plentiful than ever. **And for a fleeting moment, we can experience the same powerful emotions of unconditional love anchored with that hug and grandma's cookie. This is also a trance!**

Imagine with me for a moment that you have a grandchild the same age as the little boy or girl who you saw on the movie screen and this child is the same gender as you. You walk into the kitchen

and there is your grandchild furiously eating a plate of cookies. One glance and you know that something is wrong; something is upsetting your grandchild. What would you say? Might you sit down and start talking to find out what has upset your grandchild? Would you suggest going for a walk or some other activity? Might you touch, hug or hold your grandchild and tell your grandchild that you love him or her? You certainly wouldn't shame or guilt your grandchild for thoughts, emotions or even for eating, and I hope you wouldn't offer ice cream to go with the cookies!

Let's look at how this works. Borrowing from Eric Berne's Transactional Analysis, and *I'm OK, You're OK*, by Thomas Harris, look at the three circles on the next page.

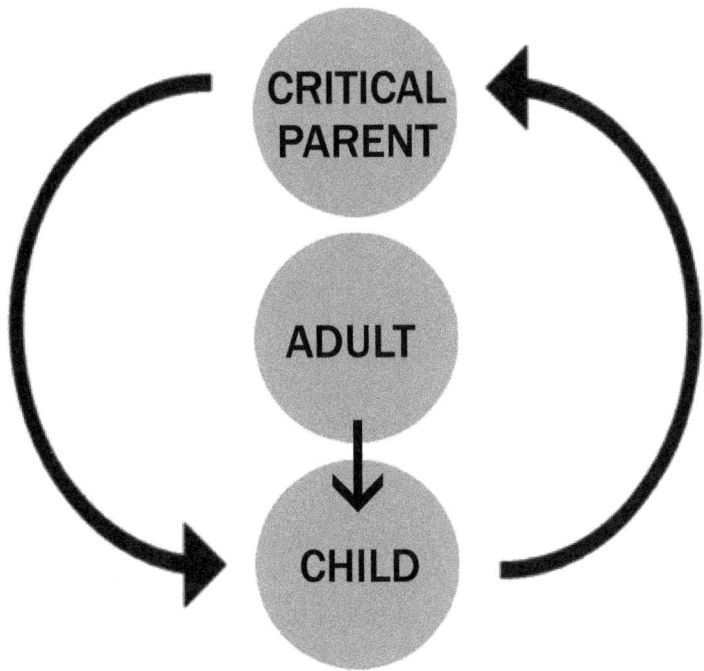

In the center is the loving, nurturing adult you of today. On the bottom is the child part of you that is cellular memory or the child trance that is looking for love, for attention or to simply numb out and to not feel at all. And there on the top is that critical parent, that shaming and guilting part of you. We live most of our lives moving back and forth from the trance of that child looking for love and protection and the critical parent that shames and guilts us—that "shoulds" on us.

All it takes is a tone of voice, a word, a look, a song, a gesture, or a scent and we move into a trance. Our job is to learn to recognize the trance and to take control of the trance we are in.

> **There will never be enough love, safety, attention or even cookies to meet the needs of that young child in you. This little child does not exist to anyone else but you. You are the only one that can do that for you.**

It is not a child's job to choose its parent's meals. It is not the job of your inner child to choose what and how much you eat. *I feel*

It is not the job of your inner child to choose what and how much you eat.

like having cookies for dinner! Nor is it the job of that critical parent to tell you what you can and cannot eat. *Don't you dare eat that cookie—you're on a diet!* A cookie is just a cookie. Cookies are neither right or wrong or good or bad. They are simply cookies. I've yet to meet a store-bought cookie that was worth eating, let alone slowing someone down from releasing more pounds.

But when you're at your neighbor's house for a cup of coffee and she brings out the fresh homemade chocolate chip cookies, of course you can enjoy a cookie. Not the bowl of raw dough, the whole bag of chocolate chips, and not *twelve* cookies! Cookies are a part of life. As people, we commune together through the breaking of bread. What you eat and how much you eat is the job of the center circle, that loving, nurturing adult (the grandparent part of you).

So how do you love that child in you? How do you meet the needs of this young child? One way is to look in the mirror.

When was the last time you looked into your eyes in the mirror? If you are like most people, you can't remember. Oh sure, you glanced around as you brushed your teeth, put in your contacts or combed your hair. But I bet you really didn't look into your eyes and notice what you saw. If you were a little child, how loved would you

feel if you couldn't remember the last time someone looked at you? I bet not very loved at all. But weren't you in front of a mirror when you brushed your teeth this morning? And you've been in a room with a mirror since then, right?

Solution for addressing your inner child:
Look into your eyes, not just all around them. In the morning as you are brushing your teeth, look into your eyes and say "Good morning" and "I love you" to the younger parts of yourself. Throughout the day, remind your inner child that he or she is not the one who has to deal with challenges at work, or traffic, or your spouse or pay the bills. When you pass a mirror throughout your day, encourage a positive interaction between you, thank your inner child for a laugh you may have shared, and assure your child self that he or she is safe.

Talk to your inner child

The next time you become aware of your inner child needing comfort, ask the child what's going on and what he or she needs. Not surprisingly, this suggestion is often met with skepticism. Yet which is more crazy—listening to yourself and giving yourself kind loving thoughts, or continuing the usual negative dialogue that you've been used to having with yourself?

CD NOTE

Solution for communicating with your inner child:
If you have the CD set, be sure to listen to the Inner Child Track (CD #5 tracks 4 & 5). Grab a piece of paper and a pen, pencil, marker, crayon or paint brush, and respond with your dominant hand. Ask your inner child these questions:
· Why are you upset?
· What would make you happy?
· What are you afraid of?

Next, using your other hand, allow the child to write back. The goal here is to get a healthy dialogue going with your child.

I'm sure that you parents have experienced times when you had to undress your screaming child and put him to bed or strap him into a car seat when he wasn't cooperative. As parents we do whatever it takes to ensure our children grow up safe and healthy. That's also the role of the loving, nurturing adult part of you. There are times when your inner child wants a cookie or an extra helping and you just need to say, "No." We set boundaries with our children, we tell them it's okay to play in the fenced backyard, but that they must not play on the freeway. And it's sometimes okay to have a cookie, but not the whole bag!

For many of us, if we fed our children what we have in the past fed ourselves, it would be considered child abuse!

Your job is to learn to give love and care to yourself and to be your own loving, nurturing, responsible parent.

How stressed are you?

Now for the other big category of problem eating. We live in a fast-paced, high anxiety world. It's as if we are constantly being chased by tigers. Our tigers can be spouses, children, career,

finances, relatives, school, politics, the national economy, global warming and man's inhumanity to man. It's rare for me to see a client who does not indulge in stress eating. The vast majority of overweight people use food to deal with stress. Once in a while, I do come across a client who will go through a time of stress, eating very little. When stressed, they are preoccupied with the stressful events. But once the stress event is resolved, they eat . . . and eat . . . and eat.

For stress eaters, the story goes something like this: The stuff starts hitting the fan at work and it's off to the vending machine for a Snickers bar, bag of chips or that liquid candy known as a soda. Or perhaps it's a trip to the coffee cart for a double venti latte and a scone. (A venti latte is equivalent to 340 calories; 160 from fat.)

For some women the story plays out like this: She's Wonder Mom, fighting traffic after work to pick her children up at school, taking one to soccer practice

It's as if we are constantly being chased by tigers.

and the other to dance lessons; then to the grocery store; then home to make dinner and get it on the table. After cleaning up dinner, helping with homework and starting a load of laundry, she sees that the kids get to bed. Then finally, the house is quiet, and Mom sits down with a bowl of ice cream, a bag of cookies, chips or her cheese and crackers. And so to bed with a heavy stomach, to grab a few hours of sleep before doing it all over again.

Stress is, in and of itself, addicting. Your body becomes addicted to the rush of adrenalin poured into your bloodstream by the fight-or-flight response. You become addicted to the sheer intensity of it all. The stress may not trigger pleasant feelings, but at least they're not boring. But to soothe the unpleasant feelings, many of us depend on empty foods that we think make us feel better, which as we shall see in Chapter Five, actually have the opposite effect.

Chocolate, cheese and today's processed high-fat, high-sugar foods provide immediate feel-good satisfaction mixed with pleasurable tastes. During an exhausting stress-filled day, we often consume a candy bar at work, or cheese, crackers and wine while preparing dinner, or that late-night pint of Cherry Garcia—all without conscious acknowledgment.

Plus, the act of dieting is itself a stressful experience for most people. On top of everything else going on in their lives, my weight loss clients are adding in sessions with me, listening to hypnosis CDs, exercising, figuring out what besides lettuce there is to eat, and buying and preparing healthy meals and snacks. Then the copier runs out of paper, the cell phone is racking up urgent messages, and the boss wants that report in ten minutes—just a typical 21st century day. It's clear to me why some people just give in, go get a mochachino and a muffin and give up.

HOT

In 1973, Canadian researcher Hans Selye proved that stress always attacks the weakest link of the body first. Actually, unabated stress weakens the body's ability to protect itself, so that it's more vulnerable to its weaknesses. **Stressed people have higher incidences of heart disease, cancer, bad backs, strained muscles, headaches and other illnesses.**

POINT   **And yet stress was meant to be a life *saver*.** Millennia ago, saber-toothed tigers would chase us across the grassy plains. Naturally, that caused stress and adrenalin would kick in so we could outrun the tiger. (Or else the tiger might sneak up behind us and bite into us.) On those occasions the stress sent us into shock and we therefore died a fairly painless death.

Today, we have our own tigers, both real and imagined. Some people feel chased—they are nervous, tense and anxious—while others go into the death mode of shock, shutting down and becoming depressed. But today, stress triggers different results. Historically, outrunning the tiger used up the toxins created by the stress. If a person is literally being eaten by a tiger, death comes quickly. Now, instead, stress builds up in the body and becomes toxic, allowing for the vulnerability of disease. In our world today, cardio activity is an even more essential element for healthy living than it was for our

ancestors because it helps dissipate any built-up toxins in our bodies.

Solutions for stress eating:

Learning and using stress-reduction techniques are essential survival skills for daily living. Actually, the notion of stress reduction is a misnomer. No matter what techniques we use, the stress will continue. Employers, employees and clients have temper tantrums. We will be caught in traffic. The plane flight will be delayed. The toilet will overflow. Life does not go according to our plans and schedules. It never has and it never will. Even today in our modern world, we are still being chased by saber-toothed tigers of a different stripe. All we can do is take charge of our *reaction* to the events we experience each day. One former client effectively keeps a small sign on her phone and her monitor reading: **Response is <u>my choice</u>.** She says it keeps her from knee-jerk negative reactions to unexpected events. "I focus on that sign many times a day, and it has saved me from many hasty, unwise actions," Joyce reports.

Stress and emotional eating are bad habits, not character flaws. I am surprised at how many people are unaware they eat in reaction to stress.

journal exercise

What are you stressing about?

Once you realize that you do stress eat, it's important to identify the situations in your life that create stress. So make a list of every trigger you can think of that sends you racing for the refrigerator or the vending machine. Examine your life from the moment you wake until the moment you fall asleep, and see when you feel the urge for comfort food. Look at both workdays and days off. It may help to carry a little notebook around for a week and jot down what kinds of events set you off toward a Big Mac attack. Once you become aware of your stressors, then you can develop a plan of action to create alternative behaviors when you are stressed.

_____

_____

_____

_____

_____
_____
_____
_____
_____
_____
_____
_____

At Slender for Life™, we teach three stress-reduction techniques in addition to self-hypnosis. In the very first session clients are taught the **Stress Reduction Response**, which is especially useful because it can be done in almost any situation—even covertly during meetings when you might need it the most!

Instructions: Squeeze your thumb and forefinger together, take a deep breath in through your nose, then slowly exhale through your mouth while releasing your thumb and forefinger. This technique is used whenever stress events occur.

I also teach a **Waking Trance or Learning Trance**, a simple form of eye fixation described by James Braid in the 1850s. Using this technique alters your physiology, taking you out of stress, anger, fear and/or depression and may synchronize the left and right hemispheres of your brain. This waking trance also works wonders at ending the Siren's song of the chocolate, cookie or whatever food is calling out to you.

Instructions: Pick a spot on the wall above eye level that you can gaze at, so that your eyes have to go up. As you do this now, just let your mind relax. Notice that in a matter of moments, as you focus on that single spot, you can allow your awareness to expand outward into the periphery. Notice you can begin to see things in the periphery. In fact, you are sharply aware of the things on the left side of your peripheral vision … and now, the things on the right side of your peripheral vision … as you stay focused on that spot. You can now move your eyes around while staying in peripheral vision with a slightly upward look. (Refer to CD 2, Track 6 to listen to this exercise.)

The Stress Reduction Response can be done in almost any situation.

Another method of caging those tigers is the **Floating Perspective** exercise. **Instructions:** Imagine floating up so high that as you look down on your life now, all time as you know it is condensed into a timeline only an inch long. By doing this you gain a new perspective on that moment. With all time only an inch long, the stressful moment you were experiencing can't be seen—it doesn't even compare to a grain of sand on the beach of time. In the grand perspective of the universe, it is nothing. By realizing that whatever is going on in your life is not even as significant as a thread in the carpet, you can float back down into your body and focus on solutions rather than awfulizing the situation. (Refer to CD 2, Track 7 to listen to this exercise.)

You can stop stress eating

Since eating—and especially eating junk food—as a response to stress is so prevalent, it will take conscious effort on your part to squelch that impulse and substitute healthier behaviors.

CD NOTE

There are three steps in overcoming stress eating. The first step is to learn new stress coping skills. Using CD 2 Track 7 as well as listening to CD 6 Track 2 and 3 (Stress Buster) will allow you to become calm and relaxed in difficult situations.

Step 1. Learn the Relaxation Response. That is, any time you begin to feel any tension, anxiety or fear, you automatically take a deep breath. As you exhale, you feel a wave of calmness and relaxation come over you and you are in control. This hypnotic suggestion is installed into your subconscious behavior strategies by listening to your CDs.

Step 2. For each kind of situation that usually causes you to become stressed or upset, create three positive new activities you can do instead of eating. You then select from one of the three new behaviors and by doing so, take your mind away from the cause of the stress.

Most people have three or four primary causes or situations that trigger their stress eating. Under each category on the worksheet (see Page 126), list at least three different activities that would be appropriate to choose from in each of the different circumstances. For

instance, if one of your top three stress triggers is dealing with your boss, then under dealing with your boss you might list: run an errand, make a cup of tea, drink a glass of water. Other examples of home-based activities might be: going for a walk, calling a friend, listening to music, reading a book or playing your Slender for Life™ CDs. And of course, using your Light Switch Self-hypnosis.

Stewart tended to get easily upset by traffic problems during his long, daily commutes. Unfortunately, his route took him past an endless array of fast food fixes. He frequently told himself, as he whipped into the Dairy Queen drive-through, "Well as long as I have to wait, I might as well enjoy it." After he did the worksheet, he realized he had other options. Now Stewart enjoys books on tape while he commutes, and he altered his route to bypass the biggest concentration of temptations. And several days a week he goes in early, so he can leave early and cut his driving time in half.

Sandra, like so many others, succumbed every evening to the visual stimulation of food commercials on TV. Once she started monitoring her behavior, she noticed the desire to snack was worse when she watched certain programs. She was able to find a very creative solution that also meant she spent less time parked in front of the tube. She bought a TiVo, a digital video recording device that allows her to zip past the commercials and yet still watch programs on the night they air. She also figured out a number of other things she can do while she watches TV that keep her hands busy and keep her mind from wandering to the refrigerator. One night a week she makes a big production of doing her nails, another night she grooms her dog in her lap, and on another she does mending and sewing projects she's put off for ages. By multi-tasking those chores she's also creating some quality time for herself.

> **The key to success with this is to have multiple alternatives in place, so when you feel yourself weakening from stress, you'll already know what else you can do besides eat.**

Step 3. Whenever you interrupt an old behavior pattern you create an opportunity for a conscious choice to control your actions. By developing a stop/interrupt response, you create a kind of back-up insurance measure by retraining your mind to visualize a stop sign any time you think of or reach for food in a stressful situation. This interrupts your behavior long enough for you to decide if it would be wise and appropriate to eat that particular food at that time.

Try using the stop/interrupt response prior to taking the first bite of a meal or a snack. In so doing, you are brought into the present time so you may eat consciously, rather than wandering off somewhere else in another trance.

WORKSHEET

Write in your top three stress situations and choices for new behaviors.

1. Stress Situation: _____

Trigger

⬇

Tension
Anxiety
Fear   ➡   Think of Food or Eating   ➡   Stop Sign

Take a Deep Breath

⬇

Calm & Confident

↙ ↘

Solve Problem OR 3 Positive Behaviors

1. _____

_____

2. _____

_____

3. _____

_____

_____

2. Stress Situation: _____

Trigger

↓   Tension
           Anxiety   →   Think of Food or Eating   →   Stop Sign
           Fear

Take a Deep Breath

↓

Calm & Confident

↙ ↘

Solve Problem OR 3 Positive Behaviors

1. _____
   _____

2. _____
   _____

3. _____
   _____

3. Stress Situation: _____

Trigger

↓   Tension
           Anxiety   →   Think of Food or Eating   →   Stop Sign
           Fear

Take a Deep Breath

↓

Calm & Confident

Solve Problem OR 3 Positive Behaviors

1. _____

2. _____

3. _____

Another good use of this technique is to stop **binge eating,** a classic response to high stress. When you're eating too much too fast, you are in the binging trance. You need to get out of that trance and return to a conscious state of mind, aware of your body—aware of your feet on the floor and your behind in the chair—and seize control of what you're eating, how much you are eating and ultimately your weight.

Don't forget your greatest ally: self-hypnosis

Finally, here are some additional hypnotic suggestions you can use when working on overcoming emotional eating and having healthier responses to stress.

Emotional eating
- I am in control of my emotions.
- I chose to experience love and joy in my life.
- I am at peace with myself, the world and everyone in it.
- I am excited about today.
- I am excited about my life.
- I love my life.
- Food nourishes my body; love nurtures my heart and soul.
- I eat only when I am physically hungry.

Stress control
- I am calm and relaxed in all situations.
- I see things in their true perspective and keep them in proper proportion.

- Whenever I feel the beginning of any tension, anxiety, or fear, I automatically use the Relaxation Response taking a deep breath and exhaling slowly. I instantly feel a wave of relaxation cover over me and through me from the top of my head down to the tips of my toes.
- I am more relaxed each and every day.
- I am free of stress.
- I remain calm, cool and collected at all times.
- I am balanced, relaxed and poised always.
- I am relaxed and calm in all situations.
- I feel profound peace.
- I relax frequently throughout each day by breathing deeply.
- I give time to myself.
- I recognize and control my negative emotions.
- Peace and inner calmness pervade my being.
- The past is gone; I am creating my future now.
- I am living in the present moment.
- I stop worrying about the future.
- I am becoming more aware in the present moment.
- I stop several times each day to breathe deeply and to focus on my important goals.
- I do everything with love, joy and laughter.
- I give myself time to relax.
- I enjoy what I am doing.
- I am emotionally calm and settled.
- My mind is becoming clear, calm and composed.
- I confront and handle any problem calmly and easily.

By this point in the process, you should have better insights into your eating history and current patterns—and have clarity about your readiness to get slender for the rest of your life. In the next chapter we're going to open your refrigerator and cupboards and study which foods will help your cause to release weight and which foods will hinder it. And if you approach eating with an open mind—and mouth—**you might even become a flexitarian!**

CHAPTER FIVE

Do You Really Know How To Eat Well?

Chapter Five At A Glance

- Dealing with immediate resistance
- Recommended foods
- Foods to minimize
- Perhaps you'd like to be a flexitarian
- How much protein is too much
- Other problem foods
- Carbs—good and bad
- Eating out without pigging out
- What to do if you don't like veggies
- Hypnotic suggestions for eating well
- Top ten tips for making healthy eating easy

IMPORTANT: Do not change your diet if you are seriously ill or on medication, except under the care of a medical doctor.

A phrase I often hear from my clients who are in the midst of this program is: **"It's Not About the Food."** When they say that, I know they will be successful. So, if it's not about the food, then why talk about food? Because there is so much misinformation out there and because marketers have done such an amazing job of promoting ill-health in the name of weight-loss. True, you can lose weight on almost any program that has you burning more calories than you take in. But what about keeping the weight off? What about your long term health?

If you are like most dieters, you think that you know it all, since you've been on every diet and failed. At times, clients will argue with me about food and what they believe to be healthy eating. I respond by asking: If what you believe to be true is working for you, then why are you here seeking assistance?

For many of you who have struggled with food, feeling your emotional pain was never an option. You simply buried your pain inside glazed donuts or drowned it with fettuccine Alfredo. You didn't even realize you were sad, lonely, depressed or exhausted. The numbing effect of high-fat, sugary foods also increased your appetite, causing you to eat more without feeling full. You're stuffed. You are zoned out. You don't feel. You are drunk with food, and it's off to bed. Sound familiar?

There is a better way. If you are following the program in order—and I sincerely urge you to do so— by now you should be getting good at self-hypnosis and have a better understanding of what's been holding you back from your goals and why you eat what you eat. Now it's time to talk about the choices you can make around food—both good and bad.

What if you're already in resistance?

I realize this is the part of the program where you're most likely to feel resistance. Who wants to give up comfort foods—at least not

CD NOTE

until you're convinced there's one helluva great reason to do so! Before you even read my dietary suggestions, if you think adopting a healthier way of eating will be especially difficult for you, then at least try this. Simply listen to Weight Control CD #6 tracks 4 & 5 once a day every day for two weeks, and do self-hypnosis five times a day every day using suggestions such as:

> · I am open to eating healthfully.
> · I am open to new ideas about my food choices.
> · I choose to give love and care to my body.
> · I give myself time for my taste buds to change.
> · I prefer to eat fruits, vegetables and whole grains.
> · I allow for changes in my life.

Then read—or reread—this chapter, keeping in mind that change is a continuum, and all you have to do now is start moving in the direction of healthier eating. If you keep progressing in the right direction, you will eventually reach your goal weight—and be able to maintain it.

Exactly what healthy eating comprises will look different for each person.

Radical changes produce radical results.
Small changes produce small results.

My recommendations for healthy eating are radical—and some would call them extreme. But look at it this way. Radical changes produce radical results. Small changes produce small results. Over the years, I have consistently seen that people who make radical changes have the greatest success and tell me it was easy. They find it easier to just change, and they discover that any desire for the fatty foods that caused them to put on their excess weight very quickly vanishes. Those who make small changes are the least likely to succeed and have the most difficulty. Moderation may work for moderate people, but not for the rest of us compulsive, passionate, obsessive people.

Moderation is killing Americans

Nutritionist Jeff Novick got this absolutely right when he wrote: "The concept of Moderation is killing Americans. On average, Americans are taking in less than **40%** of the minimum recommended amounts of whole grains, vegetables, fruits and fiber. Yet, at the same time, they are taking in over **230%** of the amount of saturated fat, added sugars, other fats, refined grains and sodium.

So, who can moderate?

Moderation would do absolutely nothing to improve these numbers.

What we do need is a dramatic increase in the amount of fruits, vegetables and whole grains while at the same time a dramatic decrease in the amount of Sat Fat, added sugars, fats, refined grains and sodium.

Moderation is only an excuse and rationalization which is being fueled by the clever marketing and advertising of the food industry to keep us doing the things we know we shouldn't be doing and to keep us consuming their products, which in the end, is actually a major contributor to our ill health and early death."

You are the fat you eat

Fat is normally measured two different ways—in grams, and in percentage of total fat calories. Usually, fat is expressed as a percentage of total calories, since food is consumed to satisfy our need for calories, not our need for weight. Groups such as the American Medical Association and the American Heart Association have recommended a 30 percent total fat calorie diet to reduce the

risk of heart disease and many types of cancer. By their recommendation, no more than 30 percent of all the calories you consume in a day should come from fat. However, we do know based on the work of dietary health experts such as Dr. John McDougall, Dr. Neil Barnard, Dr. Dean Ornish and Dr. T. Colin Campbell, that fat calories should actually be no more than 10 percent of the total calories consumed each day. Sadly today, most Americans consume as much as 40 percent of their total calories as fat.

While fat is an energy source, we hardly use any fat energy in our sedentary lifestyles. Instead, we store fat in our bodies like a pillow.

In order to begin to release weight, most men and women need to consume less than 20 percent total fat calories.

If you consumed 1200 calories in a day and if 20 percent of the calories were from fat, it would mean you consumed 240 fat calories. Since there are 9 calories in just one gram of fat, 240 divided by 9 equals 27 total grams of fat.

You may desire to release weight faster than this. If you reduce your fat consumption to 15 percent total fat calories, or 20 grams of fat per day at 1200 total calories, and you exercise, you may release about one to two pounds per week. At 5 to 10 percent total fat calories you will probably release about two to three pounds each week. Doing the math you can see that eating only 5 to10 percent total fat calories is a much more motivating way to achieve results.

Moderate change results in little benefit.

But sometimes BIG is better

Why do you suppose the chances of success are greater with the more radical change? Dr. Dean Ornish found that big, radical, comprehensive changes are often easier for people than small, incremental ones. For example, he says that people who make moderate changes in their diets get the worst of both worlds: They feel deprived and hungry because they aren't eating everything they want, but they aren't making big enough changes to quickly see an improvement in how they feel, or in measurements such as weight, blood pressure and cholesterol.

But the heart patients who went on Ornish's tough, radical program saw quick, dramatic results, reporting a 91 percent decrease in frequency of chest pain in the first month. "These rapid improvements are a powerful motivator," he says. "When people who have had so much chest pain that they can't work, or make love, or even walk across the street without intense suffering, find that they are able to do all of those things without pain in only a few weeks, then they often say, 'These are choices worth making.'"

While it's astonishing that most patients in Ornish's demanding program stick with it, studies show that two-thirds of patients who are prescribed statin drugs (which are highly effective at cutting cholesterol) stop taking them within one year. What could possibly be a smaller or easier lifestyle change than popping a pill every day? But Ornish says patients stop taking the drug because it doesn't actually make them feel any better. The drug doesn't deal with causes of high cholesterol, such as obesity, that make people feel unhealthy.

The paradox holds that big changes are easier than small ones.

Small changes equate to small, insufficient wins. Moderate change results in little benefit. Without experiencing sufficient wins that are visible, timely, unambiguous and meaningful, your efforts to change invariably run into serious problems. Change takes place at the extremes. Change does not take place at the norm—it only occurs at either end of the bell curve. Sadly, Dr. Dennis H. Novack tells us in *The New Medicine* that 50 percent of the causes of mortality in the

U.S. are related to modifiable behaviors such as diet.

The books *The McDougall Program For Maximum Weight Loss* or Dr. Neal Barnard's *Breaking the Food Seduction* are highly recommended and provide safe and nutritionally sound guidance for achieving a 5 to 10 percent fat calorie approach. If you are truly interested in exploding the dietary myths that you've held as true, I also urge you to read *The Pleasure Trap* by Douglas Lisle, PhD. and Alan Goldhamer, D.C., *The Food Revolution* by John Robbins and *The China Study* by T. Colin Campbell, PhD.

While you are the one who ultimately decides on the eating strategy that best fits your needs, according to JAMA (the Journal of the American Medical Association) 280,000 Americans are killed annually by diseases due to excess weight.

You may be really surprised at what's good for you

A starch based diet causes lifelong weight loss if you continue eating that way.

The solution to weight control is to employ a starch based eating strategy. Starch you say?! **Yes, *starch*.** A starch based diet causes permanent weight loss if you continue eating that way. The reason is pretty obvious: a large, white baked potato is only 150 calories and a cup of rice is only 200 calories. Starches are low in calories, low in fat and high in carbohydrate, which satisfies the hunger drive. There are enough calories in starches to meet your needs for energy and satisfy your hunger. I've been eating pretty close to vegan

for several years. (A vegan diet contains no animal products at all—no chicken, fish or dairy.) I feel more energetic and my energy is quickly replenished. (Of course, the key is to find new ways of eating starches. Slathering them with butter or sour cream is not what I'm talking about!)

You can use hypnosis to increase your desire for foods that burn off fat and inches while giving you lots of energy as well as improve your health.

The foods you should eat include the following:

All whole grains and whole-grain cereals: such as brown rice, quinoa, corn, oatmeal, barley, millet and wheat berries; many packaged grain cereals, puffed grains and other healthful cereals containing less than 7 grams of sugar.

Squash: such as acorn, butternut, buttercup, pumpkin and zucchini.

Root vegetables: such as potatoes, sweet potatoes and yams.

Legumes: such as peas, split peas, black eyed peas, string beans, chick peas, lentils, adzuki, navy, pinto and black beans.

Green and yellow vegetables: such as collard greens, broccoli, kale, mustard greens, cabbage, various types of lettuce and watercress, celery, cauliflower, carrots, asparagus and tomatoes.

Fruits: such as apples, bananas, berries, grapefruit, oranges, peaches and pears. (Limit these to two servings per day.)

A fiber-rich diet is essential. Fiber makes foods filling without being fattening. High-fiber foods also hold blood sugar levels steady, which prevents you from falling prey to impulse eating. Fiber makes you feel more like you've had enough to eat by filling up your stomach to a greater extent. Fiber delays the emptying of the stomach and reduces the transit time in the intestines. **Fibers are made only by plants and found only in vegetable foods.** There is no fiber in beef, pork, chicken, lobster, cheese, egg or other animal-derived foods.

Here's what my client Sonya had to say about this way of eating. "I was thinking 'Here we go again, another diet.' But I let go of two pounds this week, and I even had my family over for dinner. I served roasted vegetables with no butter and no oil and my dad went on and on about how good they were. Everyone seemed to enjoy the meal. I'm discovering this is very doable."

And Karen added, "I am enjoying experimenting with various

grains. I made tacos with bulgur and they were really good. I'd serve them to company!"

One good way to think about this is to become a *flexitarian*—someone who is not overly rigid about food choices, and allows for occasional indulgences on holidays, birthdays and so on.

That approach can stave off any feelings of deprivation that you might feel if you were the only one not eating a piece of birthday cake. This eating plan is not meant to make you feel bad about what you eat—conversely, it's meant to make you feel *good* that you're taking such great care of yourself—and getting your weight under control in the bargain!

Suzanne Havala Hobbs, a health policy professor at the University of North Carolina-Chapel Hill, credits the growth of flexitarianism to the nation's better understanding of the diet-disease connection. "Whether you make a commitment to eating strictly vegetarian or not, cutting back your dependence on meat is something most people acknowledge they know they should do," she said in the *Seattle Post-Intelligencer.*

After a lifetime of yo-yoing, Mike arrived in my office fairly skeptical, but desperate. It took him quite awhile to work out a balanced flexitarian plan for himself, but he stuck with it and finally achieved his weight release goals. "I stopped craving chocolate, I eat more fruit, and I love brown rice now. I mostly eat vegan at home, but I eat chicken a few times a week when I eat out. I haven't had a burger in two years! I have an eating style now that I can use anywhere. It's rare that I can't find something to eat when out or at a friend's. I eat better food now—mostly organic."

What we eat often impacts others.

There are many ways to be a flexitarian, so experiment and see what works for your lifestyle. What we eat often impacts others. If you're also trying to lead your family in a healthier direction—and why wouldn't you?—then you may need to bring different family members along at their own pace.

Stephen gave it a try and was surprised at the results. "I think your approach to food is bold and refreshing and will be in wonderful alignment with so many people who are already vegetarians or at least leaning that way. I think the flexitarian attitude is a winner, because it doesn't make you bad or wrong if you want to eat some meat. One thing that I got from you and adopted long ago was to view meat as a condiment. As a serious carnivore, I happily found no problem cutting the percentage of meat in my recipes by 50-70 percent, with the added benefit of being able to stretch recipes further, spend less and cook less."

During the week you may eat a mainly vegan diet, then on the weekends enjoy dining out and having meat or other food options. The scope of Slender For Life™ is not to convince you to eat a certain food plan, but to teach you how to make conscious choices—conscious decisions that will ultimately result in releasing weight and maintaining your healthier self for the rest of your life.

One essential point is to not think of this way of eating as a diet that you follow until you reach your goal weight. As we all know, that kind of thinking piles the pounds right back on the minute you revert to your old ways. No, this has to be a change for life, a change to a better life. If someone told me that I can never have ice cream again in my life, I would probably be the first one in line at the ice cream counter. And yet it's been years since I have eaten ice cream, because I simply have no desire for it.

> This has to be a change for life, a change to a better life.

Foods to minimize or eliminate

Let's review the most common problem foods. This information comes from the McDougall Program for Maximum Weight Loss. I highly recommend that you at least minimize if not eliminate them all—or as many of these fattening foods as possible from your life. Once having made your decisions, use your Slender For Life™ System to shed your desire for these fattening foods once and for all. Remember, as Dr. John McDougall will tell you, "The fat you eat is the fat you wear!" (Olive oil, when worn on the body, looks no better than any other fat.)

Meat: including beef, pork and lamb. All are rich in fat, cholesterol and cause a distinct insulin spike—sometimes greater than foods like pasta—and meats are high in sulfur-containing amino acids which leach calcium from the bones.

Poultry and fish: poultry has about the same amount of cholesterol and fat as red meat, while fish varies depending on the type. Some fish are higher in cholesterol than red meat, others lower.

Here's what Melissa learned after giving up meat. "I realized that I have not had meat, poultry or fish until this last weekend in over six weeks. I have not missed it. I feel better and I have more energy."

And Sherri had a similar reaction. "I always loved my meat, but in the last six weeks I've hardly had any. I was at a friend's house this weekend and they served delicious looking steaks, and everyone raved about how good they were. I ate a few bites and wondered why I was eating it at all. That is a huge change for me!"

But I need my protein!

Who do you know with a protein deficiency? Do you know anyone who has a disease, such as kwashiorkor, caused by a lack of protein? I don't—and I don't know that I ever have. The problem is *excess* protein. Sixty-five percent of the U.S. population is fat, and many have the diseases that come with being fat. Excess food is the problem—certainly not lack of protein.

It's extremely difficult for anyone to become protein-deficient. You would have to give up eating all together. Practically all unrefined foods are loaded with proteins. Rice is 8 percent protein, oranges 8 percent, potatoes 11 percent and beans 26 percent. A 2.7-ounce tub of instant oatmeal contains 9 grams of protein. One-half cup of uncooked quinoa has 11 grams of protein. One medium-size banana and a 1.5-ounce box of raisins each have more than one

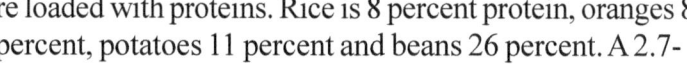

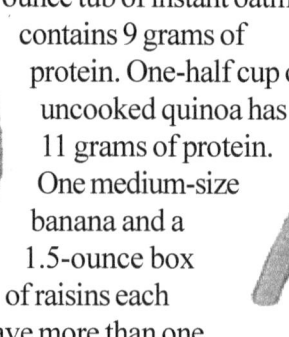

gram of protein. It is impossible to develop a protein-deficient diet based on vegetables, beans, grains and fruits. If you want extra protein, consider wheat and soy products such as seitan and tofu—more about tofu later.

> **And in spite of the tales you've been told, vegetable proteins <u>are</u> complete proteins.**

All the essential and nonessential amino acids are represented in single unrefined starches such as rice, corn, wheat and potatoes in amounts in excess of every individual's needs—even for endurance athletes or weight lifters. We don't have to seek out some complicated combinations of foods to make proteins complete. If that were true, we would never have survived as a species. There is no need to intentionally choose special combinations of foods.

A healthy adult male uses less than 20 grams of protein each day. Yet an average American consumes 160 grams of protein each day: eight times more than we need! Excess protein is not converted to carbohydrate or fat, nor is it stored. Our body has no choice but to dispose of the 140 grams of excess protein. The elimination of excess protein occurs through the kidneys and liver. Due to this excess, they become overworked, and the kidneys begin to deteriorate over time. In addition, animal proteins also contribute to kidney stones.

Excess protein causes changes in kidney metabolism and minerals, especially calcium, are lost through the kidneys in large amounts. The most damaging protein is from animals: meat, poultry, dairy and fish. This leaching of calcium from the body can lead to osteoporosis. Throughout the world, the incidence of osteoporosis correlates directly with protein intake. Countries where meat is a dietary staple have higher incidences of osteoporosis.

Excess protein causes changes in kidney metab-olism.

Although protein and carbohydrates have almost the same number of calories per gram, foods that are high in protein—particularly animal products—are also usually high in fat. Even lean cuts of meat have much more fat than a healthy body needs. And animal products always lack fiber. Fiber helps make foods more satisfying without adding many calories, and it is only found in foods from plants.

The dairy for calcium myth

Members of the Physicians Committee for Responsible Medicine recommend that you minimize or eliminate dairy products, including milk, yogurt, cheese and eggs.

All are loaded with fat and cholesterol. Cow's milk contains 50 percent more fat than mother's milk. No other species still drinks milk after the young offspring phase, and there is no other species which drinks the milk of a different species other than domesticated cats and dogs, which have been made accustomed to this. Even low-fat dairy products are not recommended because of potential health hazards including allergies, childhood diabetes, arthritis and lactose intolerance. Unfortunately, dairy industry advertisements do not reveal the unwanted side-effects, which include increased risk of prostrate and ovarian cancer, diabetes, obesity and heart disease. Use small amounts of low fat soy milk or rice milk as alternatives.

No Milk? Where do I get my calcium? Have you ever seen "Milk Builds Strong Bones" on a milk carton? No—and you won't. FDA regulations do not permit false advertising. Milk does not protect the bones.

Most of us grew up with nutritional posters on our elementary school walls that were funded by the Dairy Council. We were taught in school that milk builds strong bones and that milk was good for us. I even grew up on a dairy farm where milk was sold.

Today we know that the Dairy Council's own studies show that dairy actually takes calcium out of the body. And we know from Dr. John McDougall, the Physicians Committee for Responsible Medicine and others, that dairy foods are unhealthy and can contribute to obesity and other illnesses. In spite of the evidence to not eat dairy products, most Americans will not hear of it. They will not even look at the facts. Most Americans continue to eat cheese and feed their children milk.

Experience around the world fails to support benefits claimed by the dairy industry. Countries with the highest traditional consumption of dairy products (United States, Sweden, Israel, Finland and the United Kingdom) also have the highest rates of osteoporosis-related hip fractures. Places in the world with a traditionally low intake of dairy (Hong Kong, Singapore, countries in rural Africa) have the lowest incidence of osteoporosis. Finland has both the highest milk and milk product consumption rate and the highest diabetes rate worldwide. Spain has one of the lowest milk consumption rates and has one of the lowest diabetes rates.

Dairy actually takes calcium out of the body.

If calcium is the key and milk is such a great source, why are there still ten million Americans with osteoporosis? Long-standing recommendations to increase calcium intakes have had little or no effect on the prevalence of osteoporosis or fractures in the United States. Worldwide, the incidence of osteoporosis correlates directly and strongly with animal protein intake.

Increased dairy consumption equals increased osteoporosis.

Calcium is a mineral, and like all minerals, it comes from the ground. There are many good sources of calcium. Kale, broccoli, and other green leafy vegetables contain calcium that is readily absorbed by the body. A report in the American Journal of Clinical Nutrition found that calcium absorbability was actually higher for kale than for milk, and concluded that "greens such as kale can be considered to be at least as good as milk in terms of their calcium absorbability." Beans are also rich in calcium. **Dairy products are not required for good nutrition.**

Calcium Absorption Rates

Brussels sprouts	63.8 percent
Mustard greens	57.8 percent
Broccoli	52.6 percent
Turnip greens	51.6 percent
Kale	50 percent
Cow's milk	32 percent

Green leafy vegetables and beans are rich in calcium, without the disadvantages of dairy products. While there is somewhat less calcium in broccoli than in milk, the absorption fraction—the percentage your body can actually use—is higher from broccoli and nearly all other greens than from milk. If you are looking for calcium for whatever reason, you will find more than you need in fortified juices and soy milks.

The key in maintaining calcium balance, however, is not only to have an adequate intake, but to minimize calcium losses. That means avoiding animal protein, limiting sodium (salt) in your diet, getting adequate exercise and enough sunlight for vitamin D generation in your body.

Fats, good and bad

Minimize your use of butter and all oils, including olive, safflower, peanut and corn oil. Oil is simply a liquid form of fat. Despite misinformation to the contrary, **margarine is the worst offender of all,** since it is partially hydrogenated.

Don't I need good fat? Yes—you do need some fat in your diet—for survival, all you really need is about 3 to 4 percent of your total calories. A healthful amount for daily intake would be about 10 percent. That's all! Most people in Western countries get ten times that amount. A total of 68 percent of the population of industrialized nations dies of fat-intake illnesses, including heart and circulatory diseases. You will get all the fat you need from a diet of vegetables, fruits, beans and whole grains. Your body can synthesize the fats you need from the foods you eat. The safest and healthiest way to get your essential fatty acids is in their natural forms. Beans, vegetables and fruits have trace amounts of fat and are rich in alpha-linolenic acid. In this form, fats are found in the correct amounts in protected environments surrounded by vitamins, minerals, fibers, antioxidants and other phytochemicals to make them balanced nutritionally.

Fish oils have been popularized as an aid against everything from heart problems to arthritis. The bad news about fish oils is that omega-3s in fish oils are highly unstable molecules that tend to decompose and, in the process, unleash dangerous free radicals. Research has shown that omega-3s are found in a more stable form in vegetables, fruits and beans.

You should also minimize nuts, seeds, avocados, olives and soybean products (including tofu, soy cheese and soy milk).
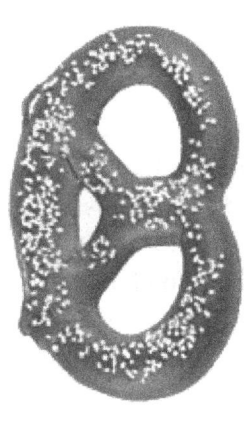
Soybean products are high in fat, unless they have been specially processed, but low-fat varieties are also not recommended. Processed soy foods such as soy burgers and soy cheese may increase your risk for cancer, impair function of your thyroid, immune system, brain, as well as cause bone loss and reproductive problems. Consuming a small amount of tofu in a stir fry or a small amount of soy milk in your oatmeal is not a concern. A new issue, though, is that more and more of the soybeans grown today are being genetically modified, which puts products made from them into the non-food category, since your body will not recognize them as real foods.

Other foods to limit

Dried fruit and fruit juices: eat your fruits as they were grown. With dried fruit and fruit juices you are mainlining sugar.

White flour products, such as breads, bagels, pretzels and white pasta: the less a food is processed, the better it is for weight release. Flour products are composed of fragments of grain, or relatively small particles, which increase absorption and slow weight release. While you are releasing weight, I recommend that you eat only about four slices of whole grain bread each week. Once you are at your ideal weight, you can eat whole grain or flourless bread on a daily basis and maintain your weight. **Sweeteners, including sugar,**

Chocolate is still not a health food!

honey, molasses, maple syrup, etc.: they all have the same negative effect on you. Sugar is sugar, and all forms react the same way in your body. Some of my clients use artificial sweeteners. Personally, I do not and would not. Many clients use estevia (or stevia), an herb, as a sweetener.

Chocolate: despite all the recent press about the alleged benefits of dark chocolate, it's still not a health food! I have previously discussed the addictive qualities of chocolate. When you do eat chocolate, make it a small piece of pure chocolate. You will get the chocolate taste with much less fat and sugar than you will from cheap chocolate candy, which is nothing more than chocolate flavored sugar.

But I'm addicted to carbs

This is one of my favorites! It's really hard for me to keep a straight face when people tell me they are addicted to carbs.

As I was researching the effects of low-carb diets, I began hearing reports on TV about the mood swings, depression, anger and concentration difficulties that can be experienced while limiting carbohydrates. The restriction of carbohydrates impacts serotonin levels resulting in these mood swings. In December 2003, the Physicians Committee for Responsible Medicine reported that of 429 participating individuals on low-carb diets, 44 percent experienced constipation, 40 percent experienced loss of energy, 40 percent reported bad breath, 33 percent reported heart-related problems, 29 percent experienced difficulty concentrating, 19 percent experienced kidney problems, 9 percent reported gallbladder problems or removal, 5 percent reported gout, 4 percent reported diabetes, 4 percent reported colorectal or other cancers and 3 percent reported osteoporosis.

HOT

POINT

Instead of looking for low-carb foods, you should be looking for products that don't have any added sugar or refined flours.

Many of the new low-carb products are just as refined and faraway from their natural state as the old low-fat products. And look at all the unnecessary ingredients like diglycerides, carrageenan, acesulfame potassium—some products have dozens of ingredients! The

ingredient label should be simple; it should contain real food like potatoes, wheat, apples or cinnamon.

Of course we really do crave carbohydrates. Our bodies need carbohydrates, even in childhood, as a nutrient. **Carbohydrates are the most efficient forms of energy that we can consume.** But I'm not talking about Oreos, Pringles and Krispy Kreme donuts. The foods our bodies crave and need for nutrition are vegetables, whole grains and fruit. No one has come to me complaining about craving brown rice, beans and apples.

You want natural food—the way it grew from the earth.

Unfortunately, when people tell me they're hooked on carbs, what they're really saying is that they're hooked on sugar. What they are craving are foods loaded with sugar or foods that rapidly disintegrate into millions of sugar molecules that rush to the bloodstream during the process of digestion. White flour and white sugar provide little nutritional value and squeeze healthier foods out of your diet. The more sugar and refined grains you eat, the less you eat nutritionally complete foods that provide essential vitamins and other micronutrients.

Mike finally kicked his sugar habit, and offers this advice. "Hang in there getting off sugar—it took me about a month to stop craving it—but now I don't think about it, and it's no big deal to turn down pastries, cookies, etc. The same goes for chips."

But let's focus on the good carbs. You want natural food— the way it grew from the earth—foods that are closest to their natural state: apples, oranges, potatoes and whole grains are packed full of life-giving nutrients. According to William Castelli, of the National Heart, Lung and Blood Institute, "Some people scoff at vegetarians, but they have only 40 percent of our cancer rate. They outlive us. On average they outlive other men by about six years now."

Charles, who had been overweight his whole life, finally released his excess weight on the Slender For Life™ program. He was surprised at how much his food preferences changed. "I became a vegan, and it is a huge success, because I was addicted to cheese. I like not feeling bloated. My cravings have disappeared, thankfully. Low-fat hummus and tofu are my new favorite foods. I am surprised that I like veggies and tofu now."

So what is a healthy, plant-based diet?

It is primarily composed of fruits, vegetables and whole grains. Food should look as if it was dug from the earth or picked off a plant or a tree. If man has sliced and diced it and put it in a package, it should be avoided. Animal products such as beef, pork, poultry and fish are for special occasions, and an appropriate serving would be the size of a deck of cards, bar of soap, or the palm of your hand.

This is the diet that we humans have evolved on. Anthropologists tell us that human communities formed 35,000 years ago depended on wild grains, vegetables and berries as their staple foods. For most human societies, the majority of food came from cultivated grains, vegetables, beans and fruits. Animal foods were in short supply and were reserved for ceremonial and celebratory feasting. We were never intended to eat the rich American diet that is so prevalent today.

For starters, Mom was right. **The most important meal of the day is breakfast**. Having a healthy breakfast regulates your appetite. In addition, researchers have found measurable reductions in stress hormone levels in people who have breakfast, compared to those who don't. Healthy protein sources are vital for ending physical cravings. Healthy protein sources include foods such as oatmeal, brown rice, quinoa, beans and legumes.

Our taste buds' memory only lasts about three weeks. By starting out each morning with a breakfast of oatmeal or other whole-grain cereal, having a piece of fruit midmorning and mid-afternoon for a snack, with lunch and dinner consisting of a fist-size serving of vegetables and a fist-size serving of high-fiber grains or legumes,

 **a person can change their physical cravings in as little as three weeks**. So for the first three weeks, I urge you to have no dairy products, no processed foods, no sweets including chocolate and sodas, and no beef, pork, poultry or fish.

 Eat breakfast, but beware of coffee drinks and their evil sidekicks. Coffee is now served as mostly sugary syrup, and baked goods such as cookies, muffins and scones that were once considered special treats are part of the daily coffee break. By the way, did you know that coffee consumption is down? Most people are only getting one or two shots of espresso with their flavored sugar syrup. (A frappacino has 530 calories—150 of them from fat!)

A typical healthy day could look something like this:

- Breakfast (within an hour of awakening): hot or cold whole-grain cereal.
- Snack (midmorning): a piece of fruit.
- Lunch (ideally the largest meal of the day): a fist-size serving of vegetables prepared in a nonfat way, a fist-size serving of brown rice or other grains and a fist-size serving of beans or legumes.
- Snack (early afternoon): another piece of fruit or some vegetables or beans.
- Snack (late afternoon): another piece of fruit or some vegetables or beans.
- Dinner (at least three hours before bedtime): a slightly smaller version of lunch.

Eating for energy

This is an athlete's way of eating—frequent small meals. Think of it like this: imagine heating your home with a wood stove. You start out the morning by stoking the stove with wood and lighting the fire. This creates a bed of hot coals that produces heat. This is breakfast, the most important meal of the day. A breakfast of whole-grain cereal gets that fire going. Throughout the day, you must put more wood in the stove to keep the fire going. If you don't, the fire goes out and the house becomes cold.

Our bodies are the same way. By eating frequent small meals, the stomach produces energy from digesting the food. This energy speeds up the metabolism, causing fat burning. If we go a long time without eating, the metabolism slows down and fat burning stops. People who skip breakfast and lunch—and then eat junk throughout the afternoon and a huge dinner at night—are setting a course for disaster with their weight.

Your body does not like to burn fat.

As a species, we once lived in caves and endured long, cold winters. Your body was created to store fat and hold it for energy for those times when there would be little or no food. Your body does not like to burn fat. It works very hard to preserve fat. When you go long periods without eating, you are signaling your body that it's a long, cold winter and to hold onto your fat reserves for survival. But in the 21st century, most of us have our kitchen cupboards loaded with food; our neighbors' cupboards are loaded with food; there are restaurants and grocery stores within five minutes of our homes. It might be a long, cold winter, but we are not going to run out of food. Snacking on cookies, chips and soda pop at work, then coming home to wine, cheese and crackers, is like filling the wood stove with rocks. Pretty soon, it becomes difficult to keep burning the fire that heats the house.

However, it is important to eat when you're hungry. When the gas tank is empty in your car, you fill it. When your stomach is empty, it's time to eat. Just as it's time to stop pumping gas when the gas pump shuts off, it is time to stop eating when your stomach signals your brain that it has enough fuel. You don't stop at each gas station you drive by to put gas in your car. So if you aren't hungry, don't eat.

Vegetables, fruits and whole grains are rich in carbohydrates and are the most efficient forms of energy we can consume. Eating these carbohydrates will fill you up and keep you from becoming hungry. Eating fat causes you to feel hungry and requires you to eat a great deal more food to feel satisfied.

Carbohydrates are the most fundamental and cleanest-burning fuel the body can obtain. Your body is designed to enjoy and efficiently use carbohydrates. Even your tongue and taste buds were designed to select carbohydrates. Your teeth are designed for carbohydrates. The front teeth are shaped with cutting edges to break off pieces of starches, vegetables and fruits, which are then ground by the flat molar teeth at the sides and back of the mouth.

Potatoes are at the top of the carbohydrate list with about 90 percent of their calories deriving from appetite-satisfying carbohydrates. Contrary to popular myth, potatoes can provide complete nutrition for children and adults. Many populations, for example, people in rural populations of Poland and Russia at the turn of the 19th century, have lived in very good health doing extremely hard work with the white potato serving as their primary source of nutrition.

There is no cholesterol or insignificant amounts of cholesterol-raising saturated fats in a potato. People in New Guinea living on diets consisting almost entirely of leaves and sweet potato tubers (with an even greater percentage of carbohydrate calories than white potatoes) have cholesterol levels on the average of 108 mg/dl. (Cholesterol levels below 150 mg/dl are associated with immunity from heart disease.) **Heart disease is unknown in these people on their sweet potato diet.** In animal experiments, potatoes have been shown to have a particularly potent cholesterol-lowering effect. The potato is such a great source of nutrition that it can supply all of the essential protein and amino acids for young children in times of food shortage. Of the calories from

Potatoes can provide complete nutrition for children and adults.

potatoes, only one percent comes from fat, and these few fats are mostly the kind that we need, called essential fats.

 The only carbs you really need to restrict are the refined ones— foods made with white sugar and flour, ranging from sodas to sugary breakfast cereals.

These processed foods fail to fill you up until you've eaten way too many calories. They contain little to no nutritional value. And they're absorbed quickly into your bloodstream, prompting your body to unleash a surge of insulin that accelerates the conversion of calories into fat.

By contrast, fruits, vegetables and whole grains are densely packed with life-sustaining compounds. They're absorbed gradually enough to prevent sudden insulin spikes. And they satisfy better, thanks to their high fiber and fluid content. Eat an apple, and you have a filling, healthful snack for 80 calories. Chow down on cookies, and you can consume 600 empty calories before you know it. Okinawa has the highest percentage of centenarians in the world, and yet Okinawans have no genetic predisposition to longevity. Their secret is locally grown vegetables, seaweed and tofu, rigorous exercise and a low-stress lifestyle. According to a 2003 article in *Newsweek*, if Americans lived more like Okinawans, "80 percent of the nation's coronary care units, one-third of the cancer units, and a lot of the nursing homes would be shut down."

To lose weight, you must burn more calories and eat fewer calories. You can burn more calories by exercising. You can eat fewer calories by consuming less food. That's why you can lose weight on any diet, but it's hard to keep it off because you feel hungry and deprived. **An easier way to consume fewer calories is to eat less fat**, because fat has nine calories per gram, whereas protein and carbohydrates have only four. So when you eat less fat, you consume fewer calories without having to eat less food.

Angela happily released 25 pounds that she had been taking on and off most of her life. She adjusted well to the eating plan. "I like feeling involved in my food choices. I don't feel so stuffed now, and I found I don't miss cookies or pastries at all." And neither will you, if you give it some time and use daily self-hypnosis.

What it looks like on your plate

To insure complete nutrition, one of the easiest to follow overall guides is the Physicians Committee for Responsible Medicine's (PCRM) New Four Food Groups. Devised in 1991, the New Four Food Groups assures an adequate mix of amino acids, essential fats, complex carbohydrates, vitamins and minerals by building the menu from grains, vegetables, legumes (beans, peas, and lentils) and fruits.

Put these groups together in the following amounts for every 1,200 calories in your daily diet:

- **Whole grains:** 3 or more servings (1 serving=1/2 cup hot cereal, 1 ounce dry cereal, 1 slice bread).
- **Vegetables:** 5 or more servings (1 serving=1 cup raw or 1/2 cup cooked).
- **Fruits:** No more than 2 servings per day (1 serving=1 medium piece of fruit, 1/2 cup cooked fruit, 1/2 cup fruit juice).
- **Legumes:** 2 to 3 servings (1 serving=1/2 cup cooked beans or peas)

In this simple plan, animal products are no longer considered dietary essentials and are best eliminated completely. It is also recommended that vegetable oils be kept to a minimum. Start with the grain. About one third to one half of your plate should be rice, noodles, corn, etc., or if you prefer, substitute a starchy vegetable, such as a potato. Next, fill about a quarter of your plate with two different vegetables, such as carrots and a green vegetable—these are vitamin powerhouses. The final quarter of your plate should be filled with legumes: beans, lentils, peas, etc. Fruits make great desserts and snacks. Add a daily multiple vitamin or any other reliable source of vitamin B12, and you're set with complete nutrition.

Meet a success story

"For the first time I feel like I have a solution to the problem, instead of just a stop gap measure," confides Phyllis, a veterinarian tech who has released 80 pounds. Prior to starting Slender For Life™, she had lost and regained the same 80 pounds three different times following a Weight Watchers diet. So how was this different? "I never felt like I was on a diet…we never used the word *diet*. I always feel like I'm eating like a horse, and it's just magically happening. Then there's the calmness and the other benefits that go along with the relaxation and having control over food. I guess the big thing is I never feel like I'm having to watch and pay attention and do this or that. I'm just doing what I've been trained to do, and it's just very easy and very natural."

> **"I never felt like I was on a diet...we never used the word *diet*."**
> **~Phyllis**

When asked if she thought she'd regain those 80 pounds this time, she replied, "No I don't." So what's different? "Well, for one thing, my cravings are gone. My office at Christmas time is unbelievable. Clients just send candy, food and so forth by the pound, and I actually ate my lunch one day at the table that was stacked absolutely high with goodies, and I was not even tempted. I had no desire to eat it! It's not a struggle; it's not a conscious battle—I just plain don't want it."

Phyllis has experienced other benefits as well. "A lot of people notice that I move easier, because I used to have a lot of difficulty with my knees and stuff getting up and down. I also believe I'm actually sleeping better, because when you carry that much weight, it's difficult to breathe. I'm not winded any more…I can do stairs, hills, walks— whatever I feel like without getting so worn out. From an energy stand point, when I come home in the evening, I am more inclined to want to do stuff instead of being worn out and wanting to sit down."

Now that she's taken control of her food issues, Phyllis is thrilled to feel she finally has control over her life. "It's extremely satisfying; it's not like a power thing, it's just very satisfying to feel like I have the knowledge and the ability to take control of something that has plagued me most of my life."

Real life as a vegetarian

It is becoming easier to be a vegetarian. More and more restaurants and even fast-food places are offering meat- and dairy-free alternatives. You can get a rice and bean burrito with no cheese or sour cream at Taco Del Mar, a salad and a potato at Wendy's, a

veggie sub on whole wheat at Subway, and pasta with tomato sauce and veggies in most restaurants. The produce sections in grocery stores are now filled year-round with a vast variety of fresh produce, and most stores carry whole grains, beans, rice and legumes.

Two common challenges to avoiding meat and dairy are being a guest in someone else's home and eating hotel banquet food. Sometimes you can put in a request for steamed vegetables and a potato or rice even at the last minute in a hotel, but when you show up as a guest in someone's home, the choices may be meat and veggies in cheese sauce. Oh well, you do the best you can.

Beware, though—there are still a lot of overweight vegetarians. Most vegetarian recipes call for olive oil and often cheese. Overweight vegetarians are also often living on packaged foods—yes, those refined flour/sugar products. Instead of stocking up on grapes, carrots or garbanzo beans, they turn to crackers, cheese, peanut butter and bread.

Another problem for vegetarians and vegans is rigidity—getting locked into diet mentality. That's why I love the term *flexitarian*. As a flexitarian, you focus most of your foods on fruits, vegetables and whole grains. Meat—if it's eaten at all—is something that's saved for special occasions, holidays and occasional meals in a restaurant. **As a flexitarian, you'll find it easier to roll with the punches and adapt to life's circumstances without guilt, failure and having blown a diet.**

Bruce, who was morbidly obese, finally found relief with

Beware, though— there are still a lot of over- weight vege- tarians.

Slender For Life™. He discovered being a flexitarian was the way to go for him. "I eat mostly vegetables, but I didn't give up meat entirely. I find that when I'm home, eating only vegetables is fine. I do not feel deprived. I really only eat meat as a guest or in restaurants."

Eating healthy is not difficult. It can be simple. Fruits, vegetables and whole grains can taste good and be delicious. An eating strategy based on fruits, vegetables and whole grains should never be boring. There are limitless ways of preparing and enjoying these healthy foods. It's easy to fall off this program if you don't understand how to prepare tasty, satisfying meals. One of the first things you should do is buy a really good vegetarian cookbook or even take a cooking class if you can find one that follows these principles. (See the Appendix for recommended reading.) Also, there are many excellent websites with vegetarian and vegan recipes.

Sally, who has had great success, offers some tips for cooking vegetarian meals. "With low-fat, meatless cooking it becomes crucial to season your food well to bring out the natural flavors. **This is a great time to start an herb garden** or invest in some new herbs and spices for your pantry. Look especially at the wonderful blends that are available—just be sure to check for sugar and high sodium content. I remember when I first gave up meat, I found my meals so bland. But after trying a lot of new spices, my food is just as tasty as ever."

> Eating healthy is not difficult. It can be simple.

Becoming a flexitarian is one of the best things you can do for your health. Now is the time to take back the power we've given to food, to people and to circumstances.

Another advantage of eating well is eliminating your guilt over *not* eating well. And that leads to lots of other good feelings. Imagine the pleasure of looking at your plate and realizing that all your food choices are good for you.

journal exercise

Who do you love?

List all the foods you love and crave, regardless of their value to your health. Now circle the ones that love you back—the ones that nurture you with positive health benefits. The remaining foods on your list signify dead-end relationships, and if you continue a long-term commitment to them, it will only end in heartbreak—or worse—in genuine heart problems for you. This list will give you a quick reality check on how far you have to go on your journey to your goal weight and improved health.

_____

_____

_____

_____

_____

_____

_____

_____

_____

_____

_____

If time is your issue

Is your health and your family's health of the highest importance to you?

I know many of you are wondering where you will find the time to prepare these foods and perhaps venture farther from home to find healthier choices. Part of the answer comes down to priorities. Is your health and your family's health of paramount importance to you? Then identify some time-wasters in your schedule (we all have them if we're honest!) and exchange those for taking the time you need to eat well.

The other part of the answer lies in choosing healthy packaged foods for times when you just plain can't do it any other way. Dr. McDougall's website has a section on approved prepared foods that is highly valuable—no matter how good your intentions are, there will always be days when we need shortcuts, so this list is great. Find it at www.drmcdougall.com and click on Packaged Foods. Nutritionist Jeff Novick's DVD *Fast Food* is also excellent. Read more about it at hypnosishealthinfo.com/jeff-novicks-fast-food. Also check out Jeff's *My Simple Recipes* on Facebook, which I link to on that page.

Drink plenty of water

Drink at least six to eight 8-ounce glasses of water throughout the day. Water flushes out bodily waste as you burn off your fat. Drinking water also removes excess retained water. If you dislike water, hypnosis can be used to increase your desire for drinking water. (Cut back as you approach bedtime to prevent an overactive bladder during the night).

Eating out without pigging out

I know this can be a potential downfall, but it doesn't need to be. My wife and I eat out at least once or twice each week. I usually find it quite easy to order. Mexican and Italian restaurants are some of my favorites. I can order black bean veggie burritos without cheese or sour cream and be a very happy camper. Even if it's not on the menu, most Italian restaurants are happy to prepare pasta with tomato sauce and veggies without dairy. Remember, you have the right to request what you want. The restaurant is working for you. If you don't see anything on the menu, ask the waitperson what the chef can prepare for you. Be courteous in your interactions, and they will usually bend over backwards to accommodate. And then I tip well!

When attending conferences, I make sure to place my meal order early and verify it with the hotel staff when I arrive. One client, who often travels internationally, orders a baked potato for breakfast from room service the night before. If I'm attending a meeting where lunch is provided, I generally bring with me some fruit and perhaps a few almonds or Wasa Crisp Bread.

In Quilcene, Washington, we stopped at a little hole-in-the-wall restaurants for lunch. I wasn't sure what I was getting into, but we were hungry and needed to eat. The establishment served breakfast all day. I spotted Vegetable Hash on the menu. It was served with 2 eggs and smothered in cheese. I thought, "this will work." When the waitress came for our order, I ordered the Vegetable Hash without the eggs and cheese. I could see into the kitchen and watch the cook at the grill. I could see that there was already enough oil on that griddle so I asked the waitress to ask the cook to please cook my veggies and potatoes "dry". "No problem," she replied. I then asked her for a side of salsa.

When my meal came it was a huge colorful platter of hash browns and vegetables that looked and smelled great. Every head in the restaurant turned to see what I had ordered. One man who was about to order asked where that was on the menu. For less than eight bucks I got two very delicious meals. **So, think outside the box when you are ordering!**

I love restaurants and grocery stores with salad bars. There are so many choices of vegetables and fruits, and I love mixing them together for a great speedy meal. Many burger chains now offer vegeburgers on whole wheat buns, so being pinched for time doesn't mean you have to blow your food plan.

A word of caution: When ordering a veggie burger, find out if it is made with cheese and find out how they prepare it. Some restaurants actually take a perfectly good veggie burger and soak it in fat to add flavor. I make sure they take the frozen patty and do nothing to it before placing it on the dry grill or open flame.

Portion Control

Think of eating as fueling your car.

Think of eating as fueling your car. When the gas pump shuts off, you stop pumping gas. And that's what you should do when your appetite tells you that you have enough food (fuel) in your body. And when do you put gas in your car? When it's nearly empty! You don't stop at every gas station you drive by to put gas in your car.

> **Fueling up only when necessary should be our relationship with food. Hunger is a good thing—it means it's time to eat.**

Try this: touch your knee for a moment. Now, how much more aware are you of your knee? Before you touched it, you probably weren't even thinking about your knee. Your hand works like a magnifying glass—it enhances awareness. You can get in touch with your level of fullness by simply placing your hand on your stomach. This allows you to be conscious—of whether or not you are hungry, and as you are eating a meal, when you are full.

Slender For Life™ uses a fullness scale of 0 to 10. Imagine that 0 on this scale is empty—you are ready to eat, you need to eat. As you do begin to eat, you almost immediately feel a release from your hunger pangs—this is level 1. As you continue to eat, you reach level 2, and you're starting to rebound—you feel your body refueling, but you are also still aware of some hunger. You reach 3 and 4 on the scale when you notice that the hunger is nearly gone and has been replaced by new energy for your tasks ahead. Depending on what time it is, you may even be happy to stop eating at level 4— think about how much fuel you will need for the rest of your day. By the time you reach levels 5 and 6, this is satisfied. You are no longer hungry, but you also feel energized by what you've just eaten, not sluggish. This is the point you should not eat beyond.

If you do continue eating, by 7 or 8 you're aware that you've overeaten, rather like you might feel after having two desserts or overindulging in a rich restaurant meal. If you go further, you'll hit 9, which is a very uncomfortable feeling—your clothes are too tight, your energy has drained and you may even feel indigestion. If you persist to level 10 on this scale, you'll feel overstuffed, like you ate way too much at Thanksgiving. It doesn't feel good; you are lethargic and bloated and probably wish you had stopped eating much sooner.

Often, deciding what a 5 or 6 feels like may be difficult. It was for me. Since I never allowed hunger, I had no idea how much fuel my body needed. I had no awareness of satisfied, since I was never satisfied. One way to begin to understand what this feels like is to wait three or four hours after eating, put two fist-sized portions of food (approximately two cups) on your plate and eat that amount. Put your hand on your stomach and check in and become aware of what this feels like. Use this feeling as a beginning understanding of a 5 or 6 on this scale.

Learn to check in with yourself throughout each meal, especially when dining out. You can be in a restaurant with family and

Learn to check in with yourself during each meal, especially when dining out.

friends laughing, talking, eating and still monitor your progress. Pick up your napkin, wipe your mouth and on the way down, touch your stomach and notice how you feel—no one will notice what you're doing. Perhaps you're at a 2. You continue eating, then touch again and realize you're now at level 3. So you eat some more, check in and find you're at level 4. Stop and think, does this restaurant have a dessert—perhaps crème brûlée—and tonight you're going to have some crème brûlée. You had better stop eating at level 4, as it only takes two or three spoonfuls of crème brûlée to get you to 5 or 6 on the fullness scale.

It's not that you can never again have birthday cake and ice cream or pumpkin pie, but they need to be factored into reaching 5 or 6. If it's your birthday and you're going to enjoy a big piece of cake and ice cream, maybe you stop eating the meal at a 2. But no matter how much birthday cake and ice cream are left on your plate, stop eating when you reach 5 or 6. And remember, birthdays and Thanksgivings are single meal events. You don't eat birthday cake and pumpkin pie for breakfast, lunch and dinner for the next three days.

Eat when your body tells you it's hungry and stop eating when you feel satisfied. If you follow this simple rule you should never be overly hungry. There is plenty of good food for you to enjoy.

 **This is not about starvation. Denial does not equal weight loss. It's a myth that in order to lose weight, you have to be hungry. Remember, you are not dieting. You are changing your eating habits.**

And most important, eat consciously and choose what you eat throughout each meal. Just because you have great tasting food on your plate does not mean you have to eat it all! Just because someone brought chocolate chip cookies into the house does not mean you have to eat them.

Your goal is to take back the power you have given to food, other people and to circumstances.

Dr. Dean Ornish asks a great question in *The Food Revolution.* "I don't understand why asking people to eat a well-balanced vegetarian diet is considered drastic, while it's medically conservative to cut people open or put them on powerful cholesterol-lowering drugs for the rest of their lives."

Did you know . . .

- Obesity rate (with a BMI of 30 or higher) among the general U.S. population: 18 percent.
- Obesity rate among vegetarians: 6 percent.
- Average weight of vegan adults compared to non-vegetarian adults: 10–20 pounds lighter.
- Fat in a single foil-packaged restaurant serving of butter: 6 grams
- As of 2006, fat in a Burger King Whopper with cheese: 47 grams. Fat in a Double Whopper with cheese: 64 grams.
- Fat in the average veggie burger found in U.S. supermarkets and natural food stores: 3 grams.
- Among the diseases associated with obesity: heart disease, certain types of cancer, Type 2 diabetes, stroke, arthritis, breathing problems and psychological disorders, such as depression.
- Harvard studied 75,000 women for a decade and the results suggest that the more fruits and vegetables women eat, the less likely they will become obese.
- Researchers at the National Cancer Institute followed over 75,000 people for ten years to find out which behaviors were most associated with weight loss and which with weight gain. They wrapped tape measures around people's waists for a decade and found that the one dietary behavior most associated with an expanding waistline was high meat consumption, and the dietary

behavior most strongly associated with a loss of abdominal fat was high vegetable consumption

· Eating vegetables and grains for health is not new information. More than 2600 years ago, Daniel said to his guard, "Please test your servants for ten days: Give us nothing but vegetables to eat and water to drink. Then compare our appearance with that of the young men who eat the royal food, and treat your servants in accordance with what you see. So he agreed to this and tested them for ten days. At the end of the ten days they looked healthier and better nourished than any of the young men who ate the royal food. So the guard took away their choice food and wine they were to drink and gave them vegetables instead.: [Daniel 1:12 – 16]

What to do if you really don't like most veggies

Listen to what Robert had to say about his journey toward broccoli. "I went seven years without biting down upon a single green thing. If there were veggies in my meal, I'd ask to have it sanitized. If I was at a party, I'd pick 'em out. But it was unhealthy and expensive and, in the end, ridiculously restrictive. There are only so many meals you can have that don't involve vegetables to some extent.

"So I set out to enjoy vegetables. It's not a slam-dunk success yet, but I can now eat asparagus without choking. Even this small step has helped make me healthier, and it's vastly expanded the things I can eat at restaurants."

So how did he do it? **Here are some techniques to use. Don't despair, even lifelong vegephobes can be rehabilitated.**

Don't discount trying a fresh baby carrot raw.

1. Decide that you're going to **rebalance your taste buds**. I know how it feels; you've avoided vegetables for so long that even putting one near your mouth causes a flutter in your belly. This is awful, you think, before the food even touches your tongue; I'm going to hate it. How are you going to enjoy anything when you've already decided not to? Part of learning to eat vegetables is to discard that initial reaction. Your tastes will evolve as you age; some folks learn to appreciate different kinds of wines, whereas others discover the joys of spicy foods.

2. Just because you tried broccoli once when you were 9 years old and hated it, doesn't mean you can't learn to like it now that you can **taste some that's been prepared properly**. (The broccoli of your childhood was probably overcooked into submission and barely resembles the texture of a lightly steamed fresh floret.) Some people were raised eating nothing but canned or frozen vegetables and have no idea how wonderful the real, fresh thing can be. Start by **exploring farmer's markets** and talking to people who grow veggies—they are a font of information about tasty ways to prepare them.

3. While you're learning to retrain your tender taste buds, **beware of restaurant veggies**. Unless you're eating in an upscale place or an actual vegetarian restaurant, there's a good chance you'll be served some poor excuse for a carrot or green bean. Don't hold that against them (the veggies). And just because you may not like cooked carrots, don't discount trying a fresh baby carrot raw. (And no, carrot cake does not count!)

4. If you managed to find one vegetable you sort of kinda like, then **eat it again, and again**. Eventually, you'll grow to appreciate them and then even crave them. Really! But you must stick with it, and not think your goal is "I can eat that once a month."

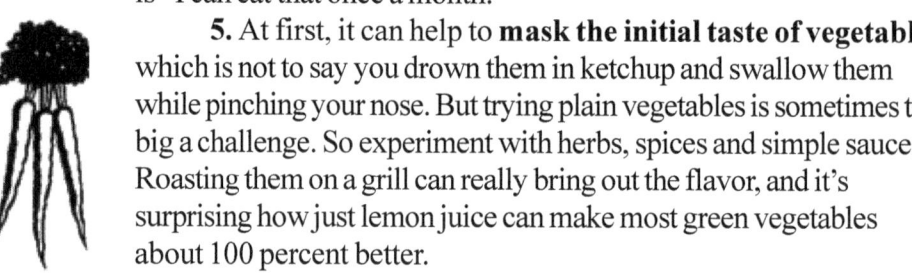

5. At first, it can help to **mask the initial taste of vegetables**, which is not to say you drown them in ketchup and swallow them while pinching your nose. But trying plain vegetables is sometimes too big a challenge. So experiment with herbs, spices and simple sauces. Roasting them on a grill can really bring out the flavor, and it's surprising how just lemon juice can make most green vegetables about 100 percent better.

6. At least learn to enjoy half a dozen or more different ones, so you can have variety. Anyone would go nuts eating two helpings of peas day in, day out. Also, **go for color variety**—they really are beautiful—start hanging out in the produce section of your store and talk to the folks who work there. They know their rutabagas. Ask friends who like veggies for tips and to show you how to prepare them properly.

7. You don't have to like them all. Lots of people never let cauliflower anywhere near their mouths (or noses). There will be vegetables that remain vile no matter what sort of preparations you put them through, and after you've tried six or seven variations, it's okay to call it quits. **Just make sure you've tried something once.**

8. If all else fails, you can manage to ingest quite a few helpings a day simply by **tucking them into other foods**. Maybe that's an answer—begin to see them as *helpers* who bring you good health. Just a thought. Make friends with your grater, and add shredded carrots, celery or zucchini to just about any soup or stew or casserole or baked loaf. This also works with veggies such as rutabaga, parsnips and jicama. For broccoli, just mince it into tiny pieces so they'll disappear into your other ingredients. A rule of thumb is, the milder the veggie, the more you can hide in another dish. A few radishes go a long way, for example. But I swear, you'll never know the veggies are in there, and you'll still get the benefits. Then after you've mastered this ploy, tip-tongue into more advanced strategies above.

> **Remember, you get all-new taste buds in about three weeks, so if you cut out the fats and sugars and focus on veggies for just three weeks, you will discover that you are beginning to enjoy vegetables!**

Don't go into overwhelm

After reading this chapter, some of you are probably in shock, denial and/or outright refusal in reaction to this new way of eating. For those of you who are currently ingesting the standard toxic American diet, the thought of this much change can be daunting or even downright terrifying. In the beginning it is common to feel that all you

are thinking about is food. You have to think ahead and plan your meals, buy healthy foods and prepare healthy meals. It is a conscious effort. I remember when I thought a healthy vegetable was a can of stewed tomatoes with a big hunk of sharp cheddar cheese melted in it. Which is why I want to reiterate that by using self-hypnosis, you can work your way through this program with much more ease than you can imagine. Soon it will become unconscious. You will find yourself choosing red, yellow, orange and green peppers or delighting in the fall squashes or the juicy berries of early summer.

Changing your eating preferences can absolutely be accomplished with hypnosis. First, through maximizing your motivation to obtain the end result by listening to Becoming Motivated (CD #5, tracks 2 &3); second by accepting hypnotic suggestions to let go of the desire for your problem foods, and third, by using the Emotion Trigger Track and self-hypnosis suggestions to take charge of your emotions and end emotional eating. When you've released the desire for a particular food, you simply don't want it anymore. There's no deprivation and, therefore, no discomfort. You can personalize hypnotic suggestions to decrease or increase desire for whatever you request. So take heart—you can do this…you can get slender for life.

In September 2010, it was revealed that Bill Clinton went vegan to reverse his heart disease. "I'm trying to be one of those experimenters," said Clinton. "Since 1986, several hundred people who have tried essentially a plant-based diet, not ingesting any cholesterol from any source, have seen their bodies start to heal themselves—break up the arterial blockage, break up the calcium deposits around the heart. Eighty-two percent of the people who have done this have had this result, so I want to see if I can be one of them." At the time of this writing, President Clinton had lost 24 pounds.

Here are some hypnotic suggestions you can use when working on various food issues.

To increase your desire
- I love to eat _____.
- My desire for _____ increases everyday.
- _____ tastes delicious.
- _____ is good for my beautiful, new, slender body.
- I enjoy the sight and taste of _____.

Eating habits control
- I enjoy eating fresh fruits, vegetables and whole grains.
- I easily listen to my body.
- I am in control of my eating.
- I only eat when my body tells me I'm hungry.
- I choose to eat appropriately.
- Food only tastes good when my body tells me it's hungry.
- I am in control of my eating habits.
- It is easy for me to eat healthfully, because I now prefer the taste of healthy foods.
- I am in control of the food I eat.
- I only eat to nourish my body.
- My appetite is quickly satisfied, because I eat delicious nutritious foods.

- I stop eating when I'm satisfied.
- I eat only those foods which assist me in releasing my excess weight.
- I prefer fresh, natural, nutritious foods.
- I listen to my intelligent mind.
- I am aware of the foods that create fat in my body and that rob me of my energy.
- My intelligent mind knows the foods that are good for me.
- It is now easy for me to move away from fat-

producing, energy robbing food.
- I stop eating at a 5 or 6 on the fullness scale.
- Sugary, greasy, fatty, oily and salty foods are unappealing to me.
- I eat only enough to safely and healthfully meet my nutritional requirements.
- I am in control of what I eat, how much I eat and ultimately my weight.
- I prefer to eat foods that create my health and beauty.
- I am removing all inappropriate food from my home.
- I choose to eat intelligently.
- I eat slowly and consciously.
- I choose to eat slowly and to savor the taste of healthy food.
- The flavors of fresh fruits and vegetables are increasingly delicious.

Increased water consumption
- I drink six to eight 8-ounce glasses of water each day.
- Water aids my body in flushing out toxins and waste products.
- When I drink water, I feel satisfied and relaxed.
- I now prefer water more than other beverages.
- I drink water when I exercise, because I know that water is the perfect fuel for my body.

The following exercise is similar to the computer screen/postage stamp technique you learned in Chapter Three and is especially helpful if you are struggling with cravings for something you no longer want to eat.

To eliminate desire for a particular food or beverage:
1. Visualize the problem food. Place a big X on top of the food.
2. Visualize a stop sign between you and the food.
3. Imagine putting the food in a blender with a foul smelling food you hate. Have the liquid in the blender take on the color, taste and smell of the bad food.

web extra

You can also go to What's On Your Desktop? at **www.hypnosishealthinfo.com/weightloss/whatsonyourdesktop** and click on What's On Your Desktop? found in the orange menu bar under Weight Loss.

Speeding up metabolism

CD NOTE

This exercise has been proven effective for many people: (CD # 7, Track 2 & 3, Control Room).

Turn off your Light Switch and allow yourself to relax . . . and just continuing to relax now deeper and deeper, imagine a door in front of you. As you open that door, you see five steps which lead you back down into the control room of your body. It's a well-lit and comfortable room of your own design, with dials and gauges all over the walls. And as you begin walking down these steps, you notice all of the gauges seemingly go on forever and ever. In fact, there are so many gauges and dials that you can't possibly see them all consciously, but as you look at them, you notice they are each labeled individually, and the one that you are most interested in now is the gauge marked **metabolism**.

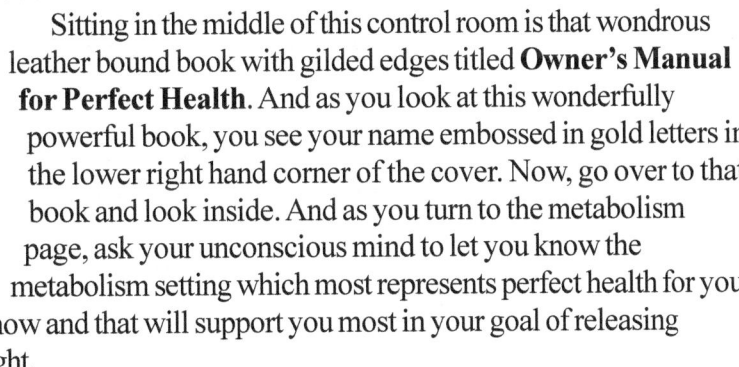

Sitting in the middle of this control room is that wondrous leather bound book with gilded edges titled **Owner's Manual for Perfect Health**. And as you look at this wonderfully powerful book, you see your name embossed in gold letters in the lower right hand corner of the cover. Now, go over to that book and look inside. And as you turn to the metabolism page, ask your unconscious mind to let you know the metabolism setting which most represents perfect health for you now and that will support you most in your goal of releasing weight.

Now, go to the wall with the gauge marked metabolism, and turn that dial to match the setting in your book of perfect health. Feel a warm tingling sensation increasing in your body.

Note: you can do this several time each day, and you can do this when falling asleep each night and sleep soundly through the night.

Now for some important warnings

For optimum diet and nutrition, the American Dietetic Association advises all vegetarians and vegans to consult a registered dietitian or other qualified nutrition professional, especially during periods of growth, breast-feeding, pregnancy, or recovery from illness. Dietary guidelines for Americans recommend that those who

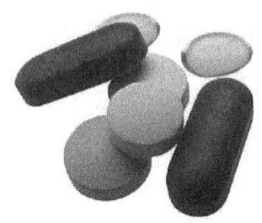

choose foods of only plant origin must supplement their diet with vitamin B12, vitamin D, calcium, iron and zinc. Adequate intake of these nutrients is even more important for growing children and pregnant and lactating women.

That said, after taking supplements for years, I have stopped. It seems to me that the plant based foods were created correctly. And as humans, we lived a long time without supplements. To make a profit, manufacturers isolate out and concentrate nutrients, like vitamins and minerals, and sell them as expensive pills. The consequence is, taking vitamins can create serious imbalances within the workings of your cells, and then diseases follow (including more cancer, heart disease and earlier death). The only supplement I routinely take is vitamin B12. You will have to decide what is best for you and your body.

Top ten tips for making healthy eating easy

1. When you have a craving for an unhealthy food, first **drink a glass of water**, then wait 15 minutes before you give in. Occupy yourself with something away from the kitchen or wherever the food is that you're hoping to avoid. Most often, a glass of water will add to a feeling of fullness, and in just that short amount of time, the craving often passes. (Or perhaps it just gives you more time to evaluate your choice and make a better one!) It's not about remaining hungry—if you are truly hungry, eat something—just try and choose something healthier.

2. Plan your meals in advance—don't wait until there is nothing healthy in the house to eat. Look at your schedule for the week and plan your meals and snacks accordingly. Be realistic in your planning—how many meals will you really cook from scratch? Will you have the energy when you get home late from work? Having salad ingredients in your refrigerator does you no good if you don't have the time or energy to prepare one.

3. Keep it simple. Fixing complicated gourmet meals every night is challenging. You can make your food both interesting and simple.

4. Cook in quantities so that you have leftovers. It's okay to eat several meals of the same food. I love to have as many as 20 lunches in the freezer, so I can go several weeks with minimal preparation when I'm pressed for time.

5. Keep your pantry and freezer full of healthy options. Life happens—you get a cold, the dog needs an emergency trip to the vet, the kids need picking up unexpectedly—and that planned shopping trip could turn into a nightmarish chore when you are already out of time and energy. Those are the days when the drive-through windows beckon with their quick fixes. But knowing you can put off the shopping trip because you have good food choices at home can ease your day considerably.

6. Make it fun! Try different recipes, enroll friends to taste new ingredients with you and cook new things together. Visit farmer's markets and ask lots of questions. Local growers often have great recipes to hand out and know the best ways to cook their produce.

7. Consider making your breakfast and/or lunch menu **automatic**. Once you find the combination of foods that you enjoy and that fuel you properly at breakfast and lunch, it often helps to make those meals the same every day—or perhaps every work day. That way you don't have to stop and wonder what to eat, or what to shop for. You already know that if you have whole grain cereal and rice milk for breakfast, you'll have all the energy you need to start your demanding day. And since it's easy to always have those things on hand, you never find yourself needing to grab a pastry at the coffee stand on your way to work.

8. Keep a **list of restaurants** of all types that you've found that can prepare food that's good for you. When friends invite you to go out for a meal, consult your list and make suggestions you know will fit your healthy new lifestyle.

9. Don't get sabotaged at the movies and other fun events. Most of us have been conditioned to wolf down a tub of popcorn or oversized boxes of candy at movies, sporting events and so on. Hot dogs and beer at the ball game. Cotton candy and Coke at amusement parks. Salt water taffy at the beach. These associations are firmly entrenched in our psyches, so it will take extra effort to enjoy those experiences without the

junk food. The solution is to bring your own delicious and nutritious snacks. It doesn't take long to fix a bag of carrot sticks. Or how about some cold cereal to crunch on? Or for a real treat, make your own trail mix. The key is to not put yourself in situations where everyone around you is indulging in unhealthy food, and you have no other options. This is not about deprivation—it's about preparation.

10. Connect spiritually with the food you eat. Acknowledge the origins of your food and the people who labored to produce it. Imagine your grains growing in the field, your apples ripening in the orchard. Feel the life force still glowing in your food and visualize it spreading throughout your body as you eat. Express gratitude for the healthy meals you enjoy. Affirm that a safe source of food continues to be readily available to you. See the farmers prospering. See yourself full of vitality thanks to the wonderful food you have on your plate.

Goal setting

Ask yourself: What do I want? What will make my life better? What will make me healthier? All too often, we focus on what we don't want, what we fear or what it is that we want to stop. Sometimes we even focus on someone else to do or change something for us.

> **One thing we can control is clearly defining what would make things better for us.**

Now, ask yourself: How could I get it? What is the smartest first step in a positive direction? Come up with a minimum of seven strategies or possibilities and then choose the path of least resistance.

Finally, ask yourself: What action am I willing to take right now? What can you do and what are you willing to do today to move towards your goal? What can you change today? What can you start or stop doing today? What are you willing to do for the next 24 hours to take you closer to your goal?

I recognize that this chapter contains for many people the greatest challenges in the Slender For Life™ program. But most likely, the reason you are reading this book is because nothing

CD NOTE

else you've tried has worked. Don't you owe it to yourself to at least try a new way of eating for a few weeks? Be sure to listen to Weight Control (CD #6 tracks 4 & 5) over and over to support your new intentions.

I urge you to make copies of the following chart and use it as a method of setting and tracking your eating and exercise goals and for measuring your progress.

In the next chapter, we'll put the last piece of the weight control puzzle in place. Some of you may be dreading this discussion, but hang in there...**I promise to offer some fun ideas for embracing the "E" word. Really!**

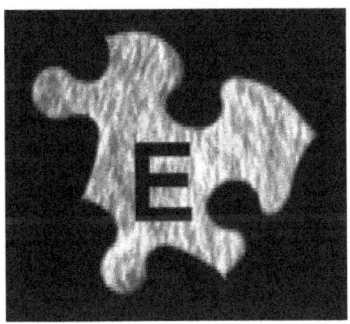

GOALS AND PROGRESS CHART

Week # _____ Starting Weight _____ Weight Goal _____ Release this week: _____

Eating Strategy - percent of total Fat Calories (circle one)   10%   15%   20%

Did you drink 6-7 glasses of water daily? __ YES __NO

Exercise   M___   T___   W___   T___   F___   S___   S___

Stopped craving for _____

Stopped craving for _____

Stopped craving for _____

Stopped craving for _____

Stopped craving for _____

Increased desire for _____

Increased desire for _____

Increased desire for _____

Increased desire for _____

Were you committed to your goals this week? __ YES __NO

Did you feel discomfort this week? __ YES __NO

Did you indulge in emotional stress eating? __YES __NO

Did you practice good portion control? __ YES __NO

Other_____

Chapter Six

Will You Get Off The Couch?

Chapter Six At A Glance

· Overcoming resistance
· How to get started
· Today is the day, not tomorrow
· You don't need to do it alone
· Making exercise fun—really!
· The price of not exercising
· Finding your own motivators
· Tips for putting more movement in your life
· Step away from your desk!
· Make it habit forming
· Hypnotic suggestions for exercising

IMPORTANT: As always, before beginning any kind of weight release program, diet change or exercise program you should consult with your personal physician, especially if you have any kind of medical condition. This program easily adapts to any recommendations from your physician.

Yes, "E" does equal exercise, which for some of you equals visions of torture in high school gym class. But it doesn't have to be that way. "E" can also equal **energy**—which you'll have a lot more of as an exerciser. "E" can equal **enthusiasm** for life, which you are bound to feel in more abundance when you are fit. And "E" can equal **enjoyment**, when you make a point of finding activities that are both fitness-enhancing and fun.

CD NOTE

What if you really looked forward to your exercise routine and loved it? What if it could be made fun, not a dreaded chore? What if moving your body became so pleasurable that you actually looked for even *more* ways to exercise? Well, that is all very possible when you use the techniques and hypnotherapy sessions on Exercise Is Better Every Day (CD 8 Tracks 2 & 3). They will help you overcome your resistance to exercise, and you will even find yourself becoming restless at times—and your only satisfaction will come when you get up and move. Then when you also add in regular self-hypnotic suggestions as motivators, you'll be amazed at how easy it will be to change even lifelong patterns of inactivity. You *can* get off the couch!

Here's what 64-year-old Arnie had to say about his newfound love of activity. "Today's status report. This morning we did our usual 18-mile bike ride. I was the first one up the hill, and then I attacked on the downhill back towards Lynwood Center. And here is the best part—I beat my two riding buddies back to Lynwood Center by two minutes. It was real quiet when we were having our oatmeal at our favorite cafe. Slender For Life™ is working for me. Being able to ride like the wind is the best! Thanks for all your help."

If you are not already enjoying regular daily exercise, stop rationalizing why you cannot or do not take the time. Put it in your schedule and make it a top priority. Exercise isn't optional. We just have to do it.

But as you'll see in this chapter, there are LOTS of ways to make it more enjoyable.

journal exercise

What's Your Excuse?

To understand your resistance to exercise, start by listing all the excuses you've ever used to not do it—then go deeper and see what's really going on. Then go back and write a way to counter each excuse. Here are some examples:

EXCUSE: I don't have enough time to go to the gym.

UNDERLYING FEELING: I'm too busy as it is. This is not a priority for me. Why not? I tell myself that because I just don't like exercising. The truth is, I haven't made my own health a high priority.

COUNTER IDEA: I could buy a treadmill or other exercise equipment that I could use at home and even multi-task. Or, I could set my alarm an hour earlier three days a week and *make* time.

EXCUSE: I can't afford a gym membership.

UNDERLYING FEELING: Why invest in something that won't pay off? I'll probably only go once in awhile. I don't believe I'm worth the expense. I don't value my health enough to make a financial sacrifice to do this. I'd like to change that thinking.

COUNTER IDEA: Walking is free, and one of the best all-around activities. I can even walk in the mall during bad weather—and I'll be in good company there if I go early before the stores open. Or I can rent all kinds of workout videos from my library, which ought to give me some new ideas.

EXCUSE: It's boring.

UNDERLYING FEELING: I'm afraid to go to a gym. I'm self-conscious about how I'd look there. I'm too busy to even think about what else I could do. That's a lie. I'm too lazy to think of something else to do! What was boring was P.E. class in high school when I had

no control. Now I can decide what kind of activity to do.

COUNTER IDEA: There are plenty of options that are *not* boring. I could take a ballroom dance class with my partner and go out dancing every Saturday night.

(See Page 183 for a lot more ideas how to make it fun.)

Getting started

Along with developing a habit for a daily exercise routine, increase your physical activity whenever you can. Walk instead of drive. Take the stairs instead of the elevator. Park your car farther away from entrances so that you walk farther. Dance around the kitchen while you cook. Get your dog up off the couch too!

Begin your exercise at the level you are at now. Exercise aerobically everyday; if walking to your mailbox is a stretch for you, then make that the goal. Gradually and carefully increase your exercise. If you are currently walking for 15 minutes and feel that you are ready to increase your exercise, then the next increment is 16 or

17 minutes. Do not jump from 15 to 30 minutes. **There is no greater way to ruin your joy of exercising than injury. Do not over do it!**

By accepting the hypnotic suggestions regarding your exercise, you begin to enjoy it so much that you make it a daily priority. Walking is an excellent form of exercise. If you're just beginning to exercise, start out in short durations and build up to 30-45 minutes a day. But don't go too fast. You want to walk fast enough that you get warm, slow enough that you can still talk or sing. This is the fat burning range. If you are going so fast that you can't talk or sing, then it's a great cardio workout and you get the "runner's high" but you are *not* burning fat. Fat is the least efficient fuel that the body has to burn, and when your heart is working that hard you are not burning fat.

The power is in today

We were never designed to sit at a computer all day.

Begin your exercise today! Exercise gets your metabolism going, burns off your excess body fat and increases your lean body mass. Starting out may be a challenge. I know it was for me and often is for many of my clients. Programs such as *Curves* have been a great way to get going for many women. But sometimes to get started, you just gotta do it!

Early one morning driving to the gym, I heard a physician on National Public Radio talking about obesity and the importance of exercise. She was very pragmatic about exercise. She said we should stop making excuses and worrying about exercise being fun or enjoyable, and instead we should consider it a prescription.

It is just something we have to do, just like taking medication for a particular condition. It isn't optional.

Our condition as humans is that we were created to hunt and gather, to walk and run, to be active most of the day. We were never designed to sit at a computer all day, lounge around in front of a TV or ride around in a car.

Putting exhilaration back in exercise

Yet despite being a requirement for health, there's no reason exercise can't be fun, too! If you're having trouble getting motivated, think back to activities you may have enjoyed as a kid. Is there something there you could try again as a first step? Going bowling or roller skating or dancing are all fine ways to return to being active. Today, most community centers, YMCAs and gyms offer all sorts of classes and activities designed to take the boredom out of exercise. Especially if you hated gym class, try not to think of your new exercise program in that light. *You* get to decide what kind of activity you'll do, and you get to set your pace. The important thing is to start somewhere.

Sherry hadn't exercised in years, but when she thought about what kind of activity used to please her, **the answer was simple: playing in the pool.** Not swimming laps, but splashing around with friends and playing water games is the pleasant image she remembered from her childhood.

"I hadn't been in a pool in years, so I was delighted to discover all the innovations in water exercise that took place while I was being a slug! I

**"Water aerobics is so much fun that it doesn't seem like exercise."
~Sherry**

immediately tried all the different types of classes at my neighborhood pool and then signed up for the one I liked best. Doing water aerobics in a big group to lively music is so much fun that it doesn't seem like exercise. And best of all, working out in the water eliminates the joint pains I used to feel whenever I attempted something on dry land.

"Now I wouldn't dream of missing my days at the pool, and I'm even planning on putting one in my backyard so I won't have any excuse not to swim every day. And you know what else? I've even learned to love lap swimming! I use a snorkel and mask so it doesn't hurt my neck, and I'm up to 30 minutes every time—and that's after a full water workout. I'm a regular mermaid!"

The buddy system works for some people, but beware of who you choose. Make sure his or her motivation is as strong—or stronger—than yours. Otherwise, your jogging partner may end up convincing you to stop before you want to, or worse, give up all together. If you prefer to workout with friends, try to enlist many people who enjoy lots of different activities. That way you aren't subject to the backsliding of just one buddy.

If you're a hard case—and you know who you are—it may take nothing short of paying good money to a personal trainer to put you through a workout. If that's what it takes, then it's money well spent. After a few weeks of establishing good exercise patterns with a trainer, you will probably be able to keep it up on your own. But there's a reason Hollywood stars look as good as they do—most of them work with a trainer five days a week to attain and maintain their optimal fitness level. I'm not suggesting you go to those extremes, but if you can't seem to make yourself get out of your recliner, then hiring a trainer is a good solution. Any gym or fitness center will be able to recommend qualified trainers.

Here's what Alice had to say about it. "I've been an on-again, off-again exerciser all my life, so when I decided to finally get serious about it, I joined my community rec center. They offered a free orientation to the weight machines, but it wasn't enough to make me feel comfortable using them. I have a history of back injuries, so I was afraid to push myself.

"That's when I decided to hire Brandon to teach me the safe way to use everything. It was the best thing I could've done! He was very patient with me and understood my concerns. After that, I also consulted my chiropractor and showed him drawings of the machines I had questions about and asked his advice as to which ones were okay for me to use. I'm glad I did, because there were a few he urged me to skip. I'm 58, and knew I had to be careful to avoid more injuries.

"By making sure I know what I'm doing and using only weight machines that are approved for me, **I can now enjoy my workouts with peace of mind.** Whenever

I feel I'm stuck and no longer progressing as I want to, I do another session with Brandon and add some new moves to my program. Plus, just seeing him in the gym helping other members reminds me what he taught me. Now when I have to miss a scheduled workout, I'm actually annoyed! That sure is a new me!"

Moving outside the box

What if all these conventional ideas just don't appeal to you? Well, you'll have to come up with a better excuse than that, because there are **plenty of alternative ways to get exercise** into your life, beyond the traditional gym, pool, walk/run, sports ideas.

- How about a class in dancing with your dog, or training your dog for agility competitions? (Those trainers have to run the course over and over just as often as the dogs do.)
- Check with your local college for folk dancing classes—and explore your heritage in the bargain. One of the best workouts around is belly dancing.
- How about fencing or martial arts classes?
- Have you heard of Frisbee golf?
- Buy a hula hoop! Or go into a big toy store and see what cool things kids have to choose from today.
- Get out and play catch with your kids.
- Borrow your daughter's scooter. Join the circus!
- Lots of cities have classes in acrobatics and trapeze work.
- Maybe you'd enjoy setting an unusual goal like walking the entire circumference of your city—in sections, of course. Or walking the length of every beach in your state. Or exploring every trail in every park in your state.

· Have you ever gone snowshoeing? It's a great workout and snowshoes can be rented at any ski area, plus you'll get to enjoy back country scenery that most people never see.
· Or join a club that takes walks to go birding or rock climbing.
· Would you believe there are paintball leagues?
· Or how about geocaching? That's a fun activity that combines orienteering and detective work to find hidden prizes all over the world. (Learn more about it online.)

I think that list should convince you that there really is a fun physical activity for everyone. Think about what your other interests are and see if there's a way to add a physical component to them. Belong to a book club? Read an adventure or sports-themed book, then hold your meeting outdoors while you go for a group stroll. Love to read? Get off your behind, switch to audio books and take you and your MP3 player out walking every day. Listening to great books while you walk will make the time fly by.

Carmen enjoys a much more active lifestyle now that she's released 130 pounds. "I definitely have more energy to spend at work, and then I can spend more time doing physical activity. I can go on hikes, and I have more energy around the house. I went white water rafting with some friends, something I wouldn't have done before, because I was too heavy."

Are you competitive by nature? **Buy an inexpensive pedometer** and track exactly how much you really do walk every day. Then set escalating goals of walking more and more each week. Keep improving your personal best. Or do the same with swimming laps. Kerry used this idea to push herself to her optimal fitness. "I used to swim laps very erratically—10 minutes one day, 20 minutes the next. I never had any good reason to stick with it. Then out of curiosity I decided to challenge myself. First I found out how long I *could* swim. Thirty minutes was my stopping point, so I told myself I would never stop before I hit that mark. Then I stretched it to 45 minutes. Now I feel like I'm letting myself down if I swim any less. Plus it has enhanced my self-esteem enormously to realize how well I'm doing."

Listening to great books while you walk will make the time fly by.

journal exercise

What did you dream of doing?

Make a list of physical activities you enjoyed as a child or teen. Then add any physical goals you may have had but abandoned. Did you ever want to climb a big mountain or enter a triathlon? Learn to line dance? List any activities your kids do that you'd like to be able to do—try inline skating? Are there any sports you enjoy watching on TV? Add those to the list. Put a star by ones that seem especially fun. Now look at your list and see what you could do today to adopt or *adapt* some of them. Perhaps you just haven't thought creatively enough about all the many ways you could find to move your body.

_____

_____

_____

_____

_____

_____

_____

_____

_____

_____

_____

Some people have moved so little in their lives that they just can't envision themselves doing anything. If you're still stuck, talk to friends who are fit and ask them what they do to stay that way. Ask if you can go along with them on a hike or visit their gym or attend a water aerobics class with them. Maybe all you need is to model someone else's activities. If you need variety, plan different activities for every day of the week. **The real point is to just start somewhere—any activity is better than none!**

Someone who loses weight without exercise loses both lean and fat tissue.

The hidden price of <u>not</u> exercising

This is an inescapable fact—physical activity is essential in any weight loss program. We live in a society with a microwave mentality that demands instant results. The American Council on Exercise is a great resource, and their Personal Trainer Manual is full of great information on exercise physiology. For example, did you know that weight loss without exercise can have a negative effect on body composition, especially if the weight is regained?

Someone who loses weight without exercise loses both lean and fat tissue. If they regain weight without exercising, more fat than lean is put back on. Exercise burns calories, speeds up metabolism and helps offset plateaus where weight loss slows down or even temporarily stops. Fat tissue is less active metabolically than lean tissue. Each time you lose weight and regain it without exercise, your metabolism requires fewer calories to function. So when you return to eating the same amount as before your last diet, you won't maintain your weight but will gain more.

You want to be healthy for the rest of your life, don't you?

Remember, *losing* your excess weight is a relatively short-term process. Staying healthy and fit should be a goal for the rest of your life. Be committed to develop a more active lifestyle for today, tomorrow and a lifetime thereafter.

I know it's tough to motivate people to exercise. When I ask clients who are struggling to exercise why they do exercise, I hear things like: "for my health" or "because I should" or "I'd feel better." *GAG!* There is no motivation there.

As I was thinking about exercise and reasons to exercise, I became intrigued with the question of what is it that is so compelling that would inspire someone to exercise. What is so compelling about exercise that I get up six out of seven mornings to do it?

I remember a woman who came to me one spring to be motivated to exercise. When I asked her why she wanted to exercise, her response was that she wanted to complete her goals. When I then asked what her goal was, I was dumbfounded by her reply. "To go to the gym five times a week." "Why," I asked, "would you ever want to go to the gym five times a week?" Her reply: "To check off my goal on the chart on my refrigerator."

I couldn't believe it. No wonder she wasn't motivated to exercise. I told her to go home and make five check marks on her refrigerator and be done with it. She came back the next week with compelling reasons why she wanted to be able to hike in the Olympic Mountains with her husband and teenage sons and why she wanted to be able to ski with them in the winter. So being able to play with her family became her compelling reasons to motivate her to exercise. Uncovering those motivators and keeping them in mind, made all the difference in her attitude and enjoyment of her workouts.

I can fall on a ski slope and stand back up.

Looking better and having better health just doesn't seem to motivate most people to get up from a warm bed at 5:00 a.m. on a cold, wet, dark morning to go to the gym.

Reflecting on my own experience, I remembered the first time I went skiing after releasing 100 pounds and after going to the gym to do weight training. When I fell down on the ski slope, I stood right back up. No help. I didn't have to struggle. No one assisted me. I didn't push up on my poles. That was way cool!

My wife would tell you that this is weird, but I even get a kick out of selecting a muscle and targeting it for sculpting. I find this to be an interesting exercise that fascinates me, but by itself is not enough to get me to the gym. So, what is it that is so compelling for me to get up out of my warm bed on a cold, wet, dark morning to work out?

As I was wrestling with this question, I made the decision to register for the Seattle Marathon. The previous week I had noticed an announcement in the men's locker room at the gym about a seminar on how to prepare for the Seattle Marathon. I started thinking about running a half marathon and then realized that I would never stop halfway, I would run the full marathon. But the Seattle Marathon was in less than four weeks. I had not been training for a marathon. I last ran 20 miles in July, and it was then the second week of November. I had only been running six miles three times a week with a few one- or two-mile and two-to-three-mile runs thrown in.

When I emailed my running coach about the idea, she said

I have the power of choice. I have options.

that if I wanted to do it, I should go for it. If I didn't finish, I could always ride the bus back. The following Sunday I ran a half marathon on my own and basically forgot about it. Later the next day I remembered that I had run over 13 miles the day before, yet I felt great and I could walk just fine. I was not sore. So that night, I registered for the Seattle Marathon with less than three weeks to prepare.

As I told this story in my first group of the week, I felt the tears well up. *I got it.* My compelling reason to exercise is that I now have more choices in my life. I can easily bend over and tie my shoes. I can fall on a ski slope and stand back up. I can climb Mount Rainier and participate in the Seattle to Portland bike ride. I have the power of choice. I have options. I can choose to run 26.2 miles or not. I have the freedom of choice.

This liberty in my life creates my compelling desire to exercise.

A woman came in for a consultation and shared with me that three years previously she had taken motorcycle lessons and had subsequently bought a Harley. At her first session she brought me a photo of the Harley. It made my heart go pitter-patter . . . it was a big hog! At her third session she was down about ten pounds in total at that point, but had not exercised. She had a gym membership but was not using it. When I asked why she would exercise anyway, I got the usual "for my health." I laughed.

I asked about her Harley and how far she rode it; she said she could only go for a couple hours because she just got too sore. Her back hurt, her legs and arms hurt too much to go any farther. She had once gone on an eight-hour ride and couldn't walk for three days. Her dream was to ride with a friend from Seattle to Washington, D.C., but she thought a trip that long would kill her. She admitted she could hardly move her bike in and out of the garage or even up off the kickstand.

"You know," I said, "I wonder if you got into the gym and started doing squats and working those adductors and abductors and getting some strength in your legs . . . and if you did some back extensions and crunches to build your core strength and maybe even some arm and shoulder exercises . . ." I could see the wheels turning. She exclaimed, "Then I could ride my Harley!" For her, exercise was about riding her Harley. She now had a compelling reason to get to the gym. After that, she hardly missed a day and several months later successfully rode her Harley to Washington, D.C. and back. You see, doing something just for good health is intangible. Her Harley is tangible. I now challenge clients to discover their "Harley."

Karen came in one day stating that she just couldn't get motivated to exercise. As we talked about exercise and motivation to exercise, I asked Karen about her dog that she dearly loved and asked if her dog pooped in her backyard that she was so proud of. Of course her dog pooped in her yard and no, she didn't like picking up after dog poop either, she replied. So I asked, "Why do you do it?" Her answers were: "So the dog doesn't track it in. So I don't step in it. It kills the grass. I love my flowers and I want my yard to look nice."

So, for the end result that she wanted, she had to do something that she didn't necessarily like to get the result that was important to her. So her challenge became: Was she willing to exercise to get the body and health that she also wanted?

Sometimes you can get motivated to move by a desire to help others. One of my clients trained for and was able to complete a 3-day Walk for the Cure event—not because she wanted to walk long distances—but because of her desire to support friends who were breast cancer survivors. For added emotional inspiration, she tied it to her 50th birthday, because she was determined to reach a certain level of fitness by that landmark. Once the event was over, she transferred her pleasure from that accomplishment to something else, and now she enjoys Pilates workouts.

Exercise is like a screwdriver. I don't know of anyone who loves to use a screwdriver. But we sure like the towel racks that we put up, the shelves that we hang and the desks that we assemble.

Anytime you find yourself sitting for more than thirty minutes, ask yourself what else you could be doing.

In order to have good health, you must use the tool of regular exercise.

Increasing motivation by focusing on your personal motivators is the key—whether it's running around the playground with your grandchildren or being able to backpack through Europe in your retirement, understanding what inspires you to hop out of your recliner will facilitate long-term commitment.

journal exercise

What's your reason to get moving?

Challenge yourself to discover what activity is so compelling that you will attain and maintain your ideal weight throughout your life. List all the physical activities you think you might like to do one day. Circle ones that give you an extra buzz. Pick one to be your first goal, and use that as your current motivator.

What you really need is a new attitude toward moving.

_____

_____

_____

_____

_____

_____

_____

_____

_____

_____

_____

_____

_____

Tips for ways to add more movement into your day

What you really need is a new attitude toward movement. Make it a game to find as many ways as you can to move throughout your day. Anytime you find yourself sitting for more than 30 minutes, ask yourself what else you could be doing. We've all come to rely way too much on drive-through everything—get out of the car and onto your feet!

- Put on music while you cook so you dance around the kitchen instead of just standing there. The same goes for housework. (Remember Mrs. Doubtfire and her vacuum?)
- Do stretches in the shower—carefully!
- Incorporate a stretching routine into your gardening activities, which is also a good way to avoid a stiff back from weeding in one position too long.
- Switch to an old-fashioned push lawn mower—plus it's better for the environment (and it makes a cool sound!).
- Do a set of lifting weights as you put away the groceries. (Think bicep curls with cans of tomato sauce.)
- Wash your own vehicle instead of going through a car wash.

- Join your kids in their games—when's the last time you played basketball, softball or rode a scooter? (For that matter, when's the last time *your kids* did anything physical?)
- Make it a family affair to go for a walk every night after dinner—and meet your neighbors in the process.
- Bring a healthy lunch from home and spend your lunch hour in a park or by the river and walk after you eat.
- On rainy days, walk up and down the stairs in your office building during your lunch hour.
- Walk your kids to school.
- Install a tether ball in your backyard or a basketball hoop over your driveway.
- Get a therapy ball and use it while you watch TV in the evening.
- If you use public transportation, get off one stop early and walk the extra distance.
- Buy some CDs of the music you loved growing up. Crank it up and get movin' all over the house. Show your kids the dances you did in high school.
- Learn isometric exercises you can do using the walls and furniture in your house. Set up your own circuit of activity in your home.

> **HOT IDEA:** Consider posting small notes or signs in strategic places in your environment to motivate you, such as on your refrigerator, TV or your dashboard. Use whatever language and images will inspire you to make better decisions about your time. If you're self-conscious about anyone else seeing them, then hide the notes in your sock drawer, day planner, journal or on your computer desktop—anywhere they can act as a gentle (or not so gentle) nudge.

For example:

· Dance more, sit less
· Couches are for pillows
· Recline = decline
· Got walk?
· Have you walked 3 miles in your shoes today?
· Have pedometer, will travel
· You there with the gut—get off the couch!
· Flab is not fab
· Flabby is shabby
· Do you want to be fat or fit?
· Get up, get moving and get on with your best life!
· Have you had some fun today?
· Got a game to play?
· Do NOT go through that drive-through
· Just say no to sugar
· Exercise is my prescription for health
· Moving gives me more energy
· There's always time to get healthy
· Just do it (still one of the all-time best motivators, because it cuts through every excuse)

Your desk is not a ball and chain

Let's face it—many of us spend our working lives sitting down. No matter how fabulous your chair is, it's still bad for your health to live so much of your live in it. "We are made to move, not sit at a desk 12 hours a day," reminds Joan Price, author of *The Anytime, Anywhere Exercise Book.* "As ergonomic as your desk or

chair may be, sitting produces back pains, headaches and listlessness. You become less productive."

In her book she suggests hundreds of ways to sneak activity into your office life, including taking one-minute aerobic breaks, which have been shown to reduce risk of heart disease and increase longevity. She also has great ideas for stretching and strength training you can do at your desk. Don't let embarrassment or fear of co-workers' kidding stop you—secretly they'll admire you for your initiative. See other books on this subject in the Appendix.

Make it a good habit you don't want to break

Set up a regular exercise schedule and stick to it. If it's the gym, say "hello" to the people you regularly see. I have been working out most every morning for ten years with the same group of people. We don't talk much, but we acknowledge each other, and we notice when someone is missing. I know the grief I will get from them the next day over sleeping in one morning isn't worth staying in bed! I know that's enough of a motivator to get me on my way.

And if you live alone, are new to an area, or are just a bit short on a social circle, making friends through a common love of activity is an added boon. This is especially important for seniors, who often become increasingly isolated as the years roll by. There are bound to be special exercise programs just for seniors in your area, so don't let embarrassment about your age or lack of physical conditioning keep you at home in the rocking chair!

Hypnotic suggestions for exercising

· I am physically active.
· I increase my amount of effort, of exercise, of walking and moving.
· My body is becoming leaner, stronger, healthier and more attractive each day.
· I look forward to exercising every day.
· I enjoy exercising every day.
· I feel strong and healthy.
· I feel wonderful as I become more alive.
· How good it feels to move and exercise.
· I have more fun every day exercising.
· I feel full of energy during and after exercising.
· I see and feel myself _____ (walking, jogging, etc.) right now.
· I make time for myself each day to exercise.
· Every day at the time of my choosing, my body becomes restless and wants to move.
· The only way to satisfy my body's restlessness is to exercise.
· Nothing is more important than keeping my body strong and healthy.
· I thrive on _____ (type of exercise).
· I see and feel the excess weight disappearing as I exercise.
· I can feel and see myself becoming more attractive as I _____ (walk, etc.).
· Each and every time I exercise I feel renewed with energy.
· With each step I take I feel empowered, filled with new energy.
· I find that the more I exercise, the more energy I have.
· I notice how clearly I think, how relaxed I am and how much energy I possess, as I exercise more and more frequently.

Well congratulations for making it this far in the program—or even just reading the book to this point. You're already way ahead of most people who attempt to change their lives for the better. If you've followed the program to this point and listened to the CDs, you now have all the tools you need to become slender for life. However, every path contains its share of rocks or even boulders, and the next chapter is designed to make you aware of potential challenges—and how to deal with them—before they sidetrack you. Plus I'll give you plenty of tips on staying the course to your weight release goal.

So don't stop now!

CHAPTER SEVEN

Are You In It For Life?

Chapter Seven At A Glance

· Bouncing back from the wall
· Making course corrections
· Focus on the small targets
· Sometimes change requires a revisit
· Taking stock—it's all related
· The Seven Steps to permanent weight control
· Strategies for releasing 100+ pounds
· Tips for staying with the program
· What to do if you have a relapse
· Squelching saboteurs
· Hypnotic suggestions for confidence and self-esteem

Once you master self-hypnosis and get into a good pattern of daily use of the CDs and your personal hypnotic suggestions, you should see fairly steady progress toward your goal weight. This presumes, of course, that you've also made whatever adjustments were needed to the food you eat and your activity level. Beware of creeping complacency, however. After you've seen some results, you may be tempted to slack off a bit, to revert to some old behaviors. If you start to notice ideas like that inching into your thoughts, it's time to review your CDs, especially the Weight Control, Emotion Trigger and Stress Buster Tracks, and **pick some stronger suggestions to work with, such as:**

CD NOTE

· I enjoy the progress I am making and keep my final goal in sight
· I am encouraged by my progress and maintain my commitment to create a healthier life
· I am diligent about following my eating and exercise plan.

More often than not, if clients are honest, these desires to slip off the program occur because they were not following it faithfully. **The great thing is, the more you master self-hypnosis, the less self-discipline you need to muster.** And if you stick with it long enough, all of this does become automatic—I promise!

In this chapter we'll look at various challenges you may encounter as you stay the course toward the new you—and of course we'll study the solutions, too. This chapter is key to your long term success, so get out your highlighter!

Bouncing back from the wall

One night Margaret came in discouraged. Her weight had held steady for the past two weeks, and she had only dropped three pounds this past month. In total, she had let go of 43 pounds in five months, so she was actually doing well, but she still had 100 pounds to go. Dejected, Margaret talked about the voice in her head that was telling her this was too hard, that she should just give up, because she'll never be successful. "At first it was so easy and natural to eat healthily, but now it's getting difficult. My portions are

Change does not occur in a straight line.

getting bigger; I'm eating more and more almonds and sneaking candy."

Margaret was recycling. Change does not occur in a straight line. She had been making changes in her life and doing very well, but then she hit the wall again. The old habits and the old pessimistic voices in her head were haunting her. Throughout life we hit these walls and many people give up, thinking they have failed. But Margaret wasn't failing. She also talked about how in the past two weeks she had increased her exercise and overall she was eating healthily. While she had not released any weight in recent weeks, she hadn't gained any either.

Margaret isn't back where she started—look how far she had come! Yes, she hit the wall and it was time for her to go to a deeper level of healing. Just like an onion with a spot—as each layer is pealed away the spot diminishes.

Remember, weight release, like most things in life, is not a straight-line event. In other words, releasing weight does not look like going from Point "A" to Point "B" in a straight line.

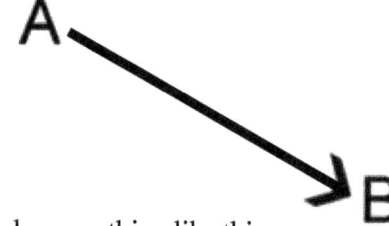

For most of us, it looks something like this:

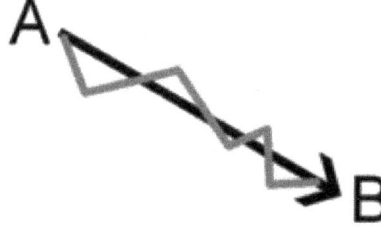

When you reach your goal and look back, you'll see that your weight loss was really a series of ups and downs, even though it will then seem like it was a straight line release.

Our weight fluctuates throughout each day and from day to day. At times, body weight may plateau for a few days while your

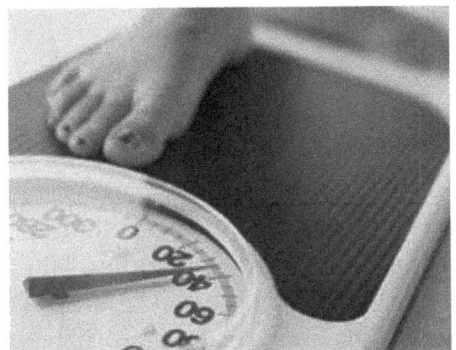

body makes other adjustments. It is not unusual for a client's weight to remain the same or be down very little one week, yet at the same time be down a dress size or in a notch or two on the belt from the previous week.

A study by the National Weight Loss Registry shows that

the most successful people who lose weight and keep it off, weigh themselves daily.

This daily weigh-in is a reality check, a way of monitoring and making sure that you stay within a healthy weight range.

Are you a secret slacker?

Maude had released 25 pounds and had another 20 to go. She plateaued for about a month and then realized that she feared if she allowed herself to reach her ideal weight, she could never be a *slacker* again. If she slacked off and didn't *try* to get to her goal, then it wouldn't be a failure. Her real fear was that if she tried to get to her goal, she might not succeed, or if she reached her goal, perhaps she wouldn't be able to maintain her ideal weight. She also acknowledged that letting go of the first 25 pounds had been too easy and that she didn't think it really counted. She was in *slacker trance*. Consciously, she knew she wanted to reach her ideal weight; unconsciously, she was stopped by her thoughts—her fears.

Paying the price

When you are pondering eating that cookie, that piece of candy or sip that glass of wine, stop and ask yourself: *Am I willing to pay the price?* Weigh your decision and ask: *What is most important— this treat or getting to my ideal weight? Is this cookie really worth slowing me down from letting go of two or more pounds this week?* You may decide that with your success at releasing weight, you are unwilling to slow down obtaining your goal weight. And if you are considering eating that cookie, that piece of candy or drinking that glass of wine, ask yourself: *If I do eat it, how will I feel afterwards? Will I feel okay with having eaten it, or will I feel bloated, guilty and like I blew it?*

Continuing on

Slender For Life™ hypnotic weight loss is a conditioning process requiring repetition and practice in the beginning. This little bit of effort is absolutely worth it. Very soon you will be amazed at how easy and effortless your new living, eating and exercise habits are becoming. Healthy new habits you are able to control for the rest of your life.

George is a good case in point. He reached his target weight goal by sticking with the program and doing self-hypnosis. "I became a light meat eater, and the transition was easy. I don't ever feel stuffed anymore, and I don't miss over-indulging in chips and desserts."

**"I don't ever feel stuffed anymore."
~George**

However, you may be thinking that once you have read this book and listened to all the CDs you are done. Think again.

If you are serious about changing your life, you need more than a few weeks to change your behaviors. It takes at least 22 weeks of consistency to make a new behavior a habit.

For best results, continue using the Slender For Life™ program throughout your life.

Clients often tell me that when they learn how to take their weight off and keep it off, they discover other areas of their life change as well. The issues that cause one to be overweight are the same issues that hold us back elsewhere in life. If someone is overeating out of fear, it's that fear that prevents successful personal relationships, greater career success or success in other areas.

This is the impact Rhonda has felt in her life since getting slender for life. "I didn't realize I was signing on for a personal spiritual journey. A lot has changed—my thinking, my behavior, my emotions and my body. In the beginning I couldn't even imagine what I'd look like at my goal weight."

Do you know how to get to Phoenix?

We talked in Chapter Three about commitment. Are you really clear on what you are committing to? As I listened to Gerry in group one night, it became clear that he had no idea where he was going. He had no clear goal in mind. He sounded lost. When I pushed him for clarity, he could not tell me about life at his goal weight or why he was going there. When I asked if he ever just got into his car and headed off down the road on a vacation with no destination in mind, he made it clear that he plans the entire itinerary and stresses when he gets off schedule. He also said that he didn't allow any unplanned or unscheduled side trips. Gerry told how he has noticed more unconscious eating and lack of focus.

I put two dots on the flip chart. One dot was Seattle and the other Phoenix. I stated that as I flew last week from Seattle to Phoenix, the pilot or the autopilot had to make continuous course corrections. There was turbulence along the way that kept blowing us off course. If there were no course corrections, we might have ended up in Oklahoma City instead of Phoenix. In life there is turbulence. There are relationship changes, job changes, holidays, birthdays and other bumps in the road of life. All too often, people move aimlessly from one bump to the next and never make course corrections. They never get to Phoenix.

Too often, people experience turbulence in life, they get off course and then use that as a reason to *continue* going off course. They never make it to Phoenix, because they are heading towards Fargo!

Your self-hypnosis is course correction. You refocus your mind and get back on track.

As we continued this discussion in the group, Patty told how she had no idea what it would be like to be at her ideal weight. People like myself who had been overweight all their lives have no frame of reference for their ideal weight. They have never been to Phoenix. The only time previously in my life that I have weighed what I do now was in grade school! This woman had dieted previously and lost a lot of weight rapidly, only to discover that her life was still there with all its challenges, and weighing less was not a ticket to the Garden of Eden. Patty had put the weight right back on. So she asked the question, "Do you believe that people can really change?" "Yes," I replied. "But you have to know what you want and you have to want it. It gets back to that issue of need and motivation."

Then Brenda asked how to deal with life's turbulences, and I asked her what it would be like for her to be a ***Principled Leader of Self***. What would it be like for her to be at *cause* and no longer at *effect*, to no longer be a victim in her life? When you have a clear goal, a clear plan for your life, then you can be that Leader of Self. You can be at cause, not a victim. You take back your power from food, people, work, events, life and circumstances.

I challenged the group to take some time in the coming week to write, draw or paint a realistic picture of what their Phoenix—their destination—would be like and to bring a copy in the next week. The next week people came in with compelling reasons for obtaining their goal weight. Some were very detailed and others vague, but everyone was clarifying their *Phoenix*. **If you didn't complete the Goals chart on Page 174, this would be a good time to do it.**

Too often, people get off course and then use that as a reason to <u>continue</u> going off course.

Look at the little picture

Letting go of weight, whether it's 20 pounds or 150 pounds, is daunting when looking at the totality. Staying focused on the next two pounds makes it more doable. I remember when I climbed Mount

Rainier—all 14,410 feet of it! After our climb to base camp carrying heavy packs, we set up our tents on a glacier. After a few sleepless hours on a bed of ice, we were up at midnight to begin the assent. At 8 a.m. I looked toward the summit. It loomed massively in front of us. We still had hours to go, and I was exhausted and discouraged. I wondered just whose idea it was for me to do this, anyway. At that moment, the fun was gone. I wanted to just sit down and tell my fellow climbers I'd be right there when they came down. I wanted to quit.

Then I recognized I was at the place when I *always* quit. I was having the exact same feelings and thoughts. That was the moment when every other time in my life I had quit. These same thoughts and feelings had held me back in most areas of my life—physically, mentally, emotionally and spiritually.

So I stopped thinking about the hours ahead of me to reach the summit and focused on my next step, and then the next and then the next. And finally, there before me was the crater on the summit. It was a beautiful, warm, sunny day—I could see forever. By taking one step at a time, I made it. I share this experience with clients as a metaphor for focusing on releasing two pounds each week.

My Slender For Life Commitment

To make sure that I release two or more pounds this next week I am willing to do the following: _____

_____

_____

_____

_____

_____

Signed _____ Date _____

What do I need to focus on this week?

So every week recommit to releasing two pounds. If you don't hit that mark, that's okay too, but you do need to recommit every week to your weight release goals. As you think about each coming week, ask yourself: What do I need to focus on this week? Is it being more calm and relaxed, is it getting in more exercise, eating more vegetables, or what? ? Remember your 52 Reasons from Chapter 3. Be sure you post a new reason for being at your goal weight each week.

Sometimes you need to take a step backward

Weight-loss clients get discouraged easily when they reach a plateau or set point. They also get discouraged when after several months of successful effort, they slip, cheat or fall onto the chuck wagon. Their old diet mentality sneaks up, along with the belief that it's a failure to have had some Cheetos.

I remind clients that change is a cyclical process and that part of the learning and healing process is to revisit issues.

I am sometimes surprised when after two or three sessions, I hear a client talking like they should have all their old eating habits behind them. That after two or three sessions they expect to have changed a lifetime of mental and emotional relationships with food. I pull out their Recommended Program Plan and show them that we have months to work together at resolving these issues. Our goal at Slender For Life™ is to stay with clients throughout the entire process of obtaining their ideal weight. For some, it's three or four months. For others, that can be two or more years. I believe that this is worth repeating: I can send smoking cessation clients out the door after one session and have them be smoke-free for the rest of their lives. But those of us with food issues do not have the luxury of never eating again. We will forever be dealing with the tastes and smells of food—with the social, cultural, religious, holiday and physical needs for food. **Being slender for life is a life-long journey.**

I urge you to view your new lifestyle as a journey and to continue exploring and learning more about yourself. From my perspective, we are all on a physical, mental, emotional and spiritual journey.

How does your life look?

Take a moment right now and evaluate your life on a scale of minus 10 to plus 10 in each of these areas, the higher number indicating your greater level of satisfaction.

Physical can include your body, your health, and if you like, your finances and anything else you choose to include of this earth.

Mental is your mental clarity, your education, your ability to use your mind.

Emotional is your level of happiness, your moodiness, how you feel about yourself, your life and your world.

Spiritual is your experience of God, Spirit, your Higher Self or a Higher Power.

[Put an X along the scale for each item, then connect the Xs with a line].

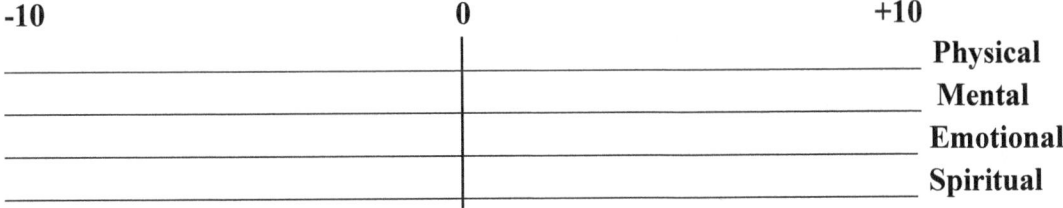

As an example, suppose that someone ranked their Physical level at a +7, their Mental level at a +4, Emotional at a -2 and Spiritual at a +2.

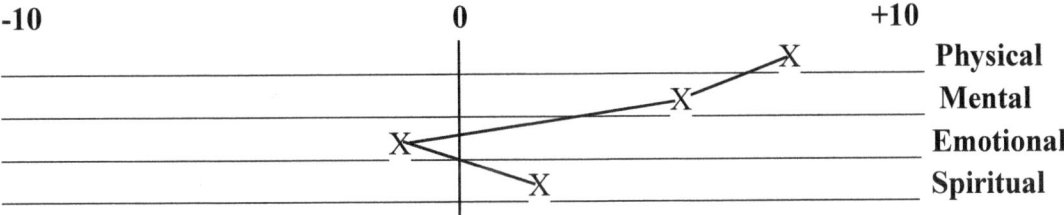

Left unaddressed, low mental, emotional and spiritual levels will drag the physical level down. Healthy eating and exercise are physical events. If we don't change what we are thinking and what we are feeling and allow our spiritual growth, then we will not likely maintain our healthy eating and exercise. In addition to healthy eating and exercise, we must challenge our thinking, stretch ourselves emotionally and express our spirituality. But don't try to focus equal attention in each area all the time. Sometimes your focus may be spiritual and other times it may be mental. Just like in an orchestra, sometimes the wind instruments dominate, while at other times, the string instruments do. What's important is that you keep growing. I urge clients to explore dance, drama, continuing education, chiropractic, acupuncture, massage, being more loving, open and vulnerable, and to allow their spiritual light to shine!

The seven steps to permanent weight control

There are seven important principals that, when followed, can virtually guarantee your success to permanent weight release. These are your seven steps to permanent weight control. These seven steps comprise all of the primary objectives of the Slender For Life™ Hypnotic Weight Management System. Through a combination of your hypnosis sessions and your own conscious determination, you can quickly and easily master these healthy lifestyle changes. Each step has been thoroughly examined in earlier chapters, but they are presented here as a summary and so you can see them all in one place.

First Step   Reduce or eliminate the foods that made you overweight

In just the last few years, nutritional science has made major breakthroughs. Many old beliefs about which foods cause excess body fat and which ones are healthy have been tossed out the window.

We now know that the primary cause of being overweight for most individuals is fat, sugar and processed foods. Researchers at the

University of Massachusetts Medical School have found that the body is able to convert dietary fat into body fat with greater ease than it can convert carbohydrates into body fat. Use Chapter Five to select a personal eating strategy that best meets your needs. Indicate your choice on your Goals and Progress Chart on Page 174.

Second Step

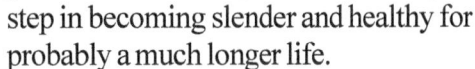

Use a starch-based eating strategy

The healthiest source of calories are complex carbohydrates. This body fuel is burned up immediately. Fats, on the other hand, are usually turned into body fat. A medium size banana and one tablespoon of peanut butter each have about 100 calories. The banana however is 96 percent carbohydrate with almost no fat. The peanut butter is 72 percent fat and only 12 percent carbohydrate. When you make starch (potatoes, rice, corn, etc.) the center of your meals instead of beef, pork, chicken, turkey or fish, you begin a vital

step in becoming slender and healthy for probably a much longer life.

If you make your larger meals from one third to one half starch and the rest of your plate is filled with delicious fresh vegetables and smaller amounts of fruit, then:

· You will not be hungry.
· You may eat as much as you want.
· You will have increased energy.
· You will release weight quickly and easily.

Should you have a dislike for any of the recommended foods, make sure you review the hypnotic suggestions at the end of Chapter Five for help and the section on Page 163. Sure, some of us are never going to enjoy cauliflower, and that's fine—as long as there are plenty of other vegetables you are eating every day. Also refer back to the exercise on Page 108 in Chapter Four, which is very effective at changing food preferences.

Read the books, *The McDougall Program for Maximum Weight Loss* by Dr. John McDougall and *Breaking the Food Seduction* by Dr. Neal Barnard. They are available in the weight loss

web extra

category here: **www.hypnosishealthinfo.com/store**.

Go online to 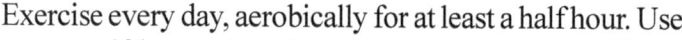www.drmcdougall.com and to www.pcrm.org for more healthy eating information and for great recipes. Be sure to check out the recipe links in the back of this book.

Third Step   Exercise

Exercise every day, aerobically for at least a half hour. Use self-hypnosis so that exercise becomes part of your daily routine. Fast walking is an excellent form of exercise. If you're just beginning to exercise, start out in short durations and build up to 30-45 minutes a day. You want to begin doing your exercise today! This gets your metabolism going to burn off your excess body fat and increase your lean body mass.

Your body is like your automobile. Take care of it, don't abuse it and it will last longer and perform better.

If you are not already enjoying regular daily exercise, stop rationalizing why you cannot or do not take the time. Put it in your schedule and make it a top priority. Along with developing a habit for a daily exercise routine, increase your physical activity whenever you can. Remember, losing your weight is a relatively short-term process. Staying healthy and fit should be for a lifetime.

> **Be committed to developing a more active lifestyle for today, tomorrow and a lifetime thereafter.**

Fourth Step: Drink more water

Drink at least six to eight glasses of water throughout the day. Water flushes out your body's waste as you burn off your fat. Drinking water also removes excess retained water. If you dislike water, give yourself hypnotic suggestions to increase your desire for drinking water. (Cut back as you approach bedtime to prevent an overactive bladder during the night).

Fifth Step

Eliminate mental roadblocks

We all have difficulty in changing habits. This is because of all the issues behind our conditioned behavioral, belief and attitudinal patterns. These side issues are our mental roadblocks and our true cause of past failures in losing weight and keeping it off. In order to bring about permanent weight release, you must not only change your eating and exercise habits, but you must also overcome these mental roadblocks.

Sixth Step: Stop eating when you are satisfied

Eat when your body signals hunger, and stop eating when you feel satisfied. If you follow the guidelines in this book and this simple rule, you should never be overly hungry. You will be eating plenty of good food. Remember, you are *not* dieting. You are changing your eating habits. **This is not about starvation. Denial does not equal weight loss. It's a myth that in order to lose weight, you have to be hungry.**

IMPORTANT: when someone has not been losing weight fast enough or at all, sometimes others will criticize their portion sizes. The truth usually is that the client is refusing to follow the eating strategy (or even come close to it).

Eat five or six times a day. Breakfast, lunch and dinner, with a healthy snack of fruit during the mid morning and mid afternoon.

Portion control should not be a problem. Imagine a scale of 0 to 10. Satisfied, is a 5 or 6 on this scale. It's just like when you put gas in your car and the gas pump shuts off. You learn to recognize that signal when your stomach says *Enough…no more!* On your CDs you were given hypnotic suggestions to become more internally aware of your appetite. This is complimented with mental conditioning to take small bites. Chew your food slowly until it liquefies. And stop eating when you feel that feeling of satisfaction. It's okay to be proud of yourself for saying "No thank you" to extra portions, and it's perfectly fine to leave food on your plate when you stop eating.

Seventh Step

Practice self-hypnosis

Learn and practice self-hypnosis so you are empowered for the rest of your life to remain in control of your habits and emotional stress. After you've been using self-hypnosis for one month, you should begin to recognize changes in your attitude and behavior. Self-hypnosis is easy to learn and use, and it's natural and completely safe.

Self-hypnosis is your course correction. Just as the airplane is constantly making course corrections flying from Seattle to Phoenix, you will also need to make course corrections throughout your life. Self-hypnosis is a powerful and effective tool for staying the course toward your goals. You will also discover that you use self-hypnosis less and less about eating carrots and exercise and more and more with issues such as happy, healthy, loving relationships; feeling calm and at ease at work; and being present and conscious in your body. When you are living consciously and creating your life goals, eating and exercise come naturally.

What if you have a whole lot to lose?

The medical term for people with 100 pounds or more to lose is morbidly obese. Now that's a scary term, and it should be. If you're in that boat—make that an ocean liner, because you have a lot of company—then you've already heard all the dire warnings about your health. (Reread Chapter One if you skipped it.) I know all too well about this category, because I spent way too many years of my life languishing in it. Which is also why I can state with every ounce of what remains of my being, that you *can* release a huge amount of weight—*if* you decide you want to.

There's no doubt, you face special hurdles. From bathroom scales that can't measure your weight, to exercise equipment built for someone half your size, to the health problems associated with being extremely overweight, frustrations are a daily reality.

There is a whole different mindset to large-scale weight loss.

Warren Huberman, PhD, a behavioral consultant for the weight loss program at New York University Medical Center, writes: "You can't just toss a very overweight person the latest diet book or piece of exercise equipment and expect it to work. There is a whole different mindset to large-scale weight loss, and a whole different approach becomes necessary."

Anyone can drop off the 10 or 20 pounds they picked up when they weren't eating consciously. **However, to permanently alter your body by 100 pounds or more requires a special commitment.** I will not lie to you and say how easy it will be. It won't be. It took you years to get in the shape you're in, and it'll take more than a year to reach any state of what feels like normalcy. You may well come from a family who also is extra heavy, and they will very likely be forced to face their own issues if you go down this path. Some of them may join you, but others may not. So you need to prepare yourself mentally and emotionally for possibly having to take this journey to better health without their help or support. If your own children are also overweight, then at least consider doing this for their sake.

You'll need to work extra hard on all the intangible factors. And that's where I can offer some encouragement. Self-hypnosis will be your new best friend—for the rest of your life. This is the tool that can make the difference between one more bounce of the yo-yo and sustaining a new you.

So where do you start, and how do you stay motivated, when your goal is to lose 100 pounds or more? **Here's a collection of tips, some from people who used to weigh over 100 pounds more than they do now.**

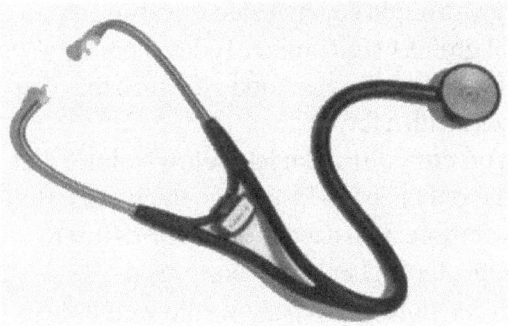

1. Seek medical supervision. Whenever you start a new diet or exercise plan, it's always wise to visit your doctor, but that's especially important if you're undertaking a radical change like releasing 100 or more pounds. Janet Finestein, MS, RD, a nutritionist and dietitian at the Comprehensive Weight Loss Center of New York-Presbyterian Hospital advises: "The more overweight you are, the more likely you need to be monitored—and the more you need some type of medical supervision, at least at the start."

Because obesity contributes to other health problems, including high blood pressure, high cholesterol, and insulin resistance, Finestein says medical care is a must. The good news is, learning how to control your insulin levels may also help you control your hunger, which in turn can make it easier for you to release your excess weight.

Some of my clients have attended Dr. John McDougall's weekend and live-in programs in Santa Rosa, California. For more information visit his website at www.drmcdougall.com.

2. Seek out a Slender For Life™ Hynotherapist. Check out the list at www.slenderforlife.com. If there is none in your area, go to www.iact.org or www.imdha.com to look for a qualified hynotherapist who deals with weight issues. You can also schedule with me via Skype at roger@hypnosishealthinfo.com.

3. Join a support group. Being in this category can be isolating enough, but when you decide you are ready to change you situation, it can get even lonelier. Whether you seek the friendship of established groups, such as Overeaters Anonymous, or whether you create your own circle of support, having peers to discuss all your challenges with will be tremendously helpful. You might ask your doctor if she has other patients who might be interested in starting an informal group. Or go online. Today there are endless sources of support and guidance that you can access with a few clicks.

4. Be careful how you cut your calories. A low-calorie diet may be right for people who only need to lose 20 or 30 pounds. But if your goal is 100 pounds or more, you need more calories just to survive. "The more you weigh, the higher your caloric needs," Finestein says, "so you can eat more than a person who weighs less, and still lose an equal amount of weight." If you can eliminate 500 calories out of your diet every day, you could see a one-pound weight loss each week, she says.

5. Get moving. Being super-sized offers special challenges when it comes to exercising, but no matter what your current fitness level is, you can always do more. Just start gradually and congratulate yourself for all progress, no matter how small it may seem to someone else. If you aren't comfortable exercising in public yet, then there are still plenty of things you can do at home until you are ready to venture out. See Chapter Six for all kinds of good ideas. Even the smallest changes to your routine will add up. Hide the remote and walk across the room to change the channel. Do some stretches before you even get out of bed in the morning. Rely less on others to do things for you.

6. Get lifting. Experts believe that one of the most important exercises for very overweight folks is lifting weights. Resistance training builds muscles, which in turn burn more calories. And you know what—many weight lifting exercises can be done sitting down, making them ideal for people who need to start from that position. Start small with things you have around the house—cans of soup, bags of rice, then liter bottles of water. (A gallon of water weighs a little over eight pounds.) Especially if you've been inactive for a long period of time, you really need to do something to convert fat to muscle. Once you feel up to going to a real gym, you'll discover a huge array of machines specifically designed to isolate and exercise each part of your body. Many people are surprised to learn that they enjoy lifting weights—partly because the results are noticeable fairly quickly.

While releasing this much weight is truly life-altering, it would be the best gift you could ever give yourself and your family—the gift of a longer, healthier life. Scientific studies continue to reveal the mysteries of obesity, and there is a lot of ongoing research into the biological causes and cures, including the genetic component, but don't use that as an excuse to wait for a magic pill. **The power is all within you.**

Tips for staying with the program

Some of these suggestions are courtesy of the U.S. Department of Agriculture and the American Dietetic Association.

- Diet Mistake # 1: Most dieters don't eat enough.Result? They get so hungry, they give up.
- Diet Mistake # 2: Most dieters want to lose weight too fast. Result? They get so impatient, they give up. Because eating too little food makes us hungry, and hunger makes us miserable, to feel better we eat cookies and cakes. The result? Goodbye eating plan.
- If you get stuck at a weight plateau, hidden fats may be a cause. Some vegetarian food products add extra fat to compensate for lack of meat flavor. Always check the label. Another solution is to eat more vegetables and fewer starches.
- Increase your workout by 10-15 minutes AND change your workout routine. Changing the type of exercise you do, or the duration, gives your metabolism an extra boost and helps to burn extra calories.

- If you are an ovo-lacto vegetarian, don't overdo the cheese and other calorie-dense dairy foods. Cheese is 30 percent fat!
- And don't go hog wild with mayo. Mayonnaise is 80 percent fat!
- If you aren't feeling full enough, maybe you aren't eating the right things. Include regular helpings of complex carbs, like whole wheat bread, whole grain cereal, oats and rice in your weight release plan. These foods fill you up and prevent you overeating fattening foods like cheese pizzas.
- If you start to regain weight, examine your recent eating behaviors. Careless vegetarian dieting can cause low levels of dietary nutrition, which in turn may lead to a slowdown in metabolic rate and actually cause weight gain.
- You may be overeating because you're wolfing down your chow. Slow down! When you eat too fast, you end up ingesting more food before your body has a chance to figure out you're satisfied.
- There are conflicting reports on whether or not this is relevant, but it won't hurt to test it for yourself. Don't eat right before going to bed. Try not to eat within three hours of retiring. Your metabolism slows down during later hours and is very low while sleeping.

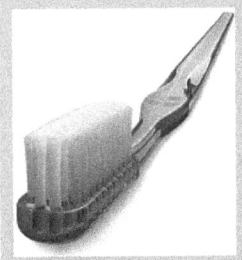

· Need a trick to help with that one? Brush your teeth right after dinner. Many people find they don't want to eat after that point in their daily routine.

· Need a good visual rule to eat by? Eat big to get small. When you choose fruits, vegetables and hearty soups, which are bulked up by fiber and water, you're consuming food that fills you up but without a lot of calories. Unhealthy foods are just the opposite—many calories packed into tiny, unsatisfying portions, such as cheese, sugary snacks, crackers and cookies. Many studies show that hunger tends to be satisfied by a certain volume of food—about four to five pounds a day. And it doesn't matter how many calories are packed into each pound. So the goal is to reach that full feeling without eating an excessive amount of calories.

· Is exercise your downfall? Even making small changes adds up eventually—if you stick with them. Experts at the Centers for Disease Control and Prevention say that if you spend 10 minutes a day walking up and down stairs, you could shed as much as 10 pounds over the course of a year.

· Avoid TV commercials like the fatty Sirens they are. Watching chocolate drip seductively off a spoon and into someone's mouth puts images back in your mind that don't reinforce your new eating plan. The same goes for the Food channel and other cooking shows—except for ones that teach healthy cooking and eating.

· If you just can't resist temptation in grocery stores, have someone else do your shopping, or go with a friend you can count on to steer you away from the cookie and cracker aisle. One client explains that the fruit juice and ice cream are in the same aisle in her store, so she makes sure she always enters and exits that aisle from the juice end. Do whatever it takes at first to install new habits. Eventually you'll be able to saunter past old Ben & Jerry without a second glance. But in the beginning, use all the tricks you need to stay on your new road.

· Make sure you've changed your attitude about all this. You are NOT on a diet. You can't diet to lose weight, you have to alter your eating habits in a way that you can live with for the rest of your life. If you are still in diet mode, looking forward to a time when the diet will end, you are setting yourself up for failure.

Everybody recycles—just don't quit because of it

There is no relapse, but it's not unusual to occasionally deviate from your weight-release program and slide back into old patterns of unhealthy eating and minimal exercise. In fact, you can expect it to happen—perfection in all things is an illusion, but that's especially true in releasing weight. But if you have a plan in place to recover when you do recycle, then you can get past it quickly. It takes time and regular reinforcement for your new healthy behaviors to become habits.

Use these tips to help you deal with occasional weight-release setbacks.

- **Skip tempting situations.** If potluck parties are just too much temptation, avoid them, at least until you feel more in control of your new eating behavior.

- **Stall.** If you're tempted to indulge in an old favorite food, first ask yourself if you're really hungry. Chances are, it's a craving and you may talk yourself out of it. If not, wait a few minutes and see if the desire passes. Or try distracting yourself from your urge to eat—call a friend or take your dog for a walk. If it's a craving, have a glass of water and wait five minutes. Often a craving for sweet or salty foods is really your body signaling you're dehydrated.

Take your dog for a walk.

- **Get some help.** Accepting help from others isn't a sign of weakness, nor does it mean you're failing. Asking for help is a sign of good judgment, not weakness. You need support from others to keep you on track when you have rough days. I urge you to work with a therapist as you make these changes in your life.

- **Be the boss.** Accept responsibility for your own behavior. Remember that ultimately only you can help yourself release weight.

- **Don't beat yourself up.** Learn self-

forgiveness. Don't let negative self-talk (*I've messed up now!* or *I'm a failure!*) prevent you from getting back on track with your eating and exercise goals. Try not to think of your slip-up as a disaster. Remember that mistakes happen and that each day is a chance to start over.

· **Move through it.** Work out your guilt and frustration with exercise. Take a walk or go for a swim. But keep your exercise and activity upbeat. Never use it as punishment for a lapse.

· **Review your goals often.** Go over your weight-release goals and Your Slender For Life™ Commitment regularly and make certain they're still realistic. Remember, healthy weight loss is not too fast—one to two pounds a week is a healthy rate.

· **Think ahead.** Note potential problems, and make a list of possible solutions. Then try a solution. If it works, you've got a strategy for preventing another lapse. If it doesn't, go on to the next solution and keep trying until you find one that works.

And what if you do experience a weight-loss setback? Although relapses are disappointing, they can help you learn to keep your goals realistic, understand what high-risk situations to avoid or realize that certain strategies don't work for you. **Above all, realize that a relapse is temporary—you are not a failure.** Reverting to old behaviors doesn't mean that all hope is lost. It just means you need to recharge your motivation, recommit to your plan and return to healthy behaviors. And most likely, also be more faithful with your daily self-hypnosis.

journal exercise

Understanding why you ate that

If you find yourself experiencing more recycling than you'd like, try journaling about your eating behavior during any of these situations you find yourself in: going out to eat; being on vacation; being under stress; feeling anger, hostility, jealousy, loneliness, fear or social anxiety; suffering from group pressure, a desire to fit in, or a need for approval; feeling financial stress, guilt, lack of trust, insecurity or an inability to take risks. Figuring out the underlying cause for your relapse and dealing with that, always makes returning to your program much easier.

_____

_____

_____

_____

_____

_____

_____

_____

_____

_____

_____

_____

_____

Not everyone may be rooting for you

As sad as this is to imagine, not all of your friends and family may be thrilled that you are releasing weight. The reasons for this are complex, and don't necessarily imply that you have mean-spirited people in your life. It is often inadvertent on the part of the saboteurs—they rarely realize what they are doing. This can be one of the toughest hurdles to leap, especially if the saboteurs are in your immediate circle. So if this is your reality, the first key to dealing with it is awareness. **Here are some signs of diet sabotage—how many have you experienced?**

· "Honey, you know I like you just the way you are."
· "I think your love handles are cute."
· "It's Christmas…you can't diet during the holidays."
· "Just have a few bites…this is the best cake I've ever tasted."
· "You're wasting away to nothing."
· "What—now you're too good for my cooking?"
· "What do you mean you're not eating meat anymore—have

you lost your mind?"
· "I wondered why you were so grumpy lately—it must be because you're on a diet."
· "The gym can wait…I haven't seen you in ages."
· "You're doing so well on your diet—let's go out for ice cream to celebrate."
· "It's too cold to go for a walk—let's watch a movie instead."
· "But I made this pie just for you—it's your favorite!"
· "Why bother dieting—you know you'll just gain it all back and then some."
· "Oh come on, have the last cookie."
· "Just finish up these potatoes—there aren't enough to save for another meal."
· "Let's celebrate your birthday at that French restaurant you love so much…you know how you adore their chocolate tortes."
· Then there are friends who repeatedly pass bowls of junky snack foods to you every time you come over.
· Co-workers who always have a candy bowl on their desk and bring donuts into the office once a week.
· Spouses who offer boxes of candy and other treats as gifts.
· Don't go getting too skinny on us now.
· You look great! You don't need to lose anymore weight.

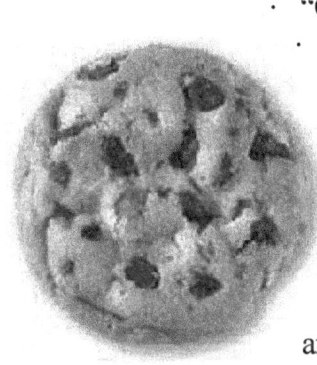

Your weight loss program forces those around you to examine their own weight.

Julie's experience is typical. "Whenever I make an effort to improve my eating and reduce my weight, my friends, my mother and even my husband seem intent on undermining me. They bring rich foods into the house, they push desserts in front of me and tell me I don't need to diet."

Your weight loss program forces those around you to examine their own weight, and that may make them uncomfortable because they aren't ready to change. Or perhaps they've witnessed your past weight loss failures and are simply trying to prevent another one. Or they could be simply jealous and fear that you may seek out new relationships to match your new body and improved self-image.

Whatever the cause, the answer is speaking your truth to those you experience trying to sabotage you. Let them know how you

Simply but firmly explain that you now place a high priority on your health.

view their actions and words and request their support. It's fair to ask your mother to fix more vegetables when you come over to eat. It's okay to tell your friends to put the Cheetos away before you stop by. It's reasonable to ask a co-worker to consider bringing healthier treats into work—or to at least put her donuts someplace less conspicuous. Even better—if it feels comfortable to do so, consider suggesting to your boss that the company adopt a healthy eating policy and dissuade employees from bringing in junk food. In any case, be sure to keep healthy snacks at the office so you can join in a birthday celebration—without the cake. When people try and shove food in your face, just say firmly: "No thanks—maybe later." A conditional response will often make them go away, when a firm "No" elicits an argument. Above all, don't be afraid to be assertive about what you need to succeed. You are the only one who gets to decide what you eat, and you need to enforce that right.

Others may need reassurances from you that you will not abandon them once you reach your target weight. Rather than nagging and pleading, be a good example for them, and some of them may well join you in your quest. Perhaps you'll need to find new ways of participating in familiar social rituals. If you're accustomed to going out for drinks after work with pals, you can still go—just order mineral water and a veggie plate instead of a pitcher of beer and a heap of onion rings. Or if you need to turn down food offered by friends and family, make sure they understand it's the Boston cream pie you're rejecting, not them.

But there's no doubt your priorities will change as you get healthier. You may prefer going to the gym after work instead of a pub. You may want to go for a nice long run on Saturday mornings rather than go out for a big greasy brunch. You may learn to love different restaurants than the ones you've been used to frequenting. All these things can be cause for concern among those who are invested in your *not* changing. When they complain to you about your new habits, simply but firmly explain that you now place a high priority on your health, and let them know they are welcome to join you. If they insist on telling you how you should eat and what worked

Don't give away the power to determine the fate of your body!

for them, simply smile, nod your head and say, "Thank you, but this is working for me." Inevitably, some friends may indeed fade away from your life—but they will be the ones who are most toxic for your long-term success—so just remain clear what matters most to you, and you'll be fine. For every potato who won't get off the couch with you, there's a new friend waiting who'll love to join you on your daily walks.

Spouses can present the worst situations. A New York diet doctor studied data from more than 6,000 of his patients, and found that 70 percent of the women had difficulty eliciting support from their mates, as opposed to 5 percent of his male patients. He learned that a man often considers his wife's diet as her problem, not his, and is unaware how his actions affect the outcome. Fears and concerns about sexual attractiveness may also be part of the mix. Communicating why you are intent on releasing your excess weight and enlisting your spouse as a partner is key. Emphasize that your motivation is better health and more time to enjoy life together—it'll be hard to argue with that.

Remember, every time you say "yes" to something you know is not good for you, when what you really want to say is "no," you can create passive anger within yourself. Passive anger can gnaw away at you in the form of guilt and depression, making lifestyle changes much more difficult. Until you can say "no" whenever you want to, "yes" means nothing. **When others sabotage you, remember that the problem lies with them and not you. You have taken charge of your life.**

If sabotage remains an ongoing issue for you, journal about it. Your reality may be that you will just have to have stronger resolve and constant clarity about your intentions. Venting about it to your journal is at least an outlet. And you are especially likely to find comfort from a support group. Just don't give away to anyone the power to determine the fate of your body!

Hypnotic suggestions to increase confidence and self-esteem

· I easily achieve my goals.
· I am more confident in myself, my choices and my abilities.
· My success is forever.
· I am walking toward my ideal body.
· I remove all inappropriate thoughts from my mind.
· I remove all inappropriate behaviors from my actions.
· I am proud of the control I have over my eating and exercise habits.
· I am walking away from my dysfunctional behavior.
· I am free from the limiting opinions of others.
· I experience joy in each step I take toward achieving my goals.
· I do the best possible things for myself.
· I am assuming the behavior of a happy, physically fit and athletic person.
· Each day I wake up happier and more content with my healthier choices.
· Each day brings new opportunities and a greater sense of purpose.
· I love myself enough to do whatever safe and healthy things it takes to ensure my ideal body weight.
· I find a greater joy in living.
· I am freeing myself from the embarrassment of excess weight.
· I am freeing myself from the misery of excess weight.
· Each day I congratulate myself for the positive steps I take toward my success.
· I make choices today to create the tomorrow I want.
· I am in charge of my life and accept responsibility for my power.
· I am in control and feel worthy and vibrant. My confidence and determination overcome any setback or obstacle. I let go of my negative emotions.
· I am free to become the magnificent me that I am meant to be.
· I am an important person.
· I consistently behave in a way that creates my wellness because I deeply love and care about myself.
· I am a person of worth and value.

- I feel good about myself.
- I accept my strengths and limitations, knowing I have the power to make changes.
- I am the master of my life.
- My inner strength grows stronger.
- I am attractive and handsome, becoming more so each day.
- I listen and trust my inner voice.
- I am empowered to act now.
- I am free from conflicting desires.
- Each day brings new opportunities and a greater sense of purpose.
- I behave with more self-assurance.
- My courage grows to help me become more sure of myself.
- I have a greater appreciation for myself.

In the final chapter, I'll tell you what you can expect during the maintenance phase of permanent weight loss…the *life* part of getting slender for life. For as many readers know, releasing your excess weight is just the beginning of the process—not the end of it. Which is why the tools you've learned to use in this program are so key to your long term success. **You've worked hard to shed your excess pounds, so don't stop until you learn how to keep them off!**

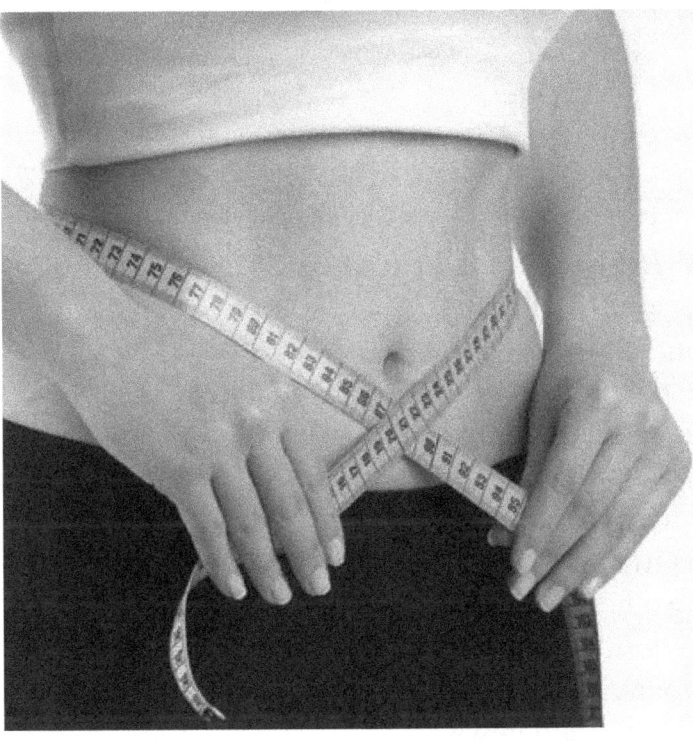

Chapter Eight

Can You Handle Success?

Chapter Eight At A Glance

· Pushing your reset button
· Give yourself the credit
· Recognizing your goal when you meet it
· Are you ready to terminate?
· Imagine your new lifestyle
· Tips for taming temptation
· Plan for pitfalls
· Handling other challenges
· Keeping holidays happy
· Living your vision
· Finally some good news

Congratulations for (almost) finishing reading this book, and I hope listening to all the CDs as well. That's an achievement in itself, as the path of good intentions is littered with unread books. If you have also reached your goal weight, then let me add my applause to that of the people in your life who support your achievement.

If all of your family and friends are indeed cheering your accomplishment, then count yourself fortunate. There are some people who reach their goal weight only to take on the additional challenge of resisting the negative influences of those around them who cannot share in their happiness. **What you are really learning to do here is take back your power.** The power you gave away to food, to other people, events and circumstances. You are becoming that *Leader of Self.* As Dr. Wayne Dyer says, "Step out of the pack and do it differently, and do it in such a way that no one notices."   But this may not be the first time you've been at this juncture in your life, enjoying reaching your goal weight, believing this time will be forever. As you well know, maintaining your new weight is what separates yo-yo dieters from people who become long-term success stories. Happily for you, you now have the tools to ensure you never relapse into that unhealthy version of yourself.

But make no mistake, the work is ongoing. **You will need to continue using self-hypnosis and all the tricks you learned in this program in order to maintain your new figure.** But it will eventually become more habitual and less difficult.

One Wednesday night in group, Molly confided how over the holidays she found herself slipping back into old behaviors. She was talking to her daughter about her awareness and her daughter said "You need a *reset button.*" She was right! So try this: as soon as you become aware of your unwanted behavior, touch your chest and say "Reset!" Thus was born another Slender For Life™ tool: the *reset button.* This physical act of touching your body (any place will work) along with speaking the words, shifts you out of your mindless trance and back into the present. You become conscious of your body and able to make new, healthier choices that support your goals.

Give yourself the credit

So exactly how do you maintain your ideal weight? All too often, the goal is to reach a certain number on the scale without regard for what comes next. Some people reach their goal and then go celebrate with a food binge! For those who have been overweight most of their lives, they have no concept of what life will be like now that they've attained their ideal weight.

Maintenance is taking all the work that went into achieving your goal and then building on that. Regression occurs when you go back to an earlier phase of your change process. Deciding to stop overeating is not enough to overcome it for good. You see, all negative habits become our friends—even, in many cases, our lovers. They play important, sometimes dominating, roles in our lives. It's really easy to slip back into old habits and not even realize it until the clothes no longer fit.

"This program works so well that I forgot I was on a program." ~Rosalie

I am continuously astounded at how many people find success difficult to accept, and their tendency is to attribute their success to others—God, a spouse, or even to me as their guide. By not accepting responsibility and credit for liberating yourself, you undermine your self-confidence, your self-esteem and your commitment. If you think others are responsible for your success, how can you maintain it yourself? Maintenance is not a time for criticizing yourself for having had weight problems. Instead, it's a time for taking both credit and responsibility for the changes you made.

Rosalie has released over 50 pounds and in the process has found a whole new outlook on life. "The combination of hypnosis and exercise has given me an edge which I never had before. To be able to stop thinking about a diet and just think about healthy eating and regular exercise as "what I do" is truly a blessing. **This program works so well that I forgot I was on a program."**

Are you there yet?

But wait, there's an important question you must answer: **What is the last thing that has to happen for you to know that you are at your goal weight?** This may sound strange, and it's one of the many times that I get odd looks from clients suggesting that I have too many holes in my head, but it is an important question for you to answer. You must be able to *certify* your success.

The obvious impulse answer is "getting on the scales!" But when people really think it through, rarely is it about a number on the scale. Sometimes I hear: "Standing in front of a dressing room mirror in my new size eight dress and seeing how it fits my lean body perfectly." Or "Wearing that new swimsuit on a white sand Maui beach and not being self-conscious." Or "Being able to play 18 holes of golf and not be tired and know that I look and feel fit." These responses are getting at what I consider to be the real answer, which is *an internal feeling*.

Sadly, some people do reach their goal weight and don't know it; they still see a fat person in their mirror. Eventually, if they stick with their maintenance plan, they reach a time when they do realize they've done it. At that point, they look back at early pictures taken when they first reached their ideal weight and realize how great they looked. This often happens to yo-yo dieters who had never before felt satisfied, never felt complete within themselves; they were always searching but never felt good enough.

You must be able to *certify* your success.

All too often people believe that when they release their extra weight, life will suddenly be wonderful. But like anything else, no matter where you go—there you are! Taking pounds off will not make an unhappy person happy. In fact, it is your emotions that dictate your weight. When you are emotionally healthy, your body will follow.

So, it is important to *certify* what it means to be at your ideal weight. **When deciding to release weight, define in tangible**

terms how you will know when you have reached your goal.

Maintenance is a time of patience and persistence. Maintenance is a lengthy process where time is an ally. You do not have to get everything right all at once or even all the time.

What have you put in your basket?

Have you ever yearned for something—more food, a cigarette, alcohol, drugs, sex, shopping, a new car, new boyfriend, new girlfriend, new spouse, new boat, new house, whatever—and then when you get it, you feel satisfied for a while, but eventually you want more, or you want something else? You may recognize it as a feeling of hunger, anxiety, restlessness, nervousness, anger or maybe as fear. Some people know it as a clenched fist feeling in their chest, an upset stomach, sore neck or back, a migraine headache or other dis-ease.

It's as if most of us are going through life with an empty basket that we are trying to fill. We buy the new toy or clothes—which seemingly fills our basket—and we feel excited for a few days, maybe even weeks. Yet, that wanting or emptiness begins to eat away at us, that feeling like something is missing, that there is more available to us. So then we try to find something else to fill us, to make us complete. Still, we feel empty.

I see this repeatedly with individuals and couples struggling with issues such as depression, stress or relationship challenges. Somewhere a couple meets, they have fun with each other, they talk, they share and they fall head over heels in love. Each partner is getting some unfulfilled need met, getting something put into their basket. It feels wonderful.

But then after awhile, something about the other person begins to bug us. So we try to change them, and they often do change to be more what we want them to be. Then we do the same thing, we change to please them. We give up a part of ourselves to fit their

> It's as if most of us are going through life with an empty basket that we are trying to fill.

expectations of us. One day, one or both people in the couple realize the unhappiness they have created in the relationship. Each has given up something important. We wonder what happened to the person with whom we fell in love. Sometimes we run from this relationship to a new one and start all over again, using the same old methods that haven't worked, yet hoping to get a different result.

You see, when we are in a relationship based on our own neediness, it takes more and more to satisfy us. The relationship is like any other dependency. It's as if our basket has no bottom; it's an empty hole. When we keep taking from the relationship, it's not long before there is nothing left to take and we are still empty. It doesn't work to be looking to people or things outside ourselves to make us happy, to make us feel loved, to meet our needs. We are just increasing our wanting and our sense of lack.

It's as if our basket has no bottom; it's an empty hole.

Often, I find that people focus on one aspect of their lives to be happy. Physically, they may have great jobs, they may have lots of money, they may have great muscular bodies. Mentally, they may be constantly learning, reading, discovering new wonders in life and going to school. Emotionally, they may have close friends and maybe even a seemingly great relationship. Spiritually, they may regularly worship a higher power and try to live a spiritual life or achieve forgiveness.

These are all outward ways we try to meet our needs, that we try to fill our baskets. Each of these can go a long way toward a better life and are great activities in and of themselves. Nevertheless, all the money in the world won't make us happy. All the education will not eliminate the negative thoughts that we have about ourselves. Friends and relationships don't take away the loneliness when we're alone. And all the good deeds will not bring us peace in our hearts and souls. Even people who seemingly have it all are often searching for something more to fill their baskets. **The only way to fill our basket is to fill it ourselves.** We will never have enough money or a good enough body if we aren't enough just as we are. We will never

Abundance starts within us, with our baskets full and overflowing.

enjoy positive thinking if we believe we aren't enough. We will never be happy if we believe we're unworthy of love and happiness. Divine forgiveness will never be enough if we don't believe we are forgivable.

Abundance starts within us, with our baskets full and overflowing. A healthy relationship exists in our overflow, not in our neediness. It's in our abundance, our mutual giving where we love unconditionally, where we can love and not worry if we are loved back. Abundance starts when we accept divine forgiveness by forgiving ourselves. When we are forgivable, we can love ourselves, have affirming mental self-talk and give gentle care to our bodies and environment.

If we want physical riches, we must see ourselves as abundant. If we want tranquility, we must be at peace in our minds. If we want love, we must be loving. And if we want forgiveness, we must be forgiving.

After maintenance comes termination

You haven't ended the process, it's simply become embedded in your behavior. You are just beginning your new life of empowerment. Some clients think that when they reach their ideal weight, they can go back to the old lifestyle that resulted in their becoming overweight. Rationally, we know this just can't work.

People who successfully maintain their weight loss shift their focus away from their previous struggles with food and exercise. They look, think and feel with genuine confidence. They just do it. The termination stage is your ultimate goal.

> **Termination is when you automatically use the skills you've learned without conscious thought.**

It's like when you learned to drive a car. Each movement from turning the key, shifting gears or braking required conscious thought. Then one day you walked out of the house, got in the car and drove away, arrived safely at your destination and didn't remember leaving home or the journey to the destination. Driving had become second nature.

For my clients, termination is the point where they automatically go to the gym without a mental fight. It is a habit. It's when they regularly use self-hypnosis and naturally choose to eat fruits, vegetables and whole grains. It is just what they do.

Sharon had been unhappy with how she looked and how she'd been eating when she came to see me. Now she's kept her excess weight off and is optimistic it will stay off forever. "I've been at my goal weight for over a year, and I'm delighted with that. This is the only program that has gotten me to the point where I don't think of dieting. All I think about is eating healthfully, and that makes me feel good. The program has given me tools to use for the rest of my life."

Learn from some long-term losers

The National Weight Control Registry (NWCR) was founded in 1994 by two university scientists who wanted to learn a lot more about how to lose weight and keep it off successfully. Anyone who is over 18, has lost at least 30 pounds, and has maintained this loss for more than one year is eligible to participate. Thus far, the NWCR has enrolled more than 4,500 people who willingly share their personal tips to weight loss success. With the rates for American obesity skyrocketing, the NWCR has made an attempt to figure out what real "losers" do to attain successful long term weight loss.

With data collected for over 11 years, here's what they've learned about how these people have effectively released weight and kept it off.

Many keep a daily food record.

· Most participants in the NWCR continuously monitor their eating habits. Many keep a daily food record to hold themselves accountable to their goals. They continuously learn how to manage their own individual "high risk" situations such as eating when stressed or "cleaning the plate" out of habit rather than hunger.

On average, NWCR enrollees enjoy 60-90 minutes of moderate to high intensity exercise daily.

· Exercise! We all know exercise is important for weight loss and health, but NWCR participants have taken exercise to new levels. On average, NWCR enrollees incorporate 60-90 minutes of moderate to high intensity exercise daily. The most popular exercise among NWCR participants is walking—on average five to six miles daily. These participants have demonstrated that you simply can't eliminate exercise from a successful weight loss program.

· Avoid fads. While many NWCR enrollees tried fad diets in the past, the majority say that a low-fat, high-carbohydrate, moderate protein diet is what got them where they are today. Now they focus more on choosing foods that are nutrient-dense and healthy.

· Have an attitude adjustment. Most NWCR participants had to change their thinking about dieting and weight loss. Some felt weight loss was impossible because "it's in my genes to be fat." Others had nearly given up because they had "failed" so many diets in the past. The key difference is that these same people finally gave up their defeatist attitude and faced this concept head on: A healthy lifestyle is a lifelong commitment and must be taken slowly, day by day.

· Hold yourself accountable. Many participants report that weighing yourself regularly, having commitments to others to exercise, or being accountable to a group is important. These extra monitoring devices help them to correct undesirable practices before they get too out of hand.

National Weight Control Registry scientists studied more than 4,500 people who lost, on average, 66 pounds and kept it off for six years. The vast majority follow a

It takes a long time to develop healthy habits, but once you do, stick to them!

diet low in fat and high in natural, fiber-rich carbohydrates like fruits and vegetables—and lots of them. They also maintain a consistent eating pattern across weekdays and weekends. It takes a long time to develop healthy habits, but once you do, stick to them! According to the NWCR, over half of successful dieters stick to their diet, lifestyle and exercise routine daily—including holidays and in restaurants. In addition, most participants frequent restaurants no more than two or three times per week because of the difficulty of sticking to their lifestyle routine while dining out.

Moreover, weight loss maintenance may get easier over time; after individuals have successfully maintained their weight loss for two to five years, the chance of longer-term success greatly increases.

Tips for taming temptation

Life changes are essential for maintenance; a new lifestyle is essential for termination. The difference is in the permanence of the change. In maintenance, you modify parts of your life—social contacts, daily schedules, behavior patterns—to overcome your old unhealthy behaviors. In termination, you institute a healthier lifestyle as a means of preserving your gains and promoting new growth.

Although you can never be problem-free, you can live in ways that reduce the recurrence of self-defeating behaviors. "I've got this beat forever" is a telltale sign of overconfidence. Overconfidence can also beget daily temptation, to which you intentionally and

unnecessarily subject yourself regularly. Dieters often buy high-calorie goodies and prepare high-calorie, high-fat meals when **entertaining**. Where did we get the notion that our family and friends won't appreciate tasty, elegantly presented healthy food?

Creating a healthier lifestyle involves altering more than your problems with food. It is simply naïve to believe you can go on living the way you did before and expect the consequences to be different. If you're going to a social event and are bringing food, then bring healthy foods. When you're going to someone's home for dinner and not bringing food, then go and enjoy it, but stop eating when your stomach tells you that you have enough fuel in your body. If you're hosting a social function, then serve healthy foods. Do we really believe that people won't appreciate leaving our homes feeling very satisfied and grateful that they don't have a food hangover?

When I attend a **social function**, I eat a little bit of brown rice before going. That way, I've taken the edge off. I am not overly hungry, and I don't have to fill up on appetizers or sit down to the meal famished. Remember, we come together with people over a meal to socialize. It is about being with people—not how much and how fast we can eat.

Eating out can present challenges, so here's a clever idea. Ask for the take home container when your food first arrives and put half of it away right from the start, then put the container out of sight. This is a great way to avoid overeating those giant restaurant meals. (Just don't use that as a license to eat three desserts!)

Be conscious, be aware during the **holidays**. Those weeks from Thanksgiving to the new year can be fraught with temptations. Ask yourself: What is my goal? Can I find ways to enjoy a few treats in moderation, or am I going to forget everything I've learned and regress to gobbling every marshmallow Santa in sight? Can I rethink my behavior so I can enjoy the holidays for years to come? Yes, the holidays are plump with special treats that should come once a year. Enjoy a taste—just not the whole pan of fudge.

Stop eating when your stomach tells you that you have enough fuel in your body.

Sure, you can be a flexitarian on Thanksgiving and have some turkey, but for many people, the holidays last six weeks or more, so we can't afford to flex *too much* for six weeks or it will just be a huge setback. According to the National Institutes of Health, pounds packed on during the holidays account for half of all weight gained annually. Don't let a few weeks of holiday gatherings undo a year's worth of hard work. (See Page 238 for more tips on eating during the holidays.)

Other challenges you may face

For some people, especially those who live in places where being a vegetarian is still viewed as something akin to being a communist or at best a kook, the psychological aspects of living a different lifestyle can cause feelings of isolation and disconnectedness from family and friends. The snide comments about eating rabbit food grow stale really fast. Depending on who you are dealing with, you can either take a sincere, thoughtful approach or fight ignorance with wit.

Here's how Dan deals with it. "I actually prefer to say I follow a vegan diet and low-impact lifestyle, rather than just say I'm a vegan. I know its only reworded, but I think the subtle change can make a huge difference in how folks hear us and accept us. To me, following a vegan diet and low-impact lifestyle means I'm doing my best for what I believe in, rather than setting myself up for critical analysis and probing by stating I'm a vegan—which can sound a bit like I think I'm better than you."

There are lots of vegetarian and vegan communities online where you can find support. One is **www.veganoutreach.org.** While I do not agree with 100 percent of the information on this website, it offers some great ideas. I am not looking for you to agree with me 100 percent. In fact, I ask all new clients to please read the information, listen to the CDs from a place of "Isn't that interesting" rather than "I agree or disagree." Take this information and use what works for you.

Another issue is dealing with people who may prefer you fat and NOT have a positive response to your success. If you missed the section on diet sabotage in Chapter Seven, be sure to see Page 218.

"I actually prefer to say I follow a vegan diet and low-impact lifestyle, rather than just say I'm a vegan."
~Dan

Plan to be sociable

Think about all the social situations you might find yourself in where making good food choices may be challenging. The key to success is to plan ahead, instead of just showing up at a party hungry and hoping there is something you can eat. For example:

· **Challenge:** Volunteering at your son's school Halloween party and being around all those cupcakes and bowls of candy.

· **Solution:** Eat a healthy meal or snacks before you go, so you won't be hungry. In addition, bring healthier treats for everyone—or even better, discuss the treats ahead of time with the other mothers and skip the cupcakes and candy all together.

· **Challenge:** Weekly Sunday dinner at your in-laws, which is always overly rich. Your mother-in-law makes you feel you're being rude if you don't eat second helpings and her famous desserts.

The key to success is to plan ahead.

· **Solution:** Have a private conversation with her in which you explain that you have decided to eat more healthily—and feed your family only healthy foods—so you don't end up with serious diseases. Offer to cook the dinner with her and gradually teach her other ways to prepare food. Give her healthy cookbooks so she can start to see what you've been learning. If all else fails, tell her that you'll still come by for a weekly visit, but you will eat elsewhere.

· **Challenge:** Business lunches at high-end restaurants notorious for their rich foods.

· **Solution:** Call ahead to the restaurant and ask what alternatives they can provide. You may even be able to pre-order a special vegetarian meal that will be the envy of your dining companions. Or, take the edge off your hunger by having some carrot sticks before you go. Then order the simplest thing on the menu, but don't eat all of it. Better still, try suggesting restaurants that you know serve healthier food. These days, most thoughtful people recognize when someone is taking good care of himself and admire that as a sign of self-esteem.

· **Challenge:** Birthday parties with the cheap store-bought cake.

· **Solution:** Don't say "*No thank you.*" All eyes will be on you with comments like: "*Aren't you being the good girl,*" and "*Are you on a diet?*" Simply accept the cake, mash it with your fork, lay you napkin on top and set it down or throw it away. Chances are no one will ever notice.

Giving good care to yourself is never something to be embarrassed about. It's a sign of a mature, intelligent adult.

journal exercise

Have fun not fat

Make a list on the left side of the page of all the social situations you might find yourself in where making good food choices may be challenging. Then opposite each situation, write as many healthy solutions as you can imagine.

_____   _____

_____   _____

_____   _____

_____   _____

_____   _____

_____   _____

_____   _____

_____   _____

_____   _____

_____   _____

_____   _____

_____   _____

How to keep holidays happy

Nearly all of us grew up associating birthdays and holidays with special food treats. Visions of sugar plums, candy canes, chocolate coins, overstuffed turkeys, heart-shaped candy boxes and

marshmallow Easter rabbits are inextricably bound up with our memories and family traditions. Plus those exotic, rich foods are all around us at those times, calling to us, seducing us, triggering lifelong desires for sugary highs. What's a person to do? How do you remain a sane voice in a sea of insane behavior and too much temptation? You just do the best you can, one day, one cupcake, one eggnog at a time. And when you do succumb to an occasional snicker doodle, you tell yourself you're simply human, you forgive yourself, and you cleanse your palate with a carrot stick! You don't use one lapse as an excuse to eat every cheese-oozing hors d'oeuvre in sight.

Be aware that stress can trigger cravings.

That said, there are things you can do to be ready for the annual feasting season.

· Be aware that stress can trigger cravings, so do whatever you can to lighten your load at that time of year. Plan breaks, pampering activities and carry healthy snacks with you to the mall.

· Be different. You don't have to bake four dozen pfeffernuesse cookies just because your mother always did.

· Don't sacrifice your sleep—exhaustion means you are more likely to overeat.

· Watch your alcohol intake—lessened inhibitions can dissolve your real intentions. Drink two 12-ounce glasses of water between each alcoholic drink.

· Find other ways to comfort yourself after emotional situations (which are often so plentiful during holiday times). A new sweater or golf club will feel much better than a raspberry cheesecake will feel thudding in your gut. Even better, distract yourself by visiting someone who'll really appreciate it, perhaps an elderly neighbor.

· Colder weather and darker days often fuel desires for empty foods. Redefine comfort foods as foods that actually make you feel better, not worse. Macaroni and cheese is not a miracle cure for anything.

· Stay active, even during the winter. Dance with the dog! Couch potatoes eat potato chips—and all the other so-called foods that come in bags, cans and bottles. Don't lose all the ground you've gained by setting aside your exercise plan just because the weather has changed. Try out a new gym. Go mall walking. What you do doesn't matter—just keep doing something.

Living your vision

I want to end by offering a true story, written by one of my former clients, Elise. This is part of her Slender For Life™ Commitment that is in Chapter 3. She is happy to share this with you, as she understands her experience may inspire others on this same path.

It felt so good to walk around without feeling the need to cover up.

"Honey, help me with this zipper, will you please?"

This was the dress. The kind I've wanted to wear for years. Black, slinky, sensually elegant and size six.

I almost can't believe I'm here and enjoying myself so much. Mike, my husband can't take his eyes, or his hands, off me. I love the way he's making me feel desirable.

Today, when we were up on the sun deck of the cruise ship, I wore a yellow bikini, which showed off my tan and my new shapely body. It felt so good to walk around without feeling the need to cover up. My scar didn't repulse anyone; in fact it seemed to draw eyes to

me. My usual buoyant personality is lifted to new heights, and both Mike and I are enjoying it.

We've both slimmed down. He's down to 180 and I'm about 130. And our energy is amazing. We can walk forever and not feel sore afterward. Our cruise companions just seem to be drawn to us, and we're invited to join everybody's party. We are confident and happy.

"There you go," Mike

I get up every morning and walk the track until breakfast is served in the dining room.

says as he slides the zipper closed. "Are you ready?" he asks. I slip my feet into my new strappy black sandals and we leave for dinner. A while ago, I wouldn't have dreamed of wearing these shoes, or this dress either, because my feet would swell in the heat and look like pillows stuffed in the straps. Now they look great. They won't swell no matter how long we stay out on the promenade deck or in the disco.

As we walk up the two flights of stairs to the dining room, I'm looking forward to the dinner. The stairs don't cause me a moment's hesitation. I'm in shape and can walk easily in the 3 1/2 inch heels. I feel elegant and graceful. I smile at an elderly lady as we pass. She's surrounded with what must be her family and looks satisfied. I want to look like that when I'm older.

Mike is talking to me. We imagine what delights are on the menu tonight. We both love the sterling presentation of the meal. We feel special when our waiters serve us. Mike jokes with them, and I'm not surprised when we seem to get special attention. The meal in itself isn't important. It's world class, of course, but we are more appreciative of the company at our table, the conversation, the mood set in the dining room. There seems to be more laughter at our table than at others. We all enjoy ourselves and genuinely like each other.

The maitre d' comes to seat us. This didn't happen to us during other cruises. He calls us by name and we thank him. This is just such a fairy tale night.

I wear the tanzanite jewelry Mike bought me in port today. It shows off my tan and seems to send out sparks of light when I move. This is the jewelry we didn't buy a few years ago. I'm glad we waited, but I've never forgotten that other cruise. It reminds me of the difference between then and now.

Now Mike and I get up every morning and walk the track until breakfast is served in the dining room.

Our whole mindset has changed, and neither of us misses fast food.

Fruit and whole-wheat cereal is so good after exercise. We haven't stopped by the pizzeria at all. We've actually made it to all the meals on time and didn't have to have the pizza. I can stay up on deck all day without feeling I need a nap. I'm so glad the waiters bring drinks around, so I don't have to leave my lounge unless I want to.

In the afternoon a quick dip in the pool cools me off. I stand at the rail on the upper deck. Straight across from me is the topless deck. Mike jokes about me sunning myself over there. I don't feel the need to expose myself any more than I am. I don't have to. I'm getting all the attention I need from him. I tell him, "You can go over there if you'd like." He looks over there, then back at me, "No, I've got better right here. And I can touch," he winks.

Straight down from our deck is the one with the large pool and slide and hot tub. I watch the people down there. Lots of young hard bodies flirting up a storm. Of course there are some older people too. That's the deck where the cruise director holds games and contests. It's fun to watch the activities. I feel very comfortable standing in plain sight in my swimsuit.

Everyone is always looking around at everyone else, checking each other out. Mike and I do too. But our eyes always come back to each other. His body is perfect for me. He's got really wide shoulders, and although I can't get him into a Speedo in public, he has relaxed. He looks tanned and in shape. Our arms and abs are getting

pretty tight. We've both worked very hard this year. The hardest was leaving the fast food. Our whole mindset has changed, and neither of us misses it. The money we've saved from not buying junk food and alcohol has really added up. This is just a new lifestyle. It's not a punishment—it's something we embrace and enjoy.

I come back to the present moment as our food is served. Beautiful lobster and crab with rice and broccoli. The plate is so pretty.

We are admiring all the plates. It all looks delicious. Mike orders several bottles of champagne for the table. We all laugh and eat at the same time. The women talk about the shopping they did in port, and the guys groan about being pulled from one store to the next. We're in high spirits. It's a good night.

I'm talking and enjoying myself too much to eat. I take a couple of bites of the lobster and crab. It's fabulous! Rich and succulent. But after a few bites of the rice and veggies, I've had enough. I don't need to eat it all and I'm satisfied. The second waiter is concerned that I don't like the meal, but I smile and tell him it's perfect, but I just can't eat the generous portion. He smiles and takes my half-full plate away. I concentrate on my water goblet. It's always full and ready.

The wine steward brings the champagne and offers Mike the first sample. He approves it and everyone gets a glass. The room's lights dim. I know from experience this means that passenger anniversaries and birthday celebrations will be honored now. Our waiters and wine steward appear with a beautiful chocolate raspberry and caramel layer cake. It's gorgeous. Everyone at the table sings as I blow out the single candle.

Instead of a wish, I say a prayer of thanksgiving. I thank my beautiful husband, my family and friends and my hypnotherapist for giving me this beautiful day and making me feel so good about myself. I'm 35 years old today, and my life is just getting started.

We are happy. And life is just getting started.

As we leave the dining room, I see the elderly lady again. She motions us over. I smile at her. She takes my hand and tells me she thinks I look so very sophisticated and elegant in my black dress. She says I'm beautiful and looks at Mike and me both. She talks about how good we look together as a couple and how happy. We look at each other and wink. Yes, life is good. We are happy. And life is just getting started.

Let's end with some good news

According to the American Journal of Clinical Nutrition, July 2005, there is a general perception that almost no one succeeds in long-term maintenance of weight loss. However, recent research has shown that 20 percent of overweight individuals are successful at

long-term weight loss when defined as losing at least 10 percent of initial body weight and maintaining the loss for at least one year. **The key is to build on your first signs of success, focus on progress not perfection, but never lose sight of the fact that you are making a permanent lifestyle change.**

As of this writing (in late 2010) there are signs that food suppliers are getting the message that we desperately need and want to eat more healthily. In late 2006 New York City instituted a bold law banning trans fats. Since then, cities like Seattle and others around the globe have been following suit. Restaurants are changing the way they operate, with most fast food chains pouring out the unhealthy oils. Even Denny's—formerly known for giant platters of fried food—announced plans to dump trans fats. Then came news that Wal-Mart of all places is going to sell organic food. That means healthier options are reaching into the smallest towns and farthest corners of America—which conveniently eliminates yet another potential excuse—that there is no healthy food in your area.

"I have lightened up both physically and emotionally."
~Leslie

Former client Leslie sums it up for many people who have stuck with the Slender For Life™ plan. "This program has given me the confidence to be myself without overeating. I have lightened up both physically and emotionally."

I wish for you the same gratifying results.

Applause, applause for finishing the book—and giving yourself the immeasurable gift

of good health. By now, you may be beginning to realize that **it's not about the food!** It's about *you* taking control of your life and creating a new relationship with yourself, where you are living consciously in the moment. It's about taking back your power—the power that you gave away to food, stress, family, other people, work, life, events and circumstances. But it is about having room in your life to savor family and other relationships. It's the love you feel when someone makes you dinner—it's the love—not what's in the skillet. It's about you loving yourself as absolutely as any pet ever did. It is about a transformation from within. **You no longer fill yourself with food— you fill yourself with living.**

May all your days be infused with enormous joy and satisfaction, a little exercise and a lot of vegetables. And please write to me and share your success...

I'd love to hear from you.

Email me at: Roger@HypnosisHealthInfo.com.
Call me at (206) 903-1232.
Find me on Skype at HypnosisHealthInfo.com.

EPILOGUE

"Let food be thy medicine and medicine be thy food."
~Hippocrates, 460 B.C.

It's not too late!

So here it is late May of 2011, and this second edition is way behind schedule. Last fall my intent was to have this published in February! Still, life happens and we must adjust. The good news is that I haven't had to turn to food to deal with the challenges and opportunities that life has provided these past few months.

The biggest event to occur in my personal life recently was having my 88-year-old Mom move in with us for a few months. In December I flew to Colorado to spend the weekend with her. Monday morning (the day I was to fly home) I woke up to the smell of smoke. Sure enough there was an electrical fire in the attic crawl space. On December 8, Mom flew home with me while her house was being repaired. (You can read my weekly blog posts about Mom at www.hypnosishealthinfo.com. Type "Mom" in the search box on the right.)

Over the next four months **I received a profound education on many levels:** family, relationships, caregiving, aging, exercise and healthy eating. For now, I will focus on aging, healthy eating and exercise.

For years my Mom has suffered with rheumatoid arthritis. It runs in our family and she has been in constant chronic pain. She's had both knees replaced and walked hunched over a walker. Prior to moving in with us, when I'd call Mom in the morning and again in the evening I could often hear the tears of pain in her voice. To make matters worse, she had gained more than twenty pounds in the year and half since my father's death.

Mom ate lots of dairy products—especially cheese and ice cream. Nearly every week Mom and my sister would stop at DQ or

McDonald's for a hot fudge sundae. Mom also ate quite a bit of meat and poultry. Consuming animal proteins and dairy products is like pouring gasoline on the fire of arthritis. As much as I talked to her about how changing her diet would help alleviate her arthritis pain, she would placate me with words of agreement, but she and I both knew the lure of a sundae would always win out over intentions.

When Mom agreed to come home with me, she said she wanted to lose at least twenty pounds. Not wanting to assume anything or force anything on her, I asked Mom what plan she had in mind and about the type of support I could offer her. **She said she wanted to eat like we eat: "like how you say to eat in Chapter 5 of your book."**

I replied that I would love to support her goal of losing twenty pounds, but I refused to play food police. If she wanted a cookie, I

wouldn't comment or try to stop her. **What transpired was truly amazing!**

For the continuance of Mom's long-term care insurance, we had to hire an in-home caregiver for at least ten hours per week. We found a gifted young woman who was skilled at exercise for seniors. Most of their time together was spent exercising. They did arm and leg strengthening exercises and crunches on the bed to build Mom's core muscles. Mom started gaining strength and stability and was practicing walking without the walker. Mom stood straighter and was able to walk further distances and faster.

Even more amazing, Mom changed her way of eating. She mostly ate vegan meals and rarely ate sweets. She started losing weight. Some weeks she lost one pound, some weeks three pounds. We kept talking to her about the importance of frequent small meals and that she should eat five or six small meals throughout the day. Mom didn't believe us, and for a bit her weight loss slowed. We convinced her one week to eat more—meaning a breakfast of whole grain cereal, a mid-morning snack of fruit, a lunch of grains and veggies, a snack of fruit and/or veggies in the afternoon and for dinner back to the veggies and grains. And guess what? She lost two pounds that week!

Mom listened to the Slender For Life™ weight loss CDs and she learned self-hypnosis. The changes in Mom were transformative. **She lost almost twenty pounds in four months and has continued to lose weight since arriving back in Colorado.** Within the first month of cutting out the dairy and other animal proteins she stopped hurting so much. It became rare to hear her complain about body aches. Her mind sharpened and her spirits lifted.

When Mom left to return to her own home, she looked and acted the best that she had for several years. She was more mobile, felt better and she was happier. It is amazing what four months of eating a plant-based diet, exercise and self-hypnosis can do! As much as I knew all this intellectually, I now realize I did not KNOW it at the deepest level. **We are never too old to improve our health. We are never too old to take responsibility for our own healthcare. We are never too old to change.**

FURTHER ACTION YOU CAN TAKE

Childhood Obesity

> **"The pain and suffering inflicted on children by the American diet is so brutal that if it were administered with a stick, parents would be put in jail."**
> **~John McDougall, MD**

The cases of child obesity are increasing day by day. **According to one survey, the number of obese children has doubled during the period of the last three decades.** Being overweight does not only mean to be over a healthy size, but it has certain complications attached to it.

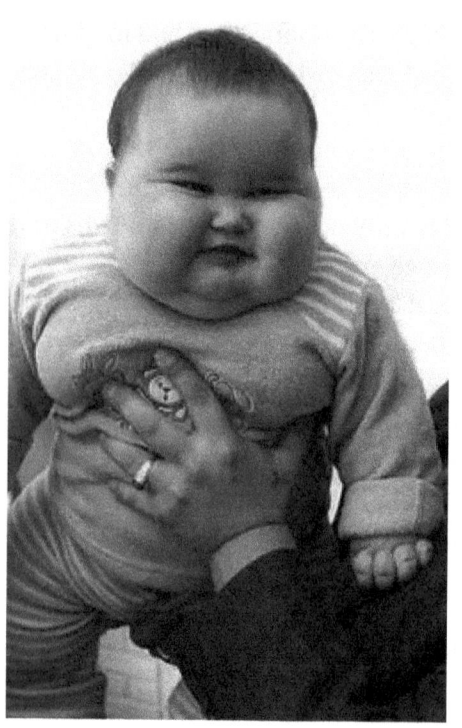

• There is an alarming increase in the number of children and adolescents developing type-2 diabetes (also termed as adult-onset diabetes) due to being overweight. More than 7% of teenagers (2 million) are estimated to be pre-diabetic, with symptoms of high blood pressure and high blood glucose levels.

• The high levels of cholesterol and high blood pressure, that are some of the main risk factors for development of heart diseases, are found in most of the obese children.

• Sleep apnea (interruption of breathing while sleeping) is considered the most severe problem faced by obese children. In rare cases, sleep apnea may lead to other problems like difficulty in learning and memory.

• Obese children are at higher risk of developing liver diseases, orthopedic problems and asthma.

• Children with higher levels of belly fat have higher

pulse pressures, which put them at risk for heart-related disorders.
• More than 70% of obese adolescents retain their overweight or obese condition during their adulthood.

Left unchecked, 75% of adults will be overweight in just 10 years.

Our kids are growing up on processed food, fast food, junk food and sodas. Our school cafeterias are filled with fatty processed

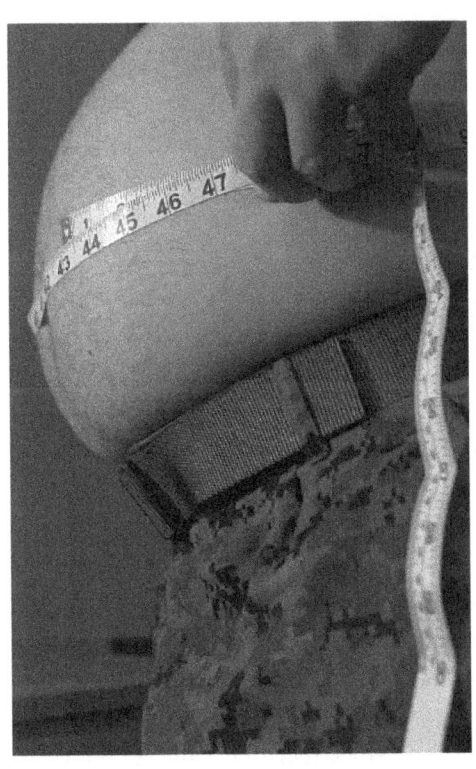

foods. 27% of Americans ages 17 to 24 are too fat to fight in the military. And with those already serving, obesity costs the military billions of dollars in job absenteeism and health care spending and has been linked to poor performance. On May 18, 2011, Chief of Staff General Martin Dempse told a Senate panel that U.S. Army recruits have had poorer diets and are less fit than past generations, making them more prone to injury from heavier loads lugged in combat. He singled out poor eating habits plus carbonated drinks as contributing factors to musculoskeletal injuries that have been a leading cause of U.S. medical evacuations from Iraq and Afghanistan. Such injuries typically include fractures, tendonitis and connective tissue disorders but not combat injuries. **The problem is that young men and women coming in the army today are not as fit or as skeletally sound as previous generations.**

This spring on *Jamie Oliver's Food Revolution*, Chef Jamie showed that milk is pushed on our kids in schools, and worse yet, 75% to 85% of it is flavored milk. One 8-ounce carton of milk contains 28 grams of sugar—the same as a 2-ounce Snickers bar! We're having our kids drink a Snickers bar as part of their school lunch. **WHAT ARE WE THINKING?!**

Childhood obesity is an unnecessary and preventable epidemic. We can change that. It is time for each of us to stand up for our kids and start a Food Revolution in our homes and in our schools.

You may be wondering why I'm supporting Jamie Oliver in having only plain milk served in schools when I truly believe that no milk should be served to our kids. That's because I just don't see the removal of all milk as a reality any time soon for our schools. The dairy council is too politically powerful for that to happen. **But I do believe we can take the first step and get the sugar out of our schools.** And to me, the great news is that for those kids who refuse to drink plain milk rather than strawberry or chocolate milk, that's even better!

It is inexcusable that for the first time since the Civil War, our children have a shorter life expectancy than older generations—all thanks to childhood obesity. We can change that. **Childhood obesity is unnecessary and preventable.** As adults, we must take action now and save our kids. As a nation, we simply cannot afford the healthcare costs of obesity, especially since it is totally preventable. **Come on folks, let's take action now.**

If you haven't already signed Jamie Oliver's petition to improve school lunches, I urge you to do so now at: **www.jamieoliver.com/jfr-beta/petition.php.**

Healthcare Reform

"Wouldn't it be great if there were a magic pill—available to everyone, with no co-pays and no deductibles—that prevents obesity and reduces its associated risks of diabetes, heart disease and depression? In fact there is such a remedy. The magical medicine is physical activity." ~Penelope McPhee

I started this edition of *Becoming Slender For Life* by writing that it's time for each of us to take personal responsibility for our health and wellness. I firmly believe that we must have healthcare reform. As a nation, we simply cannot collectively or individually afford the status quo. Studies suggest that trimming high obesity rates in the nation's most overweight cities could help local governments save more than $32 billion annually nationwide in associated healthcare costs.

Researchers estimate that direct **healthcare costs associated with obesity are about $50 million each year per 100,000**

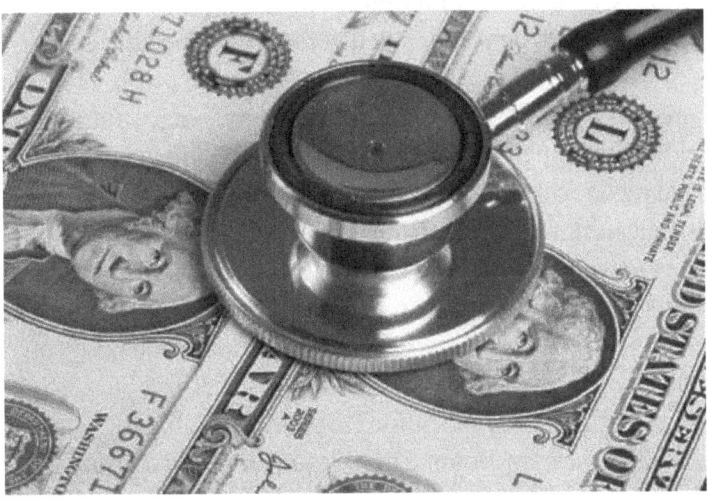

residents in U.S. cities with the highest obesity rates. If the nation's ten most overweight cities (each with more than a third of its residents classified as obese with a body mass index (BMI) over 30) reduced their obesity levels to the 2009 national average of 26.5%, they could collectively save nearly $500 million in healthcare costs

each year.

In addition to chronic health conditions, researchers say residents in the most obese cities were also more likely to be less energetic, which can lower productivity levels and may be another hidden economic cost of obesity.

More than half of all Americans may develop diabetes or pre-diabetes by 2020, unless prevention strategies aimed at weight loss and increased physical activity are widely implemented, according to a new analysis. The U.S. Diabetes Prevention Program shows that modest weight loss through dietary changes and increased physical activity could prevent pre-diabetes from progressing to diabetes.

These efforts could in theory also save about $250 billion in healthcare costs in the next ten years, suggests the analysis published by UnitedHealth Center for Health Reform & Modernization, a specialized center within UnitedHealth that focuses on healthcare reform issues.

There was a time when I would have put my energy into politics thinking that congress would and could affect change. I'm older now and realize that money and powerful lobbies will slow, or even prevent, meaningful change in the foreseeable future. **Healthcare reform must begin with personal responsibility:** Each of us must take responsibility for our own healthcare. To me, the logical place to start is with what you put in your mouth and how you move your body.

As Americans, we cannot afford to continue eating high fat, high sugar foods in the mass volume that we are currently consuming.

Many of today's healthcare costs are the result of preventable diseases causes by obesity. Americans are choosing to be fat, and it's bankrupting the nation and killing its citizens. If terrorists want to be successful in overthrowing our government, they should buy stock in McDonald's.

So, what can you do? You can vote with your fork and your wallet. Stop going to McDonald's and other fast food chains. Stop buying processed foods that are filled with fat, salt, sugar and chemicals. Don't get caught in believing that McDonald's is serving you healthy oatmeal. McDonald's oatmeal comes to you fully loaded with cream, more sugar than a Snicker's bar and eleven weird ingredients that you never keep in your kitchen—all for 290 calories.

There are so many ways that healthy plant-based meals can be prepared quickly, simply and inexpensively that also taste great. **There is simply no excuse to continue the self-destruction we are currently engaged in.**

Becoming Slender For Life offers you the opportunity to begin healthcare reform for you and your family. **True revolutionary movements start with individual change.**

> My challenge to you is to vote with your wallet, get off the couch, eat plant-based meals and reform your health. Remember, it only takes a single thought, a single action to change the world.

Resources

www.slenderforlife.com
Learn more about Slender for Life™

www.hypnosishealthinfo.com
Your resource for health and wellness information with daily blog posts, articles, radio shows, videos and products to support you.

www.rogermooreinstitute.com
For information on hypnotherapy training or training as a Slender For Life™ licensee.

www.mooreabundance.com
Find out more about Roger Moore.

www.drmcdougall.com
Great recipes and up-to-date health information.

www.pcrm.org
More tasty recipes from the Physicians Committee For Responsible Medicine.

www.fatfreevegan.com
One of my favorite recipe web sites.

www.fatfree.com
4,667 fat-free and very low fat vegetarian recipes, as well as information about healthy very low fat vegetarian diets.

www.vegsource.com
Another great resource for recipes.

www.innerdiet.com
To assist you on your journey to Becoming Slender For Life, go to this site and take the Inner Diet Assessment. It will help guide you in identifying and overcoming your mental and emotional roadblocks to taking your weight off and keeping it off.

www.fmsrelief.com
If you suffer from Fibromyalgia.

www.ibshypnotist.com
For information about Irritable Bowel Syndrome.

www.iact.org
To find a skilled therapist in your area, visit the International
Association of Counselors & Therapists or

Books

Women Food And God
Geneen Roth, Scribner Books

The McDougall Program for Maximum Weight Loss
John McDougall, M.D., Plume/Penguin Books

The McDougall Plan
John and Mary McDougall, M.D., New Win Publications, Inc.

A Challenging Second Opinion
John McDougall, M.D., New Win Publications, Inc.

The McDougall Program For Women
John McDougall, M.D., Plume/Penguin Books

The McDougall Program Twelve Days to Dynamic Health
John A. McDougall, M.D., Plume/Penguin Books

The McDougall Health-Supporting Cookbook, Vol. One
Mary McDougall, New Win Publications, Inc.

The McDougall Health-Supporting Cookbook, Vol. Two
Mary McDougall, New Win Publications, Inc.

The New McDougall Cookbook
John and Mary McDougall, Plume/Penguin Books

Breaking the Food Seduction
Neal Barnard, M.D., St. Martin's Press

The Food Revolution
John Robbins, Conari Press

Diet For A New America
John Robbins, H.J. Kramer

Eat More, Weigh Less
Dean Ornish, M.D., Harper Collins

The New Pritikin Program
Robert Pritikin, Pocket Books

Taming the Diet Dragon
Constance Kirk, Llewellyn

The Complete Idiot's Guide to Plant-Based Nutrition
Julieanna Hever, MS, RD, CPT

Women Food And God
Geneen Roth, Scribner Books

The China Study
T. Colin Campbell, Phd, Benbella Books

The Engine 2 Diet
Rip Esselstyn, Hachette Book Group

Time Line Therapy and the Basis of Personality
Tad James & Wyatt Woodsmall, Meta Publications, Inc

The Wizard Within
A. M. Krasner, Ph.D., Am. Board of Hypnotherapy Press

The Unhealthy Truth
Robyn O'Brien, Broadway Books

Other Resources

At **www.slenderforlife.com** you may download the following:
    *"I am Slender For Life™" card
    *Slender For Life™ Commitment form

Register to receive daily blog posts at
www.hypnosishealthinfo.com and checkout all the tools and
resources there to support you in your weight release journey.

Visit HypnoHealth on YouTube for hundreds of videos to help
you survive daily life. **www.youtube.com/HypnosisHealth**

You can also follow Roger on Facebook at
www.facebook.com/HypnosisHealth

Vegetarian Starter Kit PCRM **http://pcrm.org/health/
veginfo/vsk/index.html**

Plant Based Dietician's Food Guide Pyramid
**http://hypnosishealthinfo.com/plant-based-food-guide-
pyramid**

My Simple Recipes by Jeff Novick, MS, RD
http://www.facebook.com/JeffNovickRD

CD Instructions

The CD set was created to accompany the Slender For Life™ Hypnotic Weight Loss Program and the book *Becoming Slender For Life* and is available for purchase at www.slenderforlife.com. You should listen to these CDs while sitting or lying down, never while driving a car or while doing anything that requires your attention.

Most of the hypnosis therapies are meant to be listened to in two parts. The first track is a long induction session designed to induce trance, and the second track has a short deepening induction which leads into the specific therapy session. Once you've mastered the Light Switch Self-Hypnosis technique, if you prefer, you can put yourself into trance, skip the long induction track and go directly to the specific therapy track.

The CDs are divided into two groups: the first one (CDs 1 and 2) contains guided meditations and exercises based on those in the book, as well as other information derived from the book. The second group (CDs 3-10) contains the hypnotic inductions and therapies. What follows is the suggested listening order the the hypnosis CDs.

NOTE: If you are working with a licensed Slender For Life™ hypnotherapist, follow the listening recommendations given to you by your therapist.

To order the Becoming Slender For Life CD set, go to www.slenderforlife.com.

Hypnosis CD Listening Summary

This listening schedule presumes that you have already read the book or are at least reading the chapters in order, since the selections for weeks one through eight correspond to chapters one through eight.

· **Week 1 Hypnosis:** *You Are Ready & Stress Buster*
· **Week 2 Hypnosis:** Self-Hypnosis tracks on Hypnosis CD 1
· **Week 3 Hypnosis:** *Becoming Motivated, Emotion Trigger* and *Bridge of Empowerment*.
· **Week 4 Hypnosis**: *Stress Buster* and *Inner Child*
· **Week 5 Hypnosis**
       Day 1: *Weight Control*
       Day 2: *Control Room*
       Day 3: *Weight Control*
       Day 4: *Social Situations*
       Day 5: *Stress Buster*
       Day 6: *Weight Control*
       Day 7: *Control Room*
· **Week 6 Hypnosis**
       Day 1: *Exercise Is Better Every Day*
       Day 2: *Weight Control*
       Day 3: *Exercise For Your Body and Your Mind*
       Day 4: *Stress Buster*
       Day 5: *You Are Motivated to Exercise*
       Day 6: *Emotion Trigger*
       Day 7: *Exercise Is Better Every Day*
· **Week 7 Hypnosis**
       Day 1: *Baggy Pants*
       Day 2: *Weight Control*
       Day 3: *Making Friends With Your Appetite*

Day 4: *Emotion Trigger*
Day 5: *You Easily Achieve Your Goals*
Day 6: *Stress Buster*
Day 7: *Making Friends With Your Appetitive*
· **Week 8 Hypnosis**
Day 1: *Weight Control*
Day 2: *Mirror*
Day 3: *Stress Buster*
Day 4: *Weight Release Submarine*
Day 5: *Emotion Trigger*
Day 6: *Weight Control*
Day 7: *Graduation Ceremony*
· **Weeks 9, 19, 11 and 12** Use your Light Switch Self-Hypnosis technique five times each day with written suggestions. Focus your listening to the Hypnosis tracks *Weight Control, Stress Buster, Emotion Trigger, Control Room & Making Friends With Your Appetite*. Feel free to use other sessions as you choose.
· **Weeks 13 - 24** Listen to *Slender For Life* daily (found on the Hypnosis CDs) and use your Light Switch Self-Hypnosis technique five times each day with written suggestions. Use your other Hypnosis sessions as support as you need them/
· **For the rest of your life:** Use your Light Switch Self-Hypnosis technique five times each day with written suggestions. Use your Hypnosis sessions for support as you need them.

Our Clients Speak

From time to time our clients share with us their Slender For Life™ experiences. Here are excerpts from what some of them have written.

"From the first call, I felt respected, understood and listened to. I appreciated the compassion as I faced my first weigh-in. That was a hard moment for me. I left after my initial consultation convinced that this was right for me."

"The staff radiates integrity and after that first meeting I've never had doubts about my decision to participate in this program."

"The best investment I have ever made for myself. Worth every dollar spent. A path to success which carries with it benefits over and above weight loss."

"The program has worked well in keeping me on track and focused on my goals. My eating habits have changed and my cravings are gone."

"I love the ability I have gained to de-stress my world."

"I felt that I'd really found a place of hope. Food no longer controls me."

"Everything has changed. My relationship with myself is the biggest change. I'm finding so much about myself that is special and am learning to love myself, with the gift of knowing that the only thing I can change is me."

'Just thought I'd check in and let you know I'M DOING GREAT!!! I'm listening to the tracks 6:4 & 6:5 every day….very helpful.I'm working on my homework, coming up with my goals, my 52 reasons for reaching my goal weight etc. It's really making me think about these things in a way that I haven't before, and solidifying them in my mind and my actions.

Best of all: I'm eating Vegan! I've been doing it since I saw you last. I feel amazing: light, clear, focused, calm. No cravings. I feel SO MUCH BETTER not eating animals : my eating finally matches up with my ethics, my politics and my love of animals. Plus I'm amazed at how steady my energy is throughout the day, no crashes, no need for the late afternoon coffee. I'm waking up earlier and staying up later! I'm thrilled with this!

I'm excited about trying new foods and 'crowding out' the bad old foods. I've spent a fair amount of time on Dr. McDougall's website, looking at foods, recipes etc. I'm sticking with my 'only eat sugar on days that start with S (Sat/Sun) ….and that's very helpful as well. Clear boundaries work well for me…I have a tendency to be an 'all or nothing' kinda gal…so this is all working for me!

Even when I was working on this past gig in Houston, I took 15 minutes out of the 30 minute lunch break to take a fast walk around the property! This is unheard of for me; I've always found it very difficult to make myself exercise.

NOT ANY MORE!!! It all seems more do-able, not such a chore. It's gotta be the hypnosis working.

Now I'm on my vacation in Palm Springs, and my eating is going fine here too. It's a little trickier, eating out a lot, but so far, I'm managing to make the right choices. I'm so excited about all this, Roger, that I just had to write and tell you! THANK YOU SO MUCH for all that you're doing to help me!"

Biography

Roger Moore has been working with people since high school, when he volunteered on a crisis hot line. He has a BA in Criminal Justice Studies, a Masters in Applied Counseling Psychology and a Doctorate in Clinical Hypnotherapy. While an undergraduate, he began working with children who were developmentally disabled. Roger was Executive Director of Forestview Community Homes, Inc. in Minnesota, which provided residential programs to children and adults who were developmentally disabled. While attending graduate school, he was Vice President of Lutheran Social Services of Southern California, directing the emergency services, hot meal programs and senior services in Orange and San Diego Counties. In addition, he created their counseling program throughout southern California.

Since 1996, Roger has been in private practice on Bainbridge Island in in Seattle, Washington. In addition to his passion for assisting people in taking off excess weight, he specializes in Medical Hypnosis, relationship counseling and sports performance. Roger is the director and an instructor at Roger Moore's Institute of Hypnotherapy and is a regular speaker at the annual conferences of the International Association of Counselors and Therapists (IACT), the International Medical & Dental Hypnotherapy Association (IMDHA) as well as other organizations. He is a member of the International Association of Counselors and Therapists, the International Medical & Dental Hypnotherapy Association and the International Hypnosis Federation.

Index